D1569473

Public Higher Education in California

Public Higher Education in California

Edited by

NEIL J. SMELSER *and* GABRIEL ALMOND

UNIVERSITY OF CALIFORNIA PRESS
Berkeley, Los Angeles, London

University of California Press
Berkeley and Los Angeles, California
University of California Press, Ltd.
London, England

Copyright © 1974 by
The Regents of the University of California

ISBN: 0-520-02510-5
Library of Congress Catalog Card Number: 73-80833
Printed in the United States of America

Contents

Preface

This book has had a long history, and we should like to record a few details of its development in this preface.

In 1969 Talcott Parsons, then president of the American Academy of Arts and Sciences, approached Neil Smelser with a request that he devote some research time to a topic in higher education that would be relevant to the work of the Assembly on Goals and Governance in Higher Education. Parsons and Smelser explored the matter at length and decided on two lines of work. First, Smelser would collaborate with Parsons and Gerald Platt in preparing their book, *The American University* (Cambridge: Harvard University Press, 1973); for this collaboration he prepared intensive commentaries on their work as it progressed, and he wrote an Epilogue, which appears as Chapter 9 of that book. Second, Smelser agreed to undertake an independent research project on the sociological aspects of growth and conflict in the public sector of California's system of higher education.

About the same time, in 1969, the American Academy of Arts and Sciences was establishing its Western Center, in an effort to organize the activities of its members on a regional basis. Since its founding it has held nine Stated Meetings with communications on such subjects as "The President, the Press, and Urban Problems," "Technological Exaggeration," and "Economic Growth and Its Discontents" at various places in northern and southern California. It was decided from the outset that Smelser's research and any other activities associated with it would be a major project of the Western Center.

To conduct the research, Smelser secured a leave of absence from the University of California, Berkeley, for the academic year 1970–1971. To finance the research, he received a joint research grant from the Ford Foundation and the American Academy of Arts and Sciences. After the first draft of Smelser's essay was completed, it was submitted to the other contributors to this volume for papers and elaboration in 1971. The papers were discussed at a conference at the Center for Advanced Study in the Behavioral Sciences in Palo Alto, California, on February 17–18, 1972, and were subsequently revised for publication in this volume.

N.J.S.

G.A.A.

Introduction

by GABRIEL A. ALMOND

This book is the first published product of the Western Center of the American Academy of Arts and Sciences. Its subject — public higher education in California — is singularly appropriate as an inaugural of the publications of the Western Center. It is often said that new tendencies in American culture — indeed in advanced industrial culture — have a way of first breaking the surface in California. Public higher education reached its fullest development in the California of the early 1960s, and in the years that followed went into dramatic disarray in ways that were soon repeated all over the United States and in Western Europe. Thus this book has both a regional and a general import. It contains analyses of problems of public higher education in California which have implications for both public and private higher education in the United States and in other advanced industrial societies. The papers do not deal in any direct sense with the "great disturbances" of 1964 to 1969. But the undertaking as a whole is related to these events. Crises often reveal cleavages, weak points in the structure of authority, value conflicts, and ambiguities. The pride, enthusiasm, and perhaps complacency that accompanied the adoption of the California Master Plan for Higher Education in 1960 have given way to the more sober analysis and evaluation reflected in these papers. Some of the weaknesses in the system were brought to light in the confrontations and riots of 1964 to 1969. The Smelser monograph helps explain the kinds of grievances and alienations which had developed and their location among the various institutions and strata of the California system of higher education — grievances which weakened institutional solidarity and legitimacy and fueled the fires of antiwar and ethnic protest.

The central thesis of Smelser's monograph is that rapid

growth constitutes a large part of the explanation of the conflict proneness and vulnerability of the higher education system in California. The simple massive facts of a rate of growth in student population from two hundred thousand in 1950 to more than a million in 1970, the manyfold increase and proliferation of faculty and parafaculty, and the establishment of new campuses would inevitably produce a dilution of institutional loyalty and authority, uncertainty regarding roles, conflicts over privileges and burdens, and rivalry among the structural units. Although the simple fact of rapid, massive growth might explain the general instability of the system, the structural patterns of growth specific to public higher education in California explain the location of these instabilities and conflicts. Smelser draws these fault lines persuasively. He shows how the Master Plan, striving to reconcile the competing values of excellence and equality by establishing a three-tier system — of two-year community colleges, four-year state colleges, and the university — put the state colleges under particular stress. The community colleges are unambiguously egalitarian, and the universities are dedicated to excellence. The values conflict in the state colleges, creating institutional role-uncertainty and inviting a clamorous upward mobility.

Within the university system and particularly in the two oldest and largest units — Berkeley and UCLA — general growth in numbers of students and faculty was accompanied by the particularly rapid development of graduate programs and research. A new division of labor and a stratification system emerged, with a privileged senior faculty that was preoccupied with graduate training and research, a junior faculty that was loaded with undergraduate teaching, and two parafaculty strata — teaching and research assistants. The activists in the disturbances of these years recruited disproportionately from the "underprivileged" and "exploited" strata — the nontenured faculty and the teaching and research assistants.

Smelser touches on still another cleavage resulting from the pattern of growth, a substantive rather than a structural cleavage — that between the sciences and humanities. Research funds and prestigious and influential consultantships went predominantly to the sciences, to a lesser extent to the social sciences, and hardly at all to the humanities. The scientific and technological revolutions also tended to create a mood of obsolescence among humanists. Thus the disproportionate recruitment of activists from the humanities departments was doubly determined by feelings of relative deprivation and a mood of futility and irrelevance.

Parallel to these stresses and strains resulting from growth, Smelser points out, there was a complicated, multi-sited, and multi-leveled authority system to deal with conflict. Normally decision-making power was stably distributed and largely devolved to particular agencies, institutions, administrators, and faculties. But during crisis, delegated powers were taken back and decision sites competed with one another, further impairing the legitimacy of authority. Finally, Smelser concludes that if growth in considerable part caused these vulnerabilities and tensions, the rapid subsidence of growth since the late 1960s justifies an expectation of the reduction of conflict in the years ahead. He is careful to point out, however, that although internally caused tensions may subside, external conflicts and crises may continue to trouble campus life.

The various papers stimulated by Smelser's analyses and arguments fall into three groups: (1) those dealing with the institutional structure of the system; (2) those dealing with the science–humanities conflict, and the causes and implications of the defensiveness of the humanities; and (3) those taking more explicitly prescriptive positions on the values and broader social functions of higher education.

F. E. Balderston, in his treatment of the financing of higher education, explores the implications of the present financial scale and pattern for the four principle educational goals set by the Master Plan: (1) universality of opportunity for higher education; (2) greatest possible diversity of campuses, programs, and curricula; (3) maximum freedom of student choice; and (4) optimum flexibility to adapt to new situations. He shows how these goals have been affected by current financial policy and practice, and he examines alternative modes of financing higher education. These include a return to the original no-tuition system, student loan programs including the Zaccharias Plan, the Collier proposal of "learn, earn, and reimburse," and the various voucher plans which seek to introduce market principles into educational production and consumption. All these alternatives are appraised from the perspectives of the goals of the Master Plan.

T. R. McConnell introduces a comparative perspective based on organizational patterns in other states and in England. He shows that the relation between growth and conflict proneness is not a peculiarly Californian — or even American — phenomenon. He points out that growth of higher education in Britain has produced a similar pattern of relative deprivation and struggle for status among the strata and units of the system. He also points to systems of higher education in other American states which overcome some of the rigidities of California's three-tiered system. His main recommendation is for a coordinating council with teeth, which would seek to reconcile equality and excellence more effectively, facilitate movement of students when appropriate from one level of the system to another, and provide for the shifting of specific institutions from one level to the other as conditions may require.

Robert O'Neil, in his essay on law and higher education in California, deals with the question of autonomy of the university and the structure of legal powers over the system. He shows that constitutional autonomy, to the extent that it exists at all, is lodged in the regents and not in the university. In past years the regents have intervened in such delegated technical matters as faculty appointments and course offerings. The legislature through its lawmaking and appropriations powers, the governor through his appointive and veto powers, and the courts through their judicial powers are shown by O'Neil to reduce autonomy to an essentially formal norm, opening higher education to political pressures particularly in times and situations of conflict and controversy.

O. Meredith Wilson introduces a note of skepticism regarding man's capacity to plan, raising the question of whether an organizational solution such as a coordinating council is an effective solution to the organizational and power problems created by the Master Plan. Creativity and entrepreneurship in the development of higher education may be in the process of being lost as organizations are imposed on other organizations.

The second group of essays deals with the issues posed by the growth of the sciences in higher education. There is much evidence showing that the "revolutionary" elements of faculties and student bodies were recruited most heavily from the humanities, to a lesser extent from the social sciences, and least of all from the "hard" sciences. Kenneth Thimann, in his essay on the social role of the university and its science departments, demonstrates the importance of higher education for the California economy in terms of payroll and employment, the training of skilled personnel, the spinning-off of science-based industries, and the stimulation of high technology agriculture. The rapid growth of scientific research and the attraction of research funds principally from the federal government has not only meant growth in the output of students and scientific research but — through overhead charges — has contributed to the growth of the nonscience departments and general university services. Thimann's essay reflects the pride of the sciences in their extraordinary accomplishments in recent decades.

Harvey Brooks confronts the question of growth rates in the sciences and the humanities, pointing out that the popular impression — of high rates of growth in the size of the faculty and of Ph. D. production in the sciences, and lower rates of growth in the humanities and social sciences — is not supported by available evidence. He presents data showing that the relative growth rates in faculty and Ph. D.s was higher during the past two decades in the humanities and the social sciences. What does appear to be clear is that the rapidly growing support for research in the sciences, and to a lesser extent the social sciences, has provided privileges and opportunities — such as travel funds, research services and facilities, opportunities for outside influence, and additional earnings — not available to the humanities. In addition, Brooks points out that there is a more open relation between the sciences and the outside economy and society. More than 30 percent of the science and engineering Ph. D.s go into industry and government, but almost all of the humanities Ph. D.s go into academic life. He argues that the sense of relative deprivation in the humanities is attributable to differences and inequalities of these kinds, rather than to simple rates of faculty and student growth.

Henry Nash Smith and Roy Harvey Pearce approach these problems from a humanistic perspective, arguing that the defensiveness and sense of deprivation among humanists, although perhaps accentuated by recent patterns of growth, emerged out of an anti-humanist inclination and a pro-science, technology, and practical arts bias — a bias characteristic of American culture, and one that was introduced into the terms of reference of the state universities from their very founding. The values of the humanities — the disinterested and edificatory study of works of the intellect and the creative imagination — were viewed as aristocratic values, to be tolerated and moderately supported at best. Hence, from the very beginning the humanities have tended to be viewed as decorative luxuries, more appropriate for the education of women than of men. In the absence of any clear conception among humanists as to their roles in higher education, and given the sense of mission and public support for the science, engineering, and professional components, Henry Nash Smith confronts us with the prospect of continued attrition in morale among the humanistic disciplines and perhaps an increasing impatience among the more confident elements of the university community with humanist radicalism and alienation.

Roy Harvey Pearce advocates a continued search for an acceptable role definition of the humanistic disciplines in the university, and, particularly in the California context, of roles for humanistic education in the community colleges, the state colleges, and the university. The clues that he is pursuing in this search for a distinctive and constructive role lie in the special relationship of humanistic subjects to wholeness and values. As academic disciplines, humanistic subjects may not advocate and directly inculcate particular philosophical perspectives and value orientations. Rather, through the examination of intellectual and artistic texts and objects, the humanities convey to students at all levels some sense of the variety of human efforts to pursue the good, the true, and the beautiful, and their implications. From this perspective the humanities may contribute to the development of disciplined ways of choosing among values, life styles, forms of culture, and social–political structures.

The third set of papers are of a more prescriptive sort. Dean Maslach's paper demonstrates that, at least in engineering and with a substantial input of effort and goodwill, the rigidities of the three-tiered Master Plan can be overcome and the values of equality and excellence partially reconciled through substantial upward recruitment. He would perhaps question Thimann's recommendation that the lower tiers of higher education in California satisfy themselves fully with the education of a proud and productive artisanate.

Rosemary Park attributes much of the malaise higher education in California to essentially moral problems. She argues that
higher education is not the only institution which is being subjected to revaluation in modern times. All the great structures of
modern society — government, business, the church, the trade
unions, as well as the university — are being scrutinized from the
point of view of the values they embody and their appropriateness
in their present form. The special vulnerability of higher education
is attributable to its movement into the power structure, as the
base of the "knowledge industry" which has made so central a
contribution to material affluence and the creation of an ever larger
attentive and critical public. The knowledge industry came about
through the release of enormous powers of specialization and expertise, but in the process the values of higher education came to
be equated with the production of experts. And it is among many of
these experts and apprentice experts that questioning has now
become increasingly current. Park challenges the value of expertise as the sole criterion of the educated person, and offers the ideal
of the humane expert as the desired product of higher education.
She has no simple way of implementing these changes in higher
education, but she suggests that they may be attainable through an
integrative and collaborative search on the part of the sciences,
professions, and humanities among and between the community
colleges, state colleges, and the university instead of through the
current struggle for status and power.

John Vasconcellos and Patrick Callan press this point of view
considerably further. They suggest a conflict between a new and an
old culture of higher education — the old culture stressing work,
intellectuality, material accumulation, elitism, and conformity, and
the new rejecting the work ethic and conformity and offering a
more affective, integrative, and naturalistic conception of human
existence. The first culture grew out of scarcity and insecurity, the
second out of plenty and security. In this process of basic cultural
change, higher education in California and elsewhere will have to
respond increasingly to affective, integrative, communitarian, and
egalitarian needs and demands.

In the concluding essay, Talcott Parsons examines contemporary ideological conflict in the advanced industrial societies, particularly as it bears on the organization and functions of higher
education. He finds in the New Left attack on the university an

analogy with the radical Marxian critique of capitalism. By its stress on cognitive productivity, the modern university is said to have won a central place in the capitalist system — at the cost of alienating its faculty and students from their own labor and creativity. Just as Marxism was imbued by a strong *Gemeinschaft* (communitarian) nostalgia, offering a utopia combining these values with the productive consequences of *Gesellschaft*, so the university New Left attacks the cognitive–technical, impersonal, and instrumental culture of the university, and presents an image of an alternative university as a community of searchers for humanely useful truth. Parsons speaks of a sociocultural crisis affecting modern society and higher education. He brings the debate back to the formulation of these issues of the human costs and consequences of rationalization and bureaucratization of modern life in the work of Max Weber at the turn of the century. Parsons beckons us to the sobering task that Weber began, that of seeking realistic and responsible solutions to the problem of reconciling the enormous powers of cognitive specialization and social rationalization with the requirements of human proportion.

Growth, Structural Change, and Conflict in California Public Higher Education, 1950–1970*

by NEIL J. SMELSER

INTRODUCTION

In this essay I focus on a series of theoretical and empirical issues that have preoccupied me for many years. These issues revolve around a single question: What happens in social systems

*I should like to record my debt to those who facilitated the progress of this essay. Several people helped me work out the details of the joint research grant from the Ford Foundation and the American Academy of Arts and Sciences, under which my research was conducted — Marshall Robinson of the Ford Foundation; Talcott Parsons, Geno A. Ballotti, and John Voss, all of the academy. My research assistant, Betty Lou Bradshaw, and my secretary, Frances Brown, worked diligently and patiently with me during 1970–1971. The Institute of International Studies, University of California, Berkeley, generously supplied me with office facilities and other amenities during that academic year. Gabriel Almond was helpful in arranging the details of the conference — described in the preface — in February of 1972, as were Geno A. Ballotti, John Voss, and Jane Kielsmeier of the Center for Advanced Study in the Behavioral Sciences. I should also like to thank the participants in that conference: Gabriel Almond, Frederick Balderston, Harvey Brooks, George Maslach, T. R. McConnell, Frank Newman, Robert O'Neil, Rosemary Park, Talcott Parsons, Roy Harvey Pearce, Henry Nash Smith, Kenneth Thimann, John Vasconcellos, and O. Meredith Wilson. Their written essays and their oral contributions at the conference helped me revise the essay for final publication. In addition, several people gave especially careful critical readings of the manuscript of my essay, and their observations prompted me to modify a number of the arguments I had advanced in the earlier drafts. These were Margaret Fay, Frank Newman, Arthur Stinchcombe, Harlan Wilson, and James Wood. Finally, Grant Barnes and Sheila Levine of the University of California Press were extremely gracious and helpful in overseeing the production of the book itself.

This pudding, then, has had many cooks, but I think they have improved rather than spoilt the dish. I thank them all, but hold none of them responsible for what I have ultimately included in the essay.

that are experiencing rapid growth?[1] The system I examine is public higher education in California between the years of 1950 and 1970. In particular, I attempt to develop an account of how processes associated with rapid growth made that system especially vulnerable to conflict.

Public higher education in California between 1950 and 1970 provides an excellent case for such an inquiry. In 1950 the number of students enrolled in all its segments — university, state colleges, junior colleges — was slightly more than two hundred thousand. By 1960 this enrollment had grown to almost half a million, and by 1970 it was well over one million — a five-fold increase in enrollment in two decades.[2] The end of the twenty-year period was marked, moreover, by doubts in many quarters as to the wisdom of continuing the headlong pace of growth, and by serious reappraisal of the main framework — the Master Plan for Higher Education of 1960 — within which most of the growth occurred. The period was also marked by frequent episodes of conflict. Its beginning coincided with the famous loyalty oath controversy between the Board of Regents and the faculty of the University of California; the entire period was one of intense competition and conflict among the several segments over the system's resources; and the 1960s are famous for political disruption in the university and state colleges — disruption which reverberated in the state and national political scenes and which probably has not yet run its course.

I do not regard conflict as an automatic or inevitable consequence of rapid growth. Conflict can develop in the absence of growth, and growth is not always accompanied by conflict. Thus, to present my argument for the relationship between the growth of

---

[1] In *Economy and Society* (New York: Free Press, 1956), Talcott Parsons and I developed a model of structural differentiation to account for many of the social-structural changes that occur during periods of rapid economic development. My book, *Social Change in the Industrial Revolution* (Chicago: University of Chicago Press, 1959), was an elaboration of this model and a very detailed effort to apply it to a series of economic and social changes in Great Britain between 1770 and 1840. In *Theory of Collective Behavior* (New York: Free Press, 1962), I attempted to analyze some types of instability that are found in, but not limited to, periods of rapid change. And finally, several of the *Essays in Sociological Explanation* (Englewood Cliffs, N.J.: Prentice-Hall, 1968) deal with growth and modernization — chap. 6 ("Toward a Theory of Modernization"); chap. 7 ("Social Structure, Mobility, and Economic Development," with S. M. Lipset); and chap. 8 ("Toward a General Theory of Social Change.").

[2] For year-by-year figures, see below, Table 2.

the California system of higher education and the conflicts within it, it is necessary to regard this relationship as mediated by a network of intervening processes. My argument can be outlined in the following way:

(1) I identify the major factors that encouraged the system of public higher education to grow and shaped its pattern of growth. Some of these factors were not new in 1950; they had existed since the beginning of higher education in the state. But a particular confluence of factors that gave an unusual impetus to the system emerged in the postwar scene. In particular, I discuss the implications for growth contained in the values under which higher education in California had long been legitimized and institutionalized; the particular demographic and economic pressures to grow; the economic opportunities to grow; and the constitutional and political opportunities and constraints affecting the system.

(2) I trace the main structural responses to these pressures and opportunities to grow. This requires a more or less systematic classification of possible structural responses — increase in size of campuses, increase in numbers of campuses, structural reorganization of campuses, change in type of campuses, and so on. I then demonstrate that the system — conditioned by the constraints of constitution, legislation, vested interest groups, and economic opportunity — responded in the ways it could, but was prevented from responding in other ways.

(3) I trace the main shifts in the fortunes of various academic groups that were associated with the structural responses in these decades. One of the ways to characterize the structural responses is to describe changes in the numbers, proportions, and circumstances of those holding the social positions or roles that are part of the system's structure — lower division student, graduate student, teaching assistant, assistant professor, dean, chancellor, member of Board of Trustees, and so on.[3] One of the bases for the formation of social groups — which I define as aggregates of persons who share a common membership and can be mobilized for collective action — is a common incumbency in the roles of a social structure. Common incumbents have common experiences in relation to the activities,

[3]To describe structural change in this way, moreover, is to provide the transition from the social-structural level to the psychological level of analysis. Positions are described in terms of their significance to the individual incumbents, rather than in terms of their relations to other positions in the social structure.

duties, rights, and rewards associated with their roles. On the basis of these experiences they may develop common attitudes and organize for collective action.[4] These transitions from role membership to group membership, from group membership to common outlook, and from common outlook to group action are not automatic. For example, one category of academic role — holder of undergraduate scholarship — may encompass a large number of individuals, but these individuals may never combine into a group, develop common attitudes, or act on those attitudes. If, however, massive budgetary changes threaten to wipe out a significant number of scholarships, the scholarship students may find themselves faced with a common threat and mobilize to act in concert. Other roles, such as the teaching assistantship, may be under more or less chronic strain, and thus may be more readily mobilized for concerted action in conflict situations.

After characterizing the major structural responses to the pressures to grow, I trace the changing size, shape, composition, and circumstances of some of the academic estates, as I call them, between 1950 and 1970. I also suggest why some of these estates were more dissatisfied than others. In doing this I trace out some of the major "fault lines" of conflict in the system, indicate the kinds of conflict that were likely to occur, and suggest the orientation of the several estates in situations of conflict.

(4) I examine the ability of the system of public higher education to resolve conflicts. In particular, this means focusing on the agencies of coordination and authority of the system, to assess their

---

[4]These sociological observations are scarcely original. They are evident, for example, in the sociology of Karl Marx, who maintained that social groups (classes) crystallize on the basis of common economic positions (bourgeoisie and proletariat, for example), form a common outlook (class consciousness), and act on the basis of that outlook (revolutionary activity). Tocqueville maintained that the outlook of the major estates in eighteenth-century France depended on the complex patterning of social, economic, and political roles, and that these estates were disposed — for different reasons — to accept reformist or revolutionary outlooks and, given the appropriate historical circumstances, to act on them. Alexis de Tocqueville, *The Old Regime and the French Revolution* (Garden City, N.Y.: Doubleday Anchor, 1955). The same general logic informs the theoretical work of Ralf Dahrendorf, especially the notion that quasi groups with latent common interests arise from common positions in authority structures, that these quasi groups may become interest groups with manifest interests, and that these interest groups may become conflict groups. *Class and Class Conflict in Industrial Society* (Stanford: Stanford University Press, 1969), chap. 5.

effectiveness and to trace changes in their structure. The nature and extent of conflict in a system are determined not only by the structural and group bases of the conflicting parties, but also by the system's capacity to sustain and contain conflicts. I attempt to outline a typical cycle, including the following phases: (a) the establishment of machinery for regulation at a given point in time; (b) a period of rapid growth, competition, and conflict that gradually renders the system ungovernable by the previously established machinery; (c) a crisis of coordination and governance; (d) the establishment of new regulatory machinery. The logic underlying this cycle is that a rapidly growing system is forever threatening to outgrow its ability to regulate itself, and it is periodically forced to invent new integrative machinery in the heat of crisis.

In concluding this introduction, I should specify the level at which my analysis is pitched, and I should specify, too, what I am not trying to explain.[5] My preoccupation is with the social forces that generated the institutional vulnerability to crisis and conflict in the system of higher education in California over a period of two decades. I am not making judgments as to the rightness or wrongness of the moral or political stands of the parties to any given conflict, even though — as a citizen of the system I am analyzing — I was often involved in its conflicts and took partisan stands. I am concerned, rather, with *some* of the structural conditions and structural changes that predisposed people to enter such conflicts.[6]

In no sense is my analysis meant to encompass all the factors that made for vulnerability to conflict in California higher education. In particular, that educational system was growing in a set of

[5] The comments of Gabriel Almond and Frank Newman were helpful in setting the explanatory limits of this essay.

[6] My argument here is similar to that of the Joint Committee of Higher Education of the California Legislature, which, during its several years of investigation of California higher education under the Master Plan, was frequently under "strong pressure to divert its attention to matters of student unrest, off-campus political activities, and campus administration." In its final report, the committee explained that it had resisted these pressures "*not* because it has failed to see the relevancy of these matters, but because the majority of the members have remained convinced that the committee could contribute more to the strengthening of California's educational system by dealing with the basic *substantive issues of state policy* than by becoming entangled in all the various conflicts which have occurred over the past few years on and about the campuses." Joint Committee on Higher Education, *The Challenge of Achievement* (Sacramento, Calif., 1969), p. 2.

environments — international, national, Californian, and local campus. These environments were crucial in generating the social and political crises of the 1950s and 1960s — the crises of national foreign and defense policy and of racial, cultural, and local community issues. The issues that troubled the politics of higher education in California were not specific to California higher education or even to higher education in general, but affected all of American society. Higher education throughout the United States and elsewhere was vulnerable to some of these stresses, although the institutions of public higher education in California were probably in a position of peculiar vulnerability. It is this *particular vulnerability to conflict* that I attempt to explain by referring to the variables associated with growth, structural change, and the pattern of authority. My analysis of California's system of higher education, moreover, is not intended to be a general account of educational crises in other parts of the United States and the world. It is based, rather, on a mixture of general insights concerning social change and social conflict on the one hand, and the structural characteristics of the educational system of California on the other.[7]

Nor, finally, do I attempt to trace the development of any particular episode of conflict once it began, for that depends on the operation of more particular determinants — such as the strategic decisions of the parties in conflict, the role of mediators, the role of the press, and so on. Because my approach is macrosociological, I am relatively unconcerned with the key personages — Kerr, Savio, Sheriffs, Hayakawa — and their decisive contributions to the fate of particular conflicts at particular moments. Such concern would require the analysis of case studies of specific decisions and crises.[8]

FACTORS INFLUENCING THE PATTERN OF GROWTH OF CALIFORNIA'S SYSTEM OF HIGHER EDUCATION

The growth of a social system is always conditioned by two general sets of determinants: (1) pressures to grow, and (2) opportunities for and constraints on growth. The term *pressures to grow*

[7] The historical inheritance can be regarded as a number of "parameters," which limit the operation of general variables and within which the general social processes unfold. Therefore, although the processes of social change conform to quite general principles of change, the particular outcome in this case is likely to be quite unique because of the specific historical parameters.

[8] For an example of such a monograph, see Max Heirich, *Berkeley 1964: The Spiral of Conflict* (New York: Columbia University Press, 1970).

refers to a situation in which it is sensed that a system, as institution, is not performing up to the level of the demands being made on it. For example, if a community's high school system is expected to provide four years of secondary education for every young person in the community, and if the community doubles in size, there is obviously pressure on the system to grow. The term *opportunities for growth* refers to the availability of such facilities as financial resources, political support, and lack of legal obstacles. The term *constraints on growth* also refers to facilities, but focuses on their limits. Thus, if three million dollars becomes available to the local high school district to expand its system, this provides an opportunity for expansion, but because it is only three million dollars, it also sets an upper limit to the expansion. Opportunities and constraints are opposite faces of the same coin.

Pressure to Grow

These pressures may be either cultural or situational. Cultural pressures deal with values, outlooks, and expectations that encourage people to make choices that expand the system. Situational pressures stem from the potential clientele that expects an education to produce different kinds of skilled persons for the occupational system, generally educated and responsible citizens for the polity, and so on. How have these two aspects of the pressure to grow affected the state of California?

Two sets of values have worked to legitimize the institutions of higher education in California: competitive excellence and populist egalitarianism.[9] From the very beginning, California's university has had an other-oriented quality. One part of the resolution of 1867, asking the legislature to establish a university, expressed

> an earnest hope and confident expectation that the State of California will forthwith organize and put into operation upon this site [in Oakland], a University of California, which shall include a College of

[9] These values are not unique to California. They are California's cultural version of the more general American values of achievement and equality of opportunity, or "universalistic achievement." For a discussion of these values, see Talcott Parsons, *The Social System* (New York: Free Press, 1951), pp. 182–191. Some variant of these two types of values can also be found in other educational systems as well — for example, in the British tendencies toward aristocratic elitism and mass education, and in the Russian tendencies to educate for building a socialist society, on the one hand, and to realize the values of a "socialist democracy" on the other.

Mines, a College of Agriculture, and an Academical College, all of the same grade, *and with courses of instruction equal to those of Eastern Colleges.*[10]

This ambitious drive to be as good if not better than the elite private universities of the east and the other leading state universities has been important in the vision of many presidents and chancellors, including Clark Kerr. Kerr, more than any other individual, engineered the extraordinary university expansion of the 1950s and 1960s. The drive to excellence is also evident in the enormous pride with which the university counts its Nobel laureates and Guggenheim fellows as compared to other leading universities.[11] And this concern has also been used as an important means of securing budgetary support from the legislature and governor, as well as an important argument against budgetary reductions. Repeatedly, the administrators' and faculty's trump card is to threaten a mass exodus of distinguished faculty, and a decline in prestige, if a particular measure is not supported. Consider a recent variant of this approach — President Charles J. Hitch's testimony before the Assembly Subcommittee on Higher Education:

> What happens if the budget is approved as proposed, with no pay increase? Will there be a mass exodus of faculty? Will students have to be turned away?[12] Will the University of California overnight become a second-rate institution? . . . There will be no mass exodus. But there will be change, it will be for the worse, and no one now can quite predict how bad it will be . . . The competition for good faculty remains as intense as it ever was. Good people will leave and good people will not come, and many of these will be good young people and our future will thus be severely handicapped.[13]

These threats are not always persuasive, and they are seldom carried out, but they do reveal the importance of competitive excellence as a legitimizing basis for supporting university education.

[10] Quoted in Verne A. Stadtman, *The University of California 1868–1968* (New York: McGraw-Hill, 1970), p. 31. Emphasis added.

[11] For example, in the *University Bulletin* of April 19, 1971, a familiar type of announcement revealed that forty-three Guggenheim fellowships were awarded to scholars in the University of California; the numbers granted to scholars in other institutions (Harvard, Columbia, Yale, University of Chicago, Stanford, University of Pennsylvania, and MIT) were also mentioned.

[12] Note that the "mass exodus" argument is an appeal to the value of competitive excellence, whereas the "turning away students" argument is an appeal to the value of equal opportunity.

[13] *University Bulletin*, April 19, 1971.

Similarly, the state colleges are proud of their distinctive intellectual missions,[14] and the junior-college system is proud of its national leadership in the community-college movement.[15] To underscore this premium on California's competitive excellence, the Master Plan legislation decreed, as part of its "general provisions," that "[each] segment of public higher education [university, state colleges, and junior colleges] shall strive for excellence in its sphere."[16]

California is also characterized by a brisk internal competition — between north and south, valley and coast, country and city, one community and another. Because educational institutions are regarded as sources of local wealth and prestige, communities and regions have competed for campuses of their own. In the late 1950s, for example, when the pressure of numbers on California's system of education was very great — because the World War II babies had reached college age — the regional and local competition for expansion was correspondingly intense.

The second set of values, egalitarianism, can best be observed in the appeals for support of the junior colleges — appeals based on the argument that the junior colleges provide local access to post-secondary education for those who would otherwise be deprived of it. One of the earliest appeals to the state Board of Education for the establishment of a junior college was submitted by educators from the district around Fresno in 1910. The appeal argued that a junior college would "give young people of this section of the state . . . an opportunity to continue their studies at home" and that it would "carry students through the first two years of a college course, thus enabling them to complete a four-years' course with but two years' residence."[17]

This principle of extending educational opportunities to the general public has also been a powerful lever in legitimizing the

[14] Glenn S. Dumke, "Goals, Purposes and Functions of the California State Colleges," in *Papers Presented at the Conference on Educational Philosophy* (Los Angeles, January 18, 1966).

[15] Leland L. Medsker and George W. Clark, *State Level Governance of California Junior Colleges*, a report from the Center for Research and Development in Higher Education, University of California, Berkeley, authorized and supported by the California Coordinating Council for Higher Education (Berkeley: August 1966), pp. 1–2.

[16] *California Education Code*, Division 16.5, chap. i, Section 22503.

[17] Quoted in Ralph R. Fields, *The Community College Movement* (New York: McGraw-Hill, 1962), p. 28.

flow of resources to institutions of higher education. One of the recommendations endorsed jointly by the state Board of Education and the regents of the University of California in 1959 read as follows: "In order that a possible new institution may serve the greatest number of eligible students, it should be *placed near the center of the population served by it.*"[18] The principle of popular access was extended with the adoption of the Master Plan, which called for junior colleges to admit "any high school graduate," and even those who have not graduated from high school if it is determined that the student "is capable of profiting from the instruction offered."[19] A report on the junior colleges, submitted to the Coordinating Council for Higher Education in 1966, stated with pride that the goal of putting at least two years of college within the reach of every high school student "has nearly been reached in California."[20]

The egalitarian principle is also embodied in the famous tuition-free principle that held firm in the system of public higher education in California from its beginnings until very recently. When, in 1966–1967, the administration of Governor Ronald Reagan challenged that principle by asking for tuition from resident Californians, most of the opposition argued that tuition would deprive deserving but financially limited students of a chance for higher education. In its defense, the Reagan administration argued that part of the tuition fees would be used to provide financial aid to those who needed it. Partisan opponents of Reagan countered that this compensatory measure was not sufficient. The persuasive power of egalitarianism is so great that both sides attempted to demonstrate the legitimacy of *their* positions in terms of this principle.[21]

[18]T. C. Holy, *Summary of the Work of the Liaison Committee of Regents of the University of California and the State Board of Education, 1945–1960* (Berkeley, March, 1961), p. 11. Italics in original.

[19]*California Education Code*, Division 18.5, Section 22503.

[20]Leland L. Medsker and George W. Clark, *State Level Governance of California Junior Colleges*, a report from the Center for Research and Development in Higher Education, University of California, Berkeley, authorized and supported by the California Coordinating Council for Higher Education (Berkeley, August 1966), p. 51.

[21]Note the reasoning of the Joint Committee on Higher Education — a committee headed by a political opponent of Governor Reagan, Assemblyman Jesse Unruh — on the subject of tuition: "The most persuasive argument for tuition is as a user charge to reduce or eliminate the public subsidy to those who

These cultural factors — a commitment to values of excellence and egalitarianism and a strong competitive spirit — have acted as conditioning factors in the growth of California's educational system. By themselves, such cultural values do not produce growth. But they orient the system in the direction of growth; they predispose decision makers to think in terms of growth when pressures develop and opportunities arise.[22]

Such pressures and opportunities were exceptionally great in the 1950s and 1960s. At the beginning of that twenty-year period, California's population was 10,643,000; by the end it had grown to 19,905,000, making California the most populous state in the country.[23] Furthermore, the structure of California's population made a greater *proportion* of its citizens available for enrollment in public institutions of higher education. California's Coordinating Council for Higher Education noted in 1968 that:

> California is the largest of the fifty states in terms of total population and higher-than-average in the proportion of its total population falling into the eighteen to twenty four year-old category, a rough indicator of the potential student group. California ranks high also in the proportion of the eighteen to twenty four year-old category actually attending some institution of higher education, 13 percent as compared to a 9 percent nationwide average . . . Finally, the state ranked sixth in the proportion of total higher education enrollment handled in public institutions (91 percent).

---

attend public colleges [that is, to reduce or eliminate elitism]. The subsidy results in a flow of benefits which includes, on the average, higher lifetime earnings as well as other, nonmonetary satisfactions. However, if tuition is imposed to reduce the subsidy, it is important to provide for some system of deferred payment so that the burden of tuition falls upon the future income of the students who receive the subsidy rather than upon the current income of their parents." California Legislature, Joint Committee on Higher Education, *The Academic State, A Progress Report to the Legislature on Tuition and Other Matters Pertaining to Higher Education in California* (Sacramento: Spilman, 1968), p. ix.

[22] My methodological position is not dissimilar from Max Weber: "Not ideas, but material and ideal interests, directly govern men's conduct. Yet very frequently the 'word images' that have been created by 'ideas' have, like switchmen, determined the tracks along which action has been pushed by the dynamic of interest." H. H. Gerth and C. Wright Mills (eds.), *From Max Weber: Essays in Sociology* (New York: Oxford University Press, 1958), p. 280. My view is that the cultural outlook dominated by values of competitive excellence and egalitarianism predisposes people to respond to opportunities in ways that expand the system.

[23] Office of Analytical Studies, Vice-President — Business and Finance, University of California, *Fiscal Facts*, p. 43.

The sum total of these factors is a much greater proportion of the state population being accommodated in a public institution of higher education in California than is true, on the average, in other states. [24]

The percentage of total civilian population enrolled in higher education in California was 2.29 in 1950–1951 and about 5 in 1970; the percentage in full-time enrollment expanded from 1.55 to 2.78. [25] This higher participation rate depended on a number of factors, including the tradition of low student charges, the decentralized character of the junior-college system — making a place in a local junior college available in many instances — and the increasing affluence of the state, which enabled a higher proportion of families to send children to college. [26]

The other major increase in demand came from the occupational structure. The period from 1950 to 1970 was very prosperous economically, despite some setbacks. More important, much of the expanded demand was from occupations requiring considerable training in institutions of higher education. The national market for Ph.D.s and others holding advanced professional degrees was vigorous as the nation's educational system expanded rapidly; only toward the end of the period under study did the market for academics begin to contract. Furthermore, the development of electronic, engineering, mass media, and other industries — of which California had a large share — created the expanded need for highly qualified scientists, technicians, and other skilled personnel. The decrease in this demand toward the end of the two decades created serious unemployment problems for scientists and related personnel. Finally, the state — the most urbanized in the country — increased its needs for urban-related occupations, such as criminologists, city planners, social workers, architects, and other highly skilled service occupations. The task of training people

[24] Coordinating Council for Higher Education, *Study of Income for Public Higher Education* (Report 68–11) (Sacramento: May 21, 1968), p. 13.

[25] California Legislature, Joint Committee on Higher Education, *The Academic State: A Progress Report to the Legislature on Tuition and Other Matters Pertaining to Higher Education in California* (Sacramento: October 31, 1967), p. 10. For an indication of the consistently higher percentage of population in educational institutions in California than the rest of the nation in 1960, see *Study of Income*, p. 11.

[26] *Ibid.*, p. 11.

in increasing numbers for such roles fell mainly to the state's system of higher education, which had to expand its facilities accordingly.

Opportunities and Constraints for Growth

The opportunities and constraints for growth also fall into two general categories: the availability of financial resources, and the political–legal encouragement or discouragement of growth.

In real dollars, California's personal income grew from a total of $19,627,000,000 in 1950 to $85,250,000,000 twenty years later. This increase alone would have increased the financial support available to the system of higher education more than fivefold, if the rate of support were constant. That rate increased, however, as the percentage of personal income going to higher education in state expenditures rose from .32 percent in 1950 to .89 percent in 1970, raising the level of general and state support from $62,600,000 in 1950 to $756,800,000 in 1970. These figures are all the more remarkable because they refer only to California state operating expenditures for the system and do not include the special capital outlay expenditures (financed mainly by special bond issues). And these figures do not reflect the fact that the junior colleges — which grew the most in absolute terms from 1950 to 1970 — received most of their support not from state but from community sources.

Perhaps as important as the increased availability of financial resources was the general conviction, early in the period of expansion, that the state could easily finance that expansion. In the late 1940s the Strayer committee, which surveyed the needs of California higher education, concluded calmly that "the state of California has ample resources to meet its educational responsibilities."[27] When these needs were restudied in the early 1950s, the McConnell committee, after estimating income growth, enrollment trends, the tax structure, and a number of other factors, concluded that the amount expended on higher education in 1965 — ten years hence — "would represent no increase in relative burden as com-

[27] Committee on the Conduct of the Study, appointed by the Liaison Committee of the Regents of the University of California and the State Board of Education, *A Report of a Survey of the Needs of California in Higher Education* (Sacramento: March 1, 1948), p. 132.

pared with fiscal year 1954."[28] However, by the time the Master
Plan Survey Team completed its work in 1960, it was evident that
these estimates were much too modest. Costs for 1965 as projected
by the McConnell committee had already been surpassed by
1960.[29] Armed with these errors, with new indications of increasing costs, and with new projections of enrollment, the Technical
Committee on Costs of the Master Plan Survey Team produced a
series of cost projections for the following fifteen years — projections of greater demands on the state's general tax fund than had
heretofore been anticipated. At the same time, the state's welfare
and medical expenditures were also increasing rapidly. Growing
realization of rising pressure on the state's finances in the early
1960s resulted in serious consideration of various economy measures — such as year-round operations to make more efficient use of
capital plant, the imposition of increased student fees, and the end
of the tuition-free principle. Ultimately, the state adopted such
measures. And, in the first year of Governor Reagan's administration, the state embarked on a policy of yearly cutbacks on the level
of support sought by some of the segments of higher education,
thus retarding the rate of growth desired by the educational system.

About the same time it was becoming apparent that the state's
resources were going to be strained to sustain the rate of anticipated growth, the prospect of greatly increased federal aid to
higher education arose. Prior to 1960, the federal government had
undertaken considerable initiative in supporting higher education
with such legislation as the acts supporting the education of returning veterans, the Housing Act of 1950 which originated college
housing loan programs, and the National Defense Education Act of
1958 which provided loans, scholarships, and fellowships to higher
education. A sense of greater expectation, however, accompanied
the election of President John F. Kennedy. In January of 1961, the

[28]T. C. Holy, H. H. Semans, and T. R. McConnel, *A Restudy of the
Needs of California in Education*, prepared for the Liaison Committee of the
Regents of the University of California and the California State Board of Education
(Sacramento: California State Department of Education, 1955), p. 402.

[29]Technical Committee on Costs of Higher Education in California (for the
Master Plan Survey Team and the Liaison Committee of the Regents of the
University of California and the State Board of Education), *The Costs of Higher
Education in California 1960–1975* (Berkeley and Sacramento, January 1960), p.
96.

California Coordinating Council for Higher Education urged the president-elect and the 87th Congress to consider forms of aid such as grants-in-aid for construction, reservation of television channels for educational purposes, and continuing or increasing the support granted in the loan and fellowship programs.[30] During the Kennedy and Johnson administrations, the government did respond to such requests, particularly in the form of the Higher Education Facilities Act of 1963 and the Higher Education Act of 1965, both of which provided numerous types of support. With this legislation, "Federal programs related to higher education reached a degree of scope and magnitude never before known in this country."[31] Also, during the 1950s and 1960s the federal government expanded its support of research in the universities, first through the Department of Defense and subsequently through the Department of Health, Education, and Welfare and the National Science Foundation. After 1966, "a unique year for federal funding," financial stringency also began to be felt at the federal level. Some new acts were passed but not funded, and some existing programs were reduced or eliminated.[32] Higher education in California experienced a convergence of budgetary strictures at *both* the state and federal government levels in the second half of the 1960s.

This remarkable growth of federal — and, to a lesser extent, private foundation — financing of higher education meant that, during the two decades under analysis, extramural sources were assuming an increasing share of the cost of higher education in California. As Table 1 shows, federal grants had grown to almost a quarter of a billion dollars by the banner year, 1966, and loans exceeded fifty million dollars. The proportion of federal expenditures in California's total higher education bill was substantial. In 1967–1968, even though the rate of growth of federal spending had been somewhat curtailed, the federal government contributed 29 percent of the current operating expenditures and 19 percent of the capital outlay expenditures for the University of California; 11 percent of the current operating expenditures and 10 percent of

[30] Coordinating Council on Higher Education, *Minutes*, January 5, 1961, pp. 6–7.
[31] Coordinating Council for Higher Education, *Federal Funds and California Higher Education* (Report 64–14a), (Sacramento, August 1, 1968), p. 6.
[32] *Ibid.*, pp. 6–7.

Table 1
TOTAL GRANT AND LOAN SUPPORT TO CALIFORNIA UNIVERSITIES AND COLLEGES BY TYPE OF SUPPORT AND SEGMENT, FISCAL YEAR 1966 (in dollars)

	Facilities and Equipment		Research and demonstration		Training programs		Individual financial assistance		Institutional grants	Total	
	Grants	Loans	Grants	Loans	Grants	Loans	Grants	Loans	Grants	Grants	Loans
University	36,005,764	0	109,991,684	0	8,056,706	0	26,827,455	3,146,789	758,206	181,639,815	3,146,789
State Colleges	21,073,518	34,940,000	3,742,568	0	8,044,457	0	8,027,541	3,517,039	1,244,000	42,132,084	38,457,039
Junior Colleges	3,118,789	10,498,896	111,542	0	7,273,841	0	4,369,458	389,615	0	14,873,630	10,888,511
TOTAL	60,198,071	45,438,896	113,845,794	0	23,375,004	0	39,224,454	7,053,443	2,002,206	238,645,429	52,492,329

Source: Coordinating Council for Higher Education, *Federal Funds and California Higher Education*, p. 88.

the capital outlay expenditures of the California state colleges; and 3 percent of the current operating expenditures and 5 percent of the capital outlay expenditures of the junior colleges.[33] These figures indicate both the magnitude of the federal effort, particularly at the university level, and the degree to which the federal government was responsible for providing the facilities necessary for the system's overall growth.

Finally, let us examine some of the characteristics of the political–legal framework, with special reference to their facilitating or constraining influence on the growth pattern of the system of higher education. As I have noted, higher education in California has developed into three tiers or segments — the university, the state colleges (state universities, as a result of the statutory name change in 1972), and the junior colleges. The university had its official beginning in 1868, when the state legislature passed an act creating the University of California. The California state colleges had their beginnings even earlier, when the San Jose state normal school was established as a teacher training institution in 1862. Seven more normal schools were established by 1919. The legislature authorized the normal schools to become teachers' colleges in 1921 and to confer the bachelor's degree in 1923. By 1935, the word *teachers* was dropped, and these institutions became general state colleges. The California junior colleges had their official beginning in 1907, and the first public junior college was established in Fresno in 1910.

Throughout the history of higher education in California, these three segments have differed mainly according to their functions. Although there has been continuing competition over these functions, the state has always attempted to maintain more or less consistent lines of differentiation among the segments. Let me review some of these lines of differentiation.

When the state Council for Educational Planning and Coordination was established in 1933, it set some guidelines for functional differentiation among the junior colleges, the state colleges, and the university. The junior colleges, the council maintained, should provide training for that "considerable part of the graduates of our high schools, [which,] while disinclined toward the industrial

[33] Figures calculated from Table 2.9, *The Challenge of Achievement, op. cit.* (n. 2, above), p. 24.

trades, is not adapted to advanced academic studies";[34] they should also provide academic work for those equipped to go on to further higher education; and they should "serve as cultural centers providing adult education for the people of their communities."[35] The teachers colleges were "to prepare teachers for the elementary schools, for the intermediate or junior high schools, and for such phases of supervision of instruction and administration in the elementary schools as do not involve courses on the graduate level."[36] In carrying out this function, however, it was expected that the teachers colleges would include a broad program of liberal arts courses. The council listed the functions of the university as "(1) professional training; (2) development of the individual; (3) research in all matters that are of significance to the human race."[37] This division of functions did provide some guidance for those developing curricula in different institutions and for the governing agencies of higher education, such as the state Board of Education. But it did not prevent the major modification of function of 1935, when the teachers colleges became general state colleges, and it did not prevent continuous agitation by local communities for the establishment of new colleges or conversion of their junior colleges into four-year colleges.[38]

Once again, in 1947, the state legislature commissioned a general survey of the needs of higher education in California. There was at the time a vigorous movement on the part of two-year colleges to transform themselves into four-year institutions.[39] The

[34]California State Council on Educational Planning and Coordination, "Statement of Basic Principles and of the Respective Functions and Programs of the Junior College, the Teachers College, and the University" (November 1, 1934), p. 2.

[35]*Ibid.*, p. 3.

[36]*Ibid.*, p. 4.

[37]*Ibid.*, p. 5.

[38]Stadtman, *op. cit.* (n. 10, above), p. 263. For an attempt to delineate the functions of the three segments in 1939 — similar to the one in 1934 — see J. Herschel Coffin, *The Role of the State College in Higher Education in California* (Sacramento: California State Department of Education, Office of the Director of Education, November, 1939). Coffin was then the curriculum coordinator for California state colleges.

[39]Both the regional college movement and the four-year college movement occurred in the context of an increased demand on the educational system. California's population had increased by almost two-thirds in the 1920s, and the immediate postwar pressure on the system was created by the masses of returning veterans who wanted to complete their education.

Strayer committee attempted again to delineate the functions of the several segments. It argued firmly that the junior colleges should remain two-year institutions, providing a terminal vocational program, a lower-division transfer program, and general and adult education.[40] The Strayer committee also reiterated the primary function of the state colleges as "the training of teachers" but acknowledged the appropriateness of general or liberal education programs in some vocational areas, and of preprofessional courses for those planning to transfer to universities.[41] The university's functions, as before, were to be research, graduate and professional instruction, as well as undergraduate liberal arts instruction.[42]

The Strayer report was influential in subduing the movement to convert two-year colleges into four-year colleges. However, in 1949, shortly after the report was issued, the state colleges gained legislative authorization to grant the master's degree in education, their first foray into graduate instruction. In 1955, a follow-up committee generally endorsed the principle of differentiation set forth by the Strayer committee but qualified it by saying that some overlapping was justified. In particular, they noted

> the necessity of including a substantial, well-planned core of general and liberal education in all special curriculums, whether offered in the junior colleges, the state colleges, or the University. This is not to say that all these institutions should have uniform programs of general and liberal education. In fact, the relationship between general education and special education of different kinds and levels may lead to varied rather than uniform practices, as it has in the past.
>
> Furthermore, the state colleges and the University of California on its several campuses should continue to offer to qualified students a four-year program of liberal education . . . this is a function which the state colleges now perform for many students.[43]

The years following 1955 were marked by several legislative proposals to create new four-year colleges and to change the functions of existing institutions. Pressure from the state colleges for the right to grant the doctorate also mounted. This competitive

[40]*A Report of a Survey of the Needs of California in Higher Education, op. cit.,* (n. 27, above), pp. 4–18.

[41]*Ibid.,* p. 21.

[42]*Ibid.,* pp. 36–45.

[43]*Ibid.,* p. 93.

pressure threatened to develop into planless, headlong, and expensive growth that would lead to a substantial overlapping if not duplication of functions. The legislature, concerned over the implications of this growing competition, commissioned the Master Plan Survey Team in 1959 to design recommendations for legislation delineating the proper functions and promoting the orderly growth of higher education in California. The recommendations of the Survey Team were enacted into law in 1960 and have remained virtually unchanged since that time. They have constituted the legal framework for subsequent growth. What were the major lines of differentiation set forth in the Master Plan?

According to the Master Plan, the university was to remain "the primary state-supported academic agency for research" and was to have "the sole authority in public higher education to award the doctoral degree in all fields of learning," although it could establish joint doctoral degrees with state colleges in selected areas. In addition, the university was given "exclusive jurisdiction in public higher education over instruction in the profession of law, and over graduate instruction in the professions of medicine, dentistry, veterinary medicine, and architecture." Following the principle of "justified overlapping" recommended by the Restudy Team, however, the Master Plan legislation provided that "[the] university may provide instruction in the liberal arts and sciences and in the professions, including the teaching profession."[44]

The Master Plan legislation assigned to the state colleges the primary function of providing "instruction for undergraduate students and graduate students, through the master's degree, in the liberal arts and sciences, in applied fields and in the professions, including the teaching profession." It also authorized "faculty research . . . to the extent that it is consistent with the primary function of the state colleges and the facilities provided for that function." And to minimize overlapping with the junior colleges, the legislation authorized the continuation of specific existing two-year programs in agriculture, but limited any future two-year programs to those "mutually agreed upon by the trustees of the California State colleges and the State Board of Education."[45]

The functions of the junior colleges laid down in the Master

[44]*Education Code*, Division 16.5, chap. ii.
[45]*Ibid.*, chap. iii, Section 22606.

Plan legislation were identical in substance if not in language to those recommended in 1934 by the state Council for Educational Planning and Coordination:

> Public junior colleges shall offer instruction through but not beyond the fourteenth grade level, which instruction may include, but shall not be limited to, programs in one or more of the following categories: (1) standard collegiate courses for transfer to higher institutions; (2) vocational and technical fields leading to employment; and (3) general or liberal arts courses. Studies in these fields may lead to the associate in arts or associate in science degree.[46]

In the period after World War II, a number of California state colleges were established — at Long Beach, Los Angeles, Hayward, Sonoma, Stanislaus, and Fullerton — without lower-division instruction. As these colleges developed, however, one after another decided to introduce lower-division instruction and thus bring themselves into line with the general pattern of the four-year college with limited offerings at the master's level.[47] In 1967, a staff report to the Coordinating Council for Higher Education suggested the elimination of the lower division at some large campuses with ambitious graduate and research programs (such as Berkeley and UCLA),[48] but this recommendation was never implemented. Finally, the junior colleges have been limited largely to two-year instruction, although a few specialized programs of three and more years have been developed in special technical subjects.[49]

The legislation of the Master Plan — combined with the initiative referendum of 1946 — fixed into law the general principle that an institution could not transfer from one segment to another. A junior college could not become a state college, because it was generally prohibited from offering courses beyond the fourteenth year. A state college could not become a university campus because of the prohibition on the granting of the doctorate and professional degrees and the limitations on its research function.

[46]*Ibid.*, chap. iv, Section 22651.

[47]Coordinating Council for Higher Education, *Feasibility and Desirability of Eliminating Lower Division Programs at Selected Campuses of the University of California and the California State Colleges* (January 6, 1967), pp. 34–36.

[48]*Ibid.*, p. 157.

[49]Coordinating Council for Higher Education, *The More-Than-Two-Year Junior College Program in California* (Report 67–14), (Sacramento: October 30–31, 1967).

Furthermore, the university could not acquire a state college or a junior college campus and make it one of its own campuses.

But the Master Plan legislation did allow for some overlapping, especially in instruction. All segments were permitted to offer general or liberal arts programs in the lower division; both the state colleges and the university were permitted to offer four-year general or liberal arts programs; and considerable overlapping in instruction leading to the master's degree was permitted between the state colleges and the university. This meant that "there [were] no absolute limitations placed upon the University in providing instruction of a collegiate and graduate nature," and that "the California State Colleges [were] relatively free to offer most courses of study leading to a baccalaureate or master's degree."[50] This further implied that the three segments could compete for students at the upper division level, although the Master Plan Survey Team recommended that by 1975 both the university and the state colleges establish an overall sixty-forty ratio between upper division and lower division students.[51] The legislation also provided for some overlap in the research function, although the state colleges were restricted to research linked to undergraduate and first-stage graduate instruction. Nevertheless, the differentiation of the research function left some room for competition between the state colleges and the university.

What were the general implications of this pattern of differentiation of functions for the growth and structural responses of the system of higher education? First, the legislation did not set any limits in principle on the level of growth that could be attained *within* each functional segment. But the Master Plan legislation did set definite restrictions on the *directions* of growth permitted each sector. The principle of functional differentiation specified not only what functions a given sector could perform but also what functions it could not perform. Under the Master Plan legislation, it was possible both to increase the size of individual junior colleges and to form new junior colleges, thus increasing the junior college's

[50] Coordinating Council for Higher Education, *Feasibility and Desirability of Eliminating Lower Division Courses, op. cit.* (n. 47, above), pp. 42, 44.
[51] Master Plan Survey Team (for the Liaison Committee of the State Board of Education and the Regents of the University of California), *A Master Plan for Higher Education in California 1960–1975* (Sacramento: Assembly of the State of California, 1960), p. 14.

functions. But a junior college could not grow in the direction of adding new functions (research, upper division instruction, and so on) which were reserved for the other segments. It was possible to increase the size of individual state colleges and to form new state colleges, but it was not possible to add new functions that were reserved for the university. And because the university could not absorb other institutions, it also had to grow by increasing the size of its existing campuses or adding new ones. Although a good deal of diversity among the various campuses of the various segments was permitted, the principle of fairly rigid functional differentiation set definite constraints on the aspirations, possible structural responses, and patterns of growth of each segment.

Second, because the various functions were grouped together in a bundle for each segment by the legislation of the Master Plan — and, to a degree, by the policies followed before its enactment — some limits were placed on the degree of specialization that any given campus could attain. The fact that the Master Plan legislation called for vocational, transfer, and liberal arts courses constituted a restriction on the degree of specialization of a junior college campus; presumably, it would not become solely a vocational school with no transfer or liberal arts courses, or solely a transfer institution with no vocational or general preparation — although curricular patterns might be expected to vary in emphasis by virtue of geographical location, socioeconomic background of students, and so on.[52] The state college could expand its functions by adding new master's programs and even some research programs, but because of the tendency to retain the whole of a four-year preparation program, it could not easily shed existing functions and become a more specialized institution. The university could also expand in all of its functions — graduate training, research, professional training, undergraduate training, and so on. But it became, in practice, impossible to establish publicly supported graduate schools (with no lower division instruction), publicly supported research academies (with no formal instructional or degree-granting powers), or publicly supported upper division schools (with no lower division instruction) because these were institutionalized as a bundle. This bundling of functions by segment facilitates the prolifera-

[52] Coordinating Council for Higher Education, *Feasibility and Desirability of Eliminating Lower Division Courses, op. cit.*, p. 50.

tion of standardized, multifunctional educational institutions, although the legislation did permit differences in organization and cultural tone of individual campuses.

Furthermore, because the complexity of functions increased from junior college to state college and from state college to university, the possibility of functional overloading became greater for each segment. The junior colleges were restricted to two-year instruction with basically three types of program. The state colleges were clearly not vocationally oriented at the lower division as the junior colleges were, but they did offer a wide range of general or liberal arts programs. In addition, they had upper division programs in great variety, considerable numbers of master's programs, and a modest number of research programs. The university duplicated the liberal or general education programs of the state colleges in large degree and shared with them the education for master's degrees (although there were differences in emphasis). But the university had, in effect, sole jurisdiction over the doctorate and some professional degrees and placed much greater emphasis on research. This meant that a state college campus was likely to be more multifunctional than a junior college campus, and that a university campus was likely to be more multifunctional than a state college campus. This principle will be important when I come to the analysis of the distinctive structural responses of the system to growth and the emergence of academic estates in the 1950s and 1960s.

One final political factor that affected the growth of higher education must be mentioned. In the last analysis, the authorization for growth had to come from the state legislature. And the establishment of any new state college or junior college had to be authorized by legislative act. This meant that although decisions to grow (that is, to establish new units) depended in part on the formal recommendations of the governing or coordinating bodies (for example, the Board of Regents, the state Board of Education, the Liaison Committee between those two bodies, or the Coordinating Council for Higher Education), the political realities decreed that the several educational segments, as well as regions and communities, could exert direct influence on legislators with respect to budgetary allocations, the establishment of new campuses, and so on. Moreover, because of the peculiar character of the legislature — namely, that it is composed of representatives elected by local constituencies — it is probably less effective in restricting growth than would be a body less responsive to an electorate. Legislators are vulnerable to pressure from localities, regions, and educational segments, and so they are tempted to satisfy these demands (for example, for a new junior college) by political bartering with other legislators. Bartering, moreover, provides only limited safeguards against growth that is unregulated by considerations other than the general availability of resources, because the various representatives are eager to accommodate their constituencies by passing favorable legislation and to accommodate their fellow representatives by compromise. The legislative mechanism for authorizing growth, in short, is probably more inclined to encourage growth than are more purely administrative mechanisms. This is not to claim that administrative authorizing agencies are free from such political processes; but they are less prone to engage in them than are legislative bodies in which political compromise is institutionalized as normal business.

To summarize, the rapid growth of the California system of higher education in the 1950s and 1960s was in many ways overdetermined. By virtue of their commitment to the values of competitive excellence and egalitarianism, the leaders and citizens of the state *wanted* the system to grow; because of great demographic and economic pressures, it *had* to grow; because of the availability of substantial financial resources from many quarters, it *could* grow; and because the political forces regulating the growth were found, in the long run, in the state's representative bodies, the state was not very well equipped to *prevent* the system from growing.[53] At the same time, however, the legal and political structure of the state constituted a complex pattern of opportunities for and constraints on growth. As a result of this structure, and of the differential availability of resources and the competition among the several segments, the state's system encouraged some types of growth and structural responses and inhibited others.

[53] These four types of encouragement to grow correspond to the four functional exigencies (and types of resources) developed by Talcott Parsons and his associates. Cultural pressures correspond to the latent pattern-maintenance and tension-management system in Parsons' classification; the situational pressures correspond to a deficit in the goal-attainment system; the relative abundance of financial resources correspond to the adaptive system; and the legal–political framework corresponds to the integrative system. See Talcott Parsons and Neil J. Smelser, *Economy and Society* (New York: Free Press, 1956), chap. 5.

STRUCTURAL RESPONSES TO THE PRESSURE TO GROW

Size, Structure, and Function

The peculiar confluence of these pressures and opportunities to expand led to an explosive growth of the system of higher education in California between 1950 and 1970. The gross dimensions of this growth are shown in Table 2. The numerical total swelled

Table 2

TOTAL ENROLLMENTS IN PUBLIC INSTITUTIONS OF
HIGHER EDUCATION
(head count, exclusive of extension programs)

Year	Total enrollment	Percent increase
1950	206,921	—
1951	199,890	—3%
1952	207,002	4
1953	246,385	19
1954	274,596	11
1955	302,294	10
1956	343,804	14
1957	382,001	11
1958	426,691	12
1959	444,516	4
1960	484,292	9
1961	530,285	9
1962	579,319	9
1963	632,404	9
1964	693,784	10
1965	777,548	12
1966	826,973	6
1967	891,746	8
1968	975,832	9
1969	1,053,361	8

Source: California State Department of Finance

continuously throughout the two decades. During the very early 1950s the growth was slow — reflecting in part the departure of many veterans. But in the middle and late 1950s the growth rate was consistently higher than 10 percent, and it was almost that high in the 1960s. Table 2 represents an enormous increase in one of the central functions of higher education — educating students. And the availability of research funds also increased dramatically during most of this period.

Growth of this magnitude in any system invariably raises the question of whether the existing structures of the system can cope with it. This question has long been familiar to biologists — the question of size, shape, and function. With respect to living organisms, these three variables set definite limits on one another. For example, a creature the size of a horse but the shape of a spider could not function at all, because the enormous mass could not be supported by the relatively thin legs. To state the interrelations more generally:

> A particular shape limits the possible size; a particular function will only work well for a particular size and shape. As size increases the shape must be changed to meet the new forces implied, and the functions modified appropriately . . . the study of morphology and comparative anatomy is a study of the problem of getting a shape that will fit the size that has grown, and of adapting functions to the shape and size. The survival of the species depends on the solution of these problems.[54]

The hazards of regarding social systems as analogous to physiological organisms are too familiar to require reciting here.[55] Nevertheless, the physiological analogy does permit us to ask a number of similar questions about changes in social systems, even though we should not expect the answers to be the same.

What changes in size and structure are demanded by changes in function? The demands made on California's system of public higher education in the 1950s and 1960s necessitated, above all, an increase in the performance of activities relating to the system's major *functions* (teaching and research). In this portion of the essay I ask: what kinds of adaptations — what changes in size and structure — did the system of higher education in California experience in response to these demands?

In answering this question, I first outline, in the abstract, the responses that were theoretically *possible* for the system. Second, I

[54] Mason Haire, "Size, Shape, and Function in Industrial Organizations," *Human Organization*, 14 (1955): 18.
[55] Ernst Nagel, *The Structure of Science* (Princeton, N.J.: Princeton University Press, 1961), pp. 520–535.

argue that not all of these possible responses were *equally available* to the system because of its distinctive pattern of constraints and opportunities. Third, I trace the *actual* responses that unfolded in the system of public higher education during the 1950s and 1960s.

General Statement: Possible Structural Responses [56]

Under pressure to increase the performance of a system's functional activities, six structural responses are available:

(1) *To increase the size of the system's units, without modifying their structure.* In an educational system, this would mean increasing the numbers of students, faculty members, and administrative personnel on its campuses in equal proportions. The size of the faculty in each department would grow, the number of majors would grow, and so on, but the structure of the campuses would remain the same. No new departments would be formed, no new layers of administration. The demands for greater performance of function are met by *increases in scale.*

But sooner or later this response reaches a limit, and the quality of performance suffers. For example, one cannot teach a class of several hundred students in the same way one teaches a class of twenty or thirty; nor can a dean maintain the same kind of personal relationship with each of fifteen or twenty thousand students that is possible with three or four hundred students. To put it more generally, increases in scale soon become unmanageable and usually lead to changes toward centralizing and standardizing the direction of the system. [57]

(2) *To create new, separate units that are similar in structure*

[56] The statement that follows is a theoretical elaboration of my earlier work on the process of structural differentiation as a typical response to dissatisfaction with the performance of a system. See Neil J. Smelser, *Social Change in the Industrial Revolution* (Chicago: University of Chicago Press, 1959), especially chap. 1. Although the theory of structural differentiation does not rule out structural responses other than differentiation, these responses have never been classified systematically and related to differentiation. In this essay I examine some of these alternatives. Indeed, the essay's main theme is that the system of higher education in California failed to differentiate structurally to a significant degree during a period of exceptionally great pressure to grow, that it relied on other types of responses, and that by understanding this distinctive pattern of responses we can learn much about the system's vulnerability to conflict.

[57] Robert Michels' attempt to demonstrate the inevitability of oligarchy (that is, centralization of authority) rested largely on his contention that as the size of an organization increases, it becomes progressively impossible to realize the ideal of

to the existing units. This is the process of *segmentation.* A familiar economic example is the proliferation of wholesale outlets for automobile sales as the population of a given urban area increases. The outlets do not differ from one another significantly in structure or function, but performance is improved through an increased number of units. In an educational system, segmentation means creating new campuses that are basically similar to one another in function.

(3) *To shift the emphasis of functional activities, so that some parts of the system perform more, others less.* A given institution, such as Princeton or Cornell, may have performed several functions — undergraduate, graduate, and professional education, and research — for a long time, but with a greater emphasis on the undergraduate educational functions. Given a demand and opportunities for research, however, such institutions may shift their emphasis. In this shift no new functions have arisen, and no new structures are created.

(4) *To add or discard functions.* When a college that has traditionally been exclusively undergraduate begins to offer graduate instruction, it takes on a new function. When a residential college becomes a commuter college and converts its residential facilities into educational facilities, it discards the function of housing and feeding the student population. When a teaching institution encourages its faculties to seek external support for research activities, it takes on a new function. When a campus with a tradition of informally handling legal infractions — such as disturbing the peace or stealing books — in the office of the dean of students adopts a policy of turning all legal infractions over to the civil authorities, it has discarded one of its functions of social control.

Like increases in scale, the responses of shifting, adding, or discarding functional activities soon reach a limit in the absence of structural changes to accommodate the changing patterns. For example, a four-year college can begin offering courses in graduate instruction on an informally organized basis, but as this increases, a graduate department or a graduate division — some structure — must be fashioned for dealing with the new activities. Two types of

---

equal participation in decision-making, and that this concentrates power in the hands of the few. *Political Parties,* trans. Eden and Cedar Paul (New York: Dover, 1959), pt. I, chap. 2.

structural change are available to a system under pressure to increase its performance:

(5) *To add new structures with different functions, without substantially modifying the existing structures.* For example, if there is a demand for more applied instruction in the social sciences, the campus might add a school or department of public policy with distinctive functions of its own but not formally alter the functions of the existing social science departments. Or, if there is an increased demand or opportunity for research, a university campus might develop distinctive structures — such as organized research units, new types of libraries, or new laboratories — which would not substantially affect the formal functions of existing departments.

(6) *To differentiate units structurally.* Structural differentiation is the splitting of general-function units into two or more specialized units. A well-analyzed example of this is the changing structure of the family under conditions of industrialization, when the family loses its function of economic production to more specialized units (such as factories and offices) and itself becomes more specialized as a socializing agency.[58] An example of structural differentiation in an educational system would be to split a university into a teaching institution and a research academy. Or a four-year college would be split into two types of institutions, one dealing with the lower division. Or a general university would be subdivided into separate graduate and undergraduate institutions, with separate faculties and administrations. In each case new, more specialized units are created.

When new structural units appear — whether by differentiation, structural addition, or segmentation — they pose new integrative problems for the system. First, by which principles and mechanisms will resources be *allocated* to the new units? Second, what effect will the presence of new units have on the process of *adjudication* of demands for allocation of resources? Third, how will activities of the new units be *coordinated?* Coordination deals with overlapping and duplication of activities, setting limits to the level of activity in the various units, and regulating the rate of growth of the different parts of the system.

[58] Cf. William F. Ogburn and Meyer Nimkoff, *Technology and the Changing Family* (Boston: Houghton-Mifflin, 1955); Smelser, *Social Change in the Industrial Revolution, op. cit.* (n. 1, above).

The Availability of Structural Responses in the California System of Higher Education, 1950–1970

Let me return momentarily to the discussion of the legal and political framework embodied in the Master Plan and in the educational policies preceding its adoption, to review its adaptability to different structural responses.

The most striking feature of the principle of differentiation of functions is that, although it envisioned a fixed pattern of differentiation among the segments, it effectively prevented *further* structural differentiation within the segments as a structural response. By bundling the functions as it did, the principle of differentiation of functions foreclosed the development of more specialized institutions, such as research academies, graduate schools, vocational schools, upper division schools, and so on.[59] Some specialization was permitted, in that a new university campus was not *required* to include graduate instruction and research, and a new state college campus was not *required* to offer instruction in graduate programs or encourage faculty research. Yet new campuses in both segments were required to offer four-year collegiate programs as a base. And, in practice, even campuses established with this minimum degree of differentiation tended to move toward becoming general campuses under the pressure to grow and to gain prestige and financial support.

Similarly, the principle of functional differentiation placed constraints on the response of adding and discarding functions. The junior college had to devote at least a minimum portion of its activities to fulfilling its three major functions — vocational, transfer, and general instruction — at the lower division, but it could not, except under very special circumstances, expand or discard its functions. The state colleges, in practice, had to offer four years of liberal arts instruction, and they could expand their functions to graduate instruction and research — although there were fairly strict limits on both. Finally, the university had to offer four years of liberal arts instruction, and its campuses could expand graduate instruction and research to all realms deemed academically suitable. It must be noted, however, that during the decades being discussed, the lines of differentiation were occasionally redrawn, permitting state colleges first to offer the master's degree in educa-

[59] Some exceptions to this principle should be noted — for example, the Hastings Law School, which is a structurally separate, specialized institution.

tion (1949), then other masters' degrees (middle 1950s) and the joint doctorate (1960). Nevertheless, the general limits on adding and discarding functions remained consistent and strict throughout the two decades.

The legal framework, however, did not prohibit considerable shifts in emphasis of function. Because the education code did not specify what proportion of the university's resources should go to research, graduate instruction, and undergraduate instruction, these proportions were subject to variation in the light of policy changes and changing demands and opportunities. Furthermore, so far as the legal framework permitted the addition of functions within limits and shifts in functional emphasis, some structural additions were also permitted. That is to say, new structures (departments) could be formed if they were appropriately authorized and funded. And finally, the legal framework did not lay down any prohibitions, in principle, on the final two structural responses — increases in scale and segmentation — although policy decisions by the governing boards, coordinating agencies, and the state legislature influenced the degree to which the system relied on such increases.

During the 1950s and 1960s, then, we should expect that policy decisions concerning growth, as well as the actual pattern of growth, should have focused on the structural responses of increases in scale, segmentation, shifts in functional emphasis, and structural additions. But because the differentiation of functions was quite rigidly fixed — except for a few critical moments in which the functions were modestly redefined — the response of adding and discarding functions was relied on rarely, and that of structural differentiation not at all. Generally speaking, growth took place within a fixed system of functional specialization.

The Pattern of Structural Responses, 1950–1970

Before the enactment of the Master Plan, many of the policies relating to growth were adopted under considerable political pressure on the legislature to establish new campuses or change the functions of the existing ones. A succession of survey committees issued detailed reports, many parts of which became guidelines for the governing bodies of the several segments and for legislative action. Such was the pace of growth of the system, however, and such was the competition for new institutions in the 1950s, that each set of guidelines soon became obsolete, and a new survey committee would be appointed to come up with a new set of recommendations.

In tracing the pattern of structural responses of the system, I shall consider, first, increases in scale and segmentation; second, changes in functional emphasis; and, third, structural additions.

Increases in scale and segmentation before the Master Plan. The 1948 report of the Strayer committee recommended specific ways of tightening the lines of functional differentiation among the three segments — to limit junior colleges to two-year institutions; to give them a larger role in preparing students for upper division work elsewhere; to eliminate two-year transfer courses by the state colleges; and to reaffirm that the university emphasize professional, graduate, and research functions. All these recommendations were adopted by the Liaison Committee of the regents of the university and the state Board of Education.[60] Within those lines of differentiation, the committee opted for segmentation of new units, rather than increases in scale, as a means of accommodating new students. The committee was convinced that the enlargement of existing institutions was less economical than the establishment of new campuses, and that large student enrollments lead to conditions of impersonality, unwieldiness, mechanical instruction, and a deterioration in educational quality. Committee members also argued that a geographical spread of institutions would serve the needs of the state.

The committee called for the establishment of some new campuses to accommodate increasing numbers of students. It recommended a liberal arts program on the Davis campus, which had until then been mainly a center for agricultural training and research, and the development of a four-year university campus at Riverside (opened in 1953). It called for the establishment of three state colleges, in Sacramento, Los Angeles, and Long Beach.

Clearly the pattern of growth stressed in 1948 was that of segmentation, with clear limits on increases in scale. The university campuses adhered to a twenty thousand maximum enrollment during the Strayer period, but the state colleges clearly did not adhere to their limitations of five to six thousand, and junior colleges expanded both in average size and in numbers of institutions.

[60] Holy, *Summary of the Work, op. cit.* (n. 18, above), p. 3.

Especially in the state college segment (See Chart 1) the system could not absorb the growth it was experiencing within the limits set by the Strayer report. Some of the state colleges had surpassed those limits, and the legislature was beginning to feel the pressure of requests to establish more new colleges. Accordingly, in 1953, the legislature authorized the Restudy Team to reassess the needs for higher education in California.

Chart 1
GROWTH CURVES FOR STATE COLLEGES
ESTABLISHED BEFORE 1950

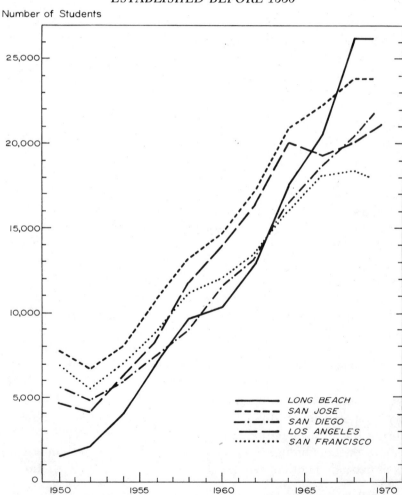

Chart 1 cont'd.

Number of Students

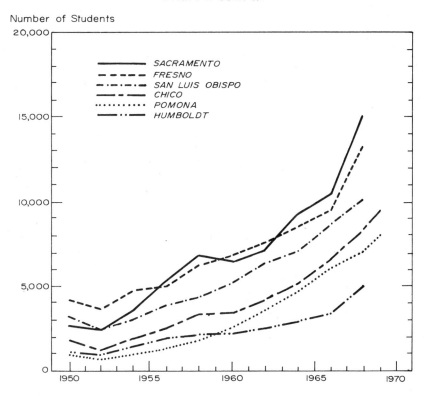

The Restudy Team challenged the assumptions of the Strayer committee, dismissing most of them as "largely qualitative judgments."[61] The team saw no evidence that the large campuses of the university offered a lower quality of education than the smaller state colleges; it pointed out that existing campuses were in areas of concentrated population in any case, and that proposed dormitory facilities could accommodate students from outlying areas; and it argued that large institutions were more economical.[62] This reasoning led the Restudy Team to recommend that no new state college or university campuses be established before 1965, and that enrollment ceilings for campuses in both segments be lifted. Thus, although the team foresaw an enrollment of 245,000 by 1965 — almost twice the number projected for 1955 — it con-

[61] Holy, *A Restudy, op. cit.* (n. 28, above), p. 38.
[62] *Ibid.*, pp. 39–40.

cluded that "no insurmountable obstacles prevent the expansion of the state colleges to accommodate the estimated enrollments," and that "the University of California seems to have available sufficient land to accommodate the estimated enrollments at all campuses, with the possible exception of the Berkeley campus."[63] The structural responses that were encouraged by the Restudy Team, then, were increases in scale for the university and state college system, and essentially no limits on either segmentation or increases in scale for the junior colleges.

These policies were adopted in 1955 by the Liaison Committee of the regents and the state Board of Education.[64] For a time the system continued to grow within the limits set by the Restudy Team's policies. The university grew exclusively by expanding the scale of operations on its existing campuses. Berkeley's enrollment grew from 16,742 in 1955 to 20,825 in 1960; enrollment at UCLA from 14,924 to 17,275; enrollment at Davis from 1,872 in 1955 to 2,872 in 1960; at Riverside from 680 in 1955 to 1,574 in 1960; and at Santa Barbara from 1,967 to 3,397 in 1960. The large urban state college campuses at Long Beach, San Jose, San Diego, Los Angeles, and San Francisco experienced an explosive growth, almost doubling their enrollments between 1955 and 1960, as shown in Chart 1. The junior colleges, encouraged by the policies of the Restudy Team, continued their brisk growth, from sixty-one campuses in 1955 with a total enrollment of 211,184 to sixty-six campuses in 1960 with a total enrollment of 340,049. The average enrollment at the junior college campuses grew from 3,462 to 4,846 in these years.

Yet even these policies did not stem the pressure for new institutions. In 1955 alone, when the Restudy Team submitted its recommendation that no new campuses be established before 1965, bills to establish nineteen new state colleges were introduced into the legislature,[65] and in response to continuing pressure, several new colleges were established between 1955 and 1960.[66] The 1957 "Additional Centers" report also raised the question of establishing several new university campuses. The regents approved

[63] *Ibid.*, pp. 19, 41.
[64] Holy, *A Summary of the Work, op. cit.*, p. 7.
[65] Stadtman, *op. cit.* (n. 10, above), pp. 385–386.
[66] Alameda County State College (later Hayward), Stanislaus State College, Sonoma State College, and Orange State College (later Fullerton).

plans for three new campuses of the university — Santa Cruz, Irvine, and San Diego — but these were not to appear until the early 1960s.[67] Support continued in the late 1950s for continued expansion of the junior colleges.

The effect of these policies — and their implementation — is indicated by the differential rates of growth of the three segments as shown in Table 3. At the very beginning of the decade, the entire system shrank slightly with the departure of many World

Table 3
TOTAL ENROLLMENTS IN CALIFORNIA PUBLIC INSTITUTIONS BY
SECTOR *(head count, exclusive of extension programs)*

Year	Junior Colleges	Percent Increase	State Colleges	Percent Increase	University	Percent Increases
1950	134,585	—	33,500	—	38,836	—
1951	133,780	−1	31,227	−7	34,883	−10
1952	139,643	4	33,589	7	33,770	−3
1953	174,419	25	38,584	12	33,382	−1
1954	194,510	12	45,206	17	34,880	4
1955	211,184	8	52,943	17	38,167	9
1956	240,709	14	62,785	19	40,313	6
1957	267,879	11	72,083	15	42,039	4
1958	302,183	13	81,030	12	43,478	3
1959	311,794	3	87,844	8	44,878	3
1960	340,049	9	95,081	8	49,162	10

Source: California State Department of Finance

War II veterans (see Table 2). After that time, however, the system as a whole grew rapidly, usually at a rate of more than 10 percent each year. However, the segments fared very differently. The junior college enrollment was two-and-one-half times as great at the end of the decade as at the beginning, which reflected both the establishment of many new campuses (segmentation) and the growth of numbers of the campuses (increases in scale). State college enrollments almost tripled, and this is accounted for mainly by the explosive growth of the large urban campuses, the more mod-

[67] In 1956 the regents voted to expand the faculty and facilities of the La Jolla campus to provide a graduate program in science and technology, with whatever undergraduate instruction was essential to support the graduate program. Such an expansion was begun in 1957–1958, but no undergraduates attended the campus until 1964.

est growth of the outlying campuses, and the establishment of
several new campuses in the second half of the decade. The
university's rate of expansion was *much* more modest, and was
accounted for mainly by the increasing scale of existing campuses.
It would appear, then, that the university's share of the educational
process was diminished by the growth of the other sectors; and the
potential growth of state college systems — given the steady pressure on the legislature to establish new campuses — must have
been alarming both to university officials and to budget-minded
state legislators.[68]

Increases in scale and segmentation after the Master Plan. The
continuing competition for new or different campuses, as well as
the absence of long-term policies for regulating the growth of the
system of higher education, led to the commissioning of the Master
Plan Survey Team in 1959, with the charge to develop a comprehensive framework within which higher education could grow
in a more orderly fashion. Like the earlier survey recommendations, the Master Plan fixed the principles of functional differentiation essentially as they had existed, although a few modest conces-
sions were made to the state colleges in the direction of research
and advanced-degree granting.[69] With respect to the accommoda-
tion of increasing numbers of students, the Master Plan changed
the direction of structural responses away from the pattern of the
late 1950s. First, it shifted most of the segmentation away from the
state colleges and toward the university. It called for the development of three new university campuses without further delay, and
for the establishment of only two new state college campuses by
1965. However, the plan called for resurveys in 1965 and 1970.[70]
And, although the pressure for new state college campuses con-

[68] Arthur Coons remarked that in the light of three or four decades of
aggressive state college growth, "[It] was small wonder . . . that other segments
of higher education, including the University of California, the junior colleges,
and the private colleges and universities, should begin to ask as to whither these
state colleges were bound. In fact, not only were enrollments and academic
standards a matter of direct concern but also the potential significance of these
regionally oriented, seemingly more politically influential, state colleges suggested the possibility of a marked transformation of the pattern of higher education in California." *Crises in California Higher Education* (Los Angeles: Ward
Ritchie, 1968), pp. 21–22.
[69] Above, pp. 28–29.
[70] Master Plan Survey Team, *op. cit.* (n. 51, above), pp. 17–18.

tinued into the 1960s, it was resisted by recommendations of the Coordinating Council for Higher Education. The provisions of the Master Plan and subsequent policy decisions, although permitting considerable segmentation of the university (three new campuses), placed a much higher premium on increases in scale as a means of accommodating the increasing number of students.

Three other provisions of the Master Plan also conditioned the pattern of growth. First, the Master Plan Survey Team, in the manner of the Strayer committee, established a set of guidelines relating to ranges of enrollment. These are shown in Table 4. Thus,

Table 4
FULL-TIME ENROLLMENT RANGES RECOMMENDED
BY MASTER PLAN SURVEY TEAM

Type of institution	Minimum[a]	Optimum	Maximum
Junior colleges	400	3,500	6,000[b]
State colleges: in densely populated areas in metropolitan centers	5,000	10,000	20,000
outside metropolitan centers	3,000	8,000	12,000
University campuses[c]	5,000	12,500	27,500

[a]These are to be attained within seven to ten years after students are first admitted.

[b]This maximum might be exceeded in densely populated areas in metropolitan centers.

[c]The minimum figure for the university assumes graduate work in basic disciplines and one or more professional schools.

Source: Master Plan Survey Team, *A Master Plan for Higher Education in California*, p. 17.

while envisioning increases in scale as a major response, the Master Plan built in some upper limits. In effect, this policy retarded the growth of the two largest campuses of the university — Berkeley and UCLA — in the middle 1960s and accelerated the growth of the smaller campuses. It aimed at achieving the same effect for the state colleges, but as we shall see, this effect was less noticeable in that segment. The policy was more flexible for the junior colleges, permitting them to exceed their maximum in crowded metropolitan areas.

Second, the Master Plan recommended that the university

select freshman students from the top 12.5 percent of graduating high school students in California, and that state colleges select them from the top 33.3 percent. (Previous policy had set the percentages at 15 percent and 45 percent, respectively.) The junior colleges were thus given exclusive access to a greater pool of the graduating high school students (67 rather than 55 percent); of potential enrollees, a greater number was excluded from the state colleges (a drop of 11.6 percent) than from the universities (a drop of only 2.5 percent). This meant in turn that the junior colleges would have to accelerate their numerical growth and that the state colleges' maximum possible pool of potential students was reduced more than that of the university.[71]

Third, the Survey Team recommended that university and state colleges reduce the percentage of lower division students (which was about 50 percent in 1960) by about ten percentage points by 1975. This policy also diverted a larger proportion of lower division students to the junior colleges, thus encouraging their numerical growth more than that of the other two segments.[72]

Under these policies, some of which were only partially implemented, segments grew substantially in the 1960s, as shown in Table 5. But the pattern of growth of the 1950s was altered. The junior colleges continued their astounding numerical growth, absorbing more students each year than the state colleges and the university combined. But their percentage rate of growth declined somewhat, because the numerical growth was building on an increasingly larger base. This expansion of the junior colleges was based on both segmentation and increases in scale. The number of junior colleges increased from sixty-six in 1960 to ninety in 1969, and the average enrollment per junior college campus increased from 4,846 to 8,027.

The state colleges also continued an impressive numerical growth. Enrollment increased by almost two-and-one-half times

[71] The Master Plan Survey Team estimated that this policy would result in the transfer of some ten thousand lower division students from the university and the state colleges to the junior colleges by 1975. Master Plan Survey Team, *op. cit.* (n. 51, above), p. 14, footnote 3.

[72] The Survey Team estimated that the number of students transferred to the junior colleges under this policy would be forty thousand students by 1975. *Ibid.*

Table 5

TOTAL ENROLLMENTS IN PUBLIC INSTITUTIONS BY SEGMENT,
1960–1969 (head count, exclusive of extension programs)

Year	Junior Colleges	Percent Increase	State Colleges	Percent Increase	University	Percent Increase
1960	340,049	9	95,081	8	49,162	10
1961	370,033	9	105,987	11	54,265	10
1962	402,646	9	118,057	12	58,616	8
1963	434,792	8	133,108	13	64,504	10
1964	473,501	9	149,016	12	71,267	10
1965	543,224	15	154,887	4	79,437	11
1966	570,907	5	169,520	10	87,033	10
1967	610,769	7	195,601	9	95,376	10
1968	665,490	9	211,653	14	98,780	4
1969	722,429	9	224,897	6	106,035	7

Source: State Department of Finance

between 1960 and 1969, and a percentage rate of growth about equal to that of the 1950s took place. But the disparity between the growth of the state colleges and that of the university segment in the 1960s was not nearly as great as in the 1950s. As we have seen, the policies of the Master Plan and the policies of the Coordinating Council for Higher Education favored the relative growth of the university in several ways. The impact of these policies is seen in Table 5. The university, which had — relatively speaking — scarcely grown at all in the 1950s, jumped to a 10 percent annual rate of growth that slowed only at the very end of the decade. Its rate of growth, moreover, was only slightly less than that of the state colleges. The Master Plan and its implementations, then, whether by design or indirectly, had changed the fortunes of these two segments slightly in favor of the university, even though both segments were growing at a rapid rate.

The increase of almost 230,000 students in the state college system was accommodated almost entirely by increases in scale of existing campuses. As Chart 1 shows, the large urban campuses at Long Beach, San Jose, San Diego, Los Angeles, and San Francisco continued their explosive growth, with all but San Francisco State College exceeding the maximum of twenty thousand suggested by the Master Plan Survey Team. The growth of the urban campuses at Sacramento and Fresno also accelerated in the 1960s.

Chart 2 — which shows the numerical growth of the state colleges
that were established after 1950 — also reveals a very rapid growth
of the campuses at San Fernando Valley, Fullerton, and Hayward
— all of them in heavily populated areas. The growth of the state
colleges in the 1960s relied almost entirely on increases in scale;
this contrasted with the 1950s, when growth relied on a combination of segmentation and increases in scale.

The university's pattern of growth in the 1960s depended
both on increases in scale and on segmentation. Enrollment at

Chart 2
GROWTH OF STATE COLLEGES
ESTABLISHED AFTER 1950

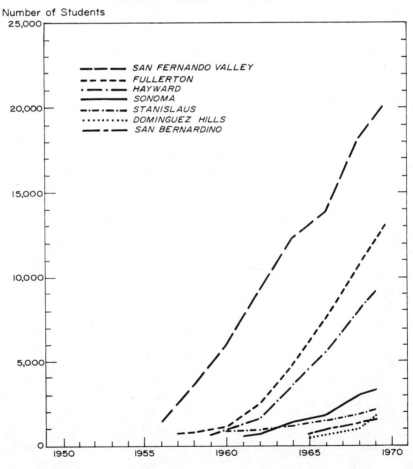

Berkeley grew from 20,825 in 1960 to 26,939 in 1964, then oscillated around its ceiling figure of 27,500 for the rest of the decade. UCLA also grew substantially, from 17,275 in 1960 to 26,250 in 1967, when it also stabilized. As the two largest campuses were moving toward their ceilings, moreover, the three campuses that had become general campuses in the late 1950s — Davis, Santa Barbara, and Riverside — began to absorb more of the increasing number of students. The enrollment at Davis increased from 2,872 in 1960 to 11,626 in 1969; that of Santa Barbara from 3,397 in 1960 to 13,254 in 1969; and that of Riverside from 1,574 in 1960 to 5,183 in 1969. Still more students were absorbed by the new campuses established after 1960. San Diego had an enrollment of 104 students in 1960; by 1969 it was 4,516; Santa Cruz, which began in 1965 with an enrollment of 1,276, had 3,092 students in 1969; Irvine also began in 1965, with 1,528 students, and increased to 3,412 in 1969. The state college system continued to rapidly expand its larger campuses. In contrast, the university — which had a number of small campuses at the beginning of the decade and three new ones added before 1965 — absorbed most of its growth in its smaller and newer campuses. And the university, which had relied on increases in scale almost exclusively in the 1950s, relied more on segmentation than did the state colleges in the 1960s.

Shifts in functional emphasis and the addition of new functions. The lines of functional differentiation laid down in the Master Plan and the policies that preceded it prevented adding or discarding functions among and within the three segments.[73] But, in three areas — the balance between lower division and upper division instruction, the balance between graduate and undergraduate education, and the distribution of research — some functional shifts did occur. And although these were not major shifts from the standpoint of the system as a whole, they occasioned some major shifts of emphasis within the university segment in particular.

(1) Lower division and upper division instruction. In line with their general policy of tightening the lines of functional differentiation, the regents of the University of California and the state Board of Education resolved in 1955 that "the University of California emphasize policies leading to the reduction of lower division enrollments in relation to those of upper and graduate divisions, and

[73] Above, pp. 39–40.

that the state colleges pursue policies which will have a similar effect."[74] In the years following 1960, the university moved toward this goal more slowly than did the state colleges. But the relatively small decrease did have considerable impact within the university system, because, as we shall see, it was experienced differently by the several campuses, and it occurred in the context of an increasing emphasis on *graduate* education in the university.

(2) Graduate and undergraduate education. Because the state colleges had been effectively barred from granting the doctorate — except for the joint doctorate authorized by the Master Plan legislation — there was almost no change of emphasis from 1950 to 1970. With respect to the granting of bachelor's and master's degrees, however, there were considerable shifts, which are shown in Table 6. In 1949–1950 the university granted more than twice the number of bachelor's degrees granted by the state colleges, but by 1969–1970 that proportion was almost precisely reversed. The

Table 6
DISTRIBUTION OF BACHELOR'S AND MASTER'S DEGREES,
UNIVERSITY AND STATE COLLEGES

	University			State Colleges		
BAs	Percent BA	Number	Percent university	Percent BA	Number	Percent state college
49-50	88	9,306	68	98	4,351	32
50-51	84	8,130	57	95	6,119	43
51-52	84	6,669	54	92.9	5,691	46
52-53	84	5,988	53	89.0	5,272	47
53-54	84	5,763	51	87.8	5,423	49
54-55	83	5,377	48	85.7	5,840	52
55-56	82	5,940	46	84.4	6,878	54
56-57	83	6,507	43	85.8	8,709	57
57-58	81	6,960	42	84.7	9,737	58
58-59	79	6,695	38	86.6	10,770	62
59-60	78	6,758	38	85.2	11,045	62
60-61	75	6,701	36	85.3	12,010	64
61-62	74	6,737	34	85.3	13,281	66
62-63	73	7,382	32	86.8	15,370	68
63-64	72	8,303	32	86.4	17,258	68
64-65	72	9,384	32	86.6	20,056	68

[74] Holy, *op. cit.* (n. 28, above), p. 44.

Table 6 *(continued)*

	University				State Colleges	
BAs	Percent BA	Number	Percent university	Percent BA	Number	Percent state college
65-66	70	9,926	32	85.0	21,533	68
66-67	71	11,848	33	84.9	23,858	67
67-68	73	12,938	32	84.7	27,271	68
68-69	73	14,545	31	84	32,558	69
69-70	75	16,437	31	85	37,409	69
MAs	Percent MA	Number	Percent university	Percent MA	Number	Percent state college
49-50	12	1,234	93	2	106	7
50-51	16	1,413	81	5	322	19
51-52	16	1,237	74	7.1	434	26
52-53	16	1,154	64	11.0	653	36
53-54	16	1,065	59	12.2	752	41
54-55	17	1,131	54	14.3	975	46
55-56	18	1,285	50	15.6	1,270	50
56-57	17	1,365	49	14.2	1,447	51
57-58	19	1,639	48	15.3	1,761	52
58-59	21	1,822	52	13.4	1,668	48
59-60	22	1,921	50	14.0	1,911	50
60-61	25	2,199	52	14.7	2,062	48
61-62	26	2,381	51	14.7	2,283	49
62-63	27	2,744	54	13.2	2,341	46
63-64	28	3,214	54	13.6	2,730	46
64-65	28	3,600	54	13.4	3,109	46
65-66	30	4,263	53	15.0	3,795	47
66-67	29	4,780	53	15.1	4,248	47
67-68	27	4,880	50	15.2	4,881	50
68-69	27	5,347	47	16	5,996	53
69-70	25	5,404	44	15	6,815	56

Sources: University Statistical Summary; State College Statistical Report Governor's Budget 68-69, p. 324, Office of Analytic Studies.

spectacular growth of the master's programs in the state colleges after 1949 produced similar results. The exceptionally rapid growth of M.A. production in the 1950s meant that the state colleges came to match and subsequently to exceed the university in numbers of M.A.s granted. Table 6 also indicates the movement of both segments toward graduate education at the expense of undergraduate education. Of all master's and bachelor's degrees granted, the proportion of master's degrees granted by the university rose from 12 percent in 1949–1950 to 25 percent in 1969–1970, and the proportion of master's degrees granted by the state colleges rose from 2 percent to 15 percent in the same period.

(3) Research. From the beginning the university has dedicated a substantial proportion of its resources to research activities, as evidenced by the development of large specialized libraries, museums, and organized research units, as well as by special funds for travel and preparation of research results. In addition, the university has normally provided sabbatical as well as other special leaves for research; indeed, a varying portion of a faculty member's basic salary is budgeted to cover departmental research.[75] The history of the other segments shows less emphasis on research. The junior colleges have devoted essentially no resources to research, and research by their faculty members has been negligible. The same applies to the state colleges, whose faculties have had heavier teaching loads (more hours in class per week) than university faculty members and have not enjoyed the same access to research funds, sabbatical leaves, and the like; also, the libraries of the state colleges have been stocked for purposes of instruction rather than research.

The period between 1950 and 1970 showed an enormous bulge in research activities at the university, and the beginnings of research at the state colleges. The organized research budget for the university increased more than tenfold in these two decades, as shown in Table 7. Most of these funds derived from extramural sources, although the regents often provided basic administrative and matching funds.[76] In addition, departmental research funds continued to grow throughout this period. Using the formula that 25 percent of the instruction and research budget is devoted to departmental research, this research expenditure also grew from

[75] For budgeting purposes the legislative analyst has reckoned that 25 percent of departmental time is devoted to research. Joint Committee on Higher Education, *The Challenge of Achievement, op. cit.* (n. 6, above), p. 22.

[76] For example, of the total of $183,393,000 spent for organized research in 1969–70, some $39,649,000 came from state funds. Office of the President of the University of California, "The Role of Organized Research Units in the University" (Report to the Regents), May 21, 1971. Attachment 5, p. 6.

Table 7

INCREASES IN EXPENDITURES ON ORGANIZED RESEARCH,
UNIVERSITY OF CALIFORNIA, 1951–70 *(in thousands of dollars)*

Year	Amount
1951–1952	16,987
1953–1954	21,133
1955–1956	26,025
1957–1958	35,461
1959–1960	47,553
1961–1962	69,599
1963–1964	92,437
1965–1966	123,144
1967–1968	157,800
1969–1970	183,393

Sources: Office of Analytical Studies, *Fiscal Facts*, p. 47; Joint Committee on Higher Education, *The Challenge of Achievement*, p. 22; Office of the President, "The Role of Organized Research in the University," Attachment 5, p. 6.

about $5.5 million in 1950–1951 to around $40 million by the end of the 1960s. The organized research budget grew faster than the total university budget, moreover, constituting about 25 percent of the total budget in the early 1950s and about 30 percent in the late 1960s.[77]

By contrast, the state colleges received formal authorization to pursue research only in 1960, when the Master Plan authorized research appropriate to their primary instructional emphasis.[78] Very little legislative support for research was forthcoming. A report to the Coordinating Council in 1962 stated flatly that "[there] is, at the present time, no research in the state colleges that can be classified as *departmental.* Such individual research as has been accomplished by state college faculty members has been conducted in addition to their normal teaching load and without additional compensation."[79] In terms of shifts in the research functions, then, the decades between 1950 and 1970 witnessed a great increase in the university's research activities. The state colleges had a foot in the research door, but financing was so modest that the university

[77] Office of Analytical Studies, *Fiscal Facts, op. cit.* (n. 23, above), p. 47.
[78] Above, p. 27.
[79] Coordinating Council for Higher Education, *Research in the California State Colleges* (Report 62–4), (June, 1962), p. 3.

maintained a virtual monopoly on organized and sponsored research.

Structural additions. The structural additions that occurred during the two decades tended to parallel the shifts in functional emphasis. As the more specialized campuses at Davis, Riverside, and Santa Barbara were converted into general campuses, they developed the usual array of courses and departments associated with a college of arts and sciences and began to develop separate graduate divisions. The same occurred at the new university campuses of San Diego, Irvine, and Santa Cruz as they moved toward becoming general campuses, although experimentation was much more in evidence — for example, in the attempt to organize the Irvine campus on divisional rather than a departmental basis. The larger campuses of Berkeley and Los Angeles remained remarkably stable structurally, although some new departments and instructional programs were formed — for example, the departments of comparative literature, demography, and ethnic studies, the graduate schools of journalism and public affairs, and the program of religious studies at Berkeley. In these instances, however, the new departments were assimilated into the existing administrative machinery and did little to alter the character of existing departments or other administrative units. Berkeley and UCLA also added experimental academic programs in the 1960s, but the effect of these programs on the structure of the two institutions was modest.[80]

The state colleges, given the right to grant master's degrees in 1949, developed a variety of professional and arts and sciences master's programs. But the joint doctoral program with the university, authorized in the Master Plan legislation of 1960, scarcely developed in the 1960s.

The most dramatic structural additions during the decades of the 1950s and 1960s were the research units, which were organized mainly to administer the increased extramural — especially federal — funds that flowed to the university in those decades. The research unit has a long history in the university; in fact the first organized research unit — the University Herbarium — was established in 1860, before the university itself was officially created,

[80] Dwight R. Ladd, *Change in Educational Policy* (New York: McGraw-Hill, 1970), chaps. 2, 11.

and was subsequently incorporated into its structure. Other research units, such as the seismographic stations and the Lick Observatory, were established before 1900. Many, including the Lick Observatory, the Lowie Museum of Anthropology, and the Scripps Institute of Oceanography, have had long and distinguished histories of contribution to knowledge.

Between 1867 — when the university was established — and 1950, forty-four organized research units had been established: twenty-five on the Berkeley campus, three at Davis, six at Los Angeles, three at San Diego, one at Riverside, and six on the San Francisco campus. The great majority of these were in the natural, life, and agricultural sciences, although about a half-dozen were in the social sciences. After 1950 the rate of growth accelerated, with Berkeley alone adding thirty new institutes and centers between 1950 and 1970. Los Angeles became as active as Berkeley, establishing twenty-nine organized research units on its campus in those two decades. Davis added only one research center in 1951, but between 1962 and 1970 eleven new organized research units were established. The large campuses with heavy emphasis on graduate training have accumulated the most organized research units. Those that have entered ambitiously into graduate training more recently — Davis, Santa Barbara, and Riverside — have an intermediate number; and the very new campuses of Santa Cruz and Irvine have barely begun. The research units vary greatly in size and budget. The Scripps Institution of Oceanography at San Diego had a budget of almost $21,000,000 in 1969, while the small International Security Studies Project at UCLA had a budget of only $21,000.[81]

Structurally, an organized research unit is attached to an administrative unit — a department, a college, or a graduate division. Its budget and personnel, however, are structurally separated from the academic departments. Typically its director is also a professor in one of the academic departments, and faculty members — both tenured and nontenured — may affiliate with the research unit, may arrange to have some of their time "bought" by the unit for nondepartmental research, and may hire research assistants through the unit. Several other classes of research personnel are attached to the organized research units — professional research-

[81]*Ibid.*, Attachment 5, pp. 3–4.

ers, who are employed by the institutes to work on research projects but do not offer instruction in the academic departments; managerial personnel, who are important in directing the day-by-day functioning of the units; and research assistants, who are typically enrolled in the graduate program of an academic department.

In the 1950s and 1960s, many of the new research units reflected the fact that extramural interests and funds followed social problem areas that emerged in those decades. Among the units established since 1960, for example, are the Air Pollution Research Center (Riverside), the Institute of Urban and Regional Development (Berkeley), the Public Policy Research Organization (Irvine), the Institute of Ecology (Davis), the Center for Administration of Criminal Justice (Davis), the Afro-American Studies Center (UCLA), the Asian-American Studies Center (UCLA), the Chicano Studies Center (UCLA), the American Indian Studies Center (UCLA), Chicano Studies (Santa Barbara), Black Studies (Santa Barbara), and the Institute of Race and Community Relations (Berkeley). The organized research units, probably more than the departments, proved to be the typical structural response to the demand for expanded knowledge in areas relevant to the larger policy concerns of the society.

The basic structural features of the colleges and universities — schools, colleges, departments, and so on — were not changed substantially during the period from 1950 to 1970. Furthermore, those structural additions that were made — such as new departments and programs and new research units — were tacked on to this basic academic structure without modifying it formally. As we shall see, however, the impact of these structural additions, in combination with other structural responses, on some of the academic estates was considerable.

We now turn to the cumulative impact of these structural changes on various roles in the academic system. Because the magnitude of the structural responses was considerable, we would expect that the role-expectations, obligations, privileges, and aspirations of the major social groups in the system would be substantially affected. Moreover, because the structural changes were often irregular in development and were concentrated in particular parts of the system, we would expect that the impact of these changes would be more drastic in some quarters than others.

My account of the impact of the structural responses on the academic estates is not exhaustive. I first develop a general statement on the relations between structural change, the institutionalization of competing normative standards, the changing fortunes of groups, and the growth of relative deprivation. Then I illustrate this general statement with reference to several topics: (a) the development of relative deprivation among the segments resulting from the simultaneous institutionalization of the normative standards of competitive excellence and egalitarianism in the system; in particular I examine the emerging pattern of conflict between the state colleges and the university, and among the various campuses of the university; (b) the development of relative deprivation occasioned by the increased size and functional shifts *within* the university segment; in particular I examine the changing fortunes of faculty, graduate students, undergraduate students, and research personnel, as well as the implications of these changing fortunes for their outlook and behavior. All of this helps to throw light on a number of themes emerging in the conflicts that gripped the university during most of the 1960s.

General Statement: Tocqueville on the Estates of Eighteenth-Century France

In his studies contrasting the social conditions of France and America in the eighteenth century, Alexis de Tocqueville developed a theoretical perspective that is helpful in understanding the impact of structural changes on group conflict in the recent past of the system of higher education in California. Although I would not argue that twentieth-century educational history in California repeats eighteenth-century French political history in any simple way, some of Tocqueville's guiding assumptions illuminate the recent history of group conflict in public higher education in California. Let me recapitulate briefly the relevant parts of Tocqueville's argument.

In Tocqueville's search for an explanation of the social and political instability in eighteenth-century France, he was preoccupied above all with the concept of equality. Furthermore, he tended always to think of two extreme ways of structuring equality in society — the aristocratic, in which equality was minimized, and the democratic, in which it was maximized.

For an example of an extreme aristocratic social organization, Tocqueville looked back to eleventh-century France, "when the territory was divided among a small number of families, who were the owners of the soil and the rulers of the inhabitants; the right of governing descended with the family inheritance from generation to generation; force was the only means by which man could act on man; and landed property was the sole source of power."[82]

For an example of a democratic society, Tocqueville looked toward the United States of America. Writing in 1835, he saw America as representing the nation where the great social revolution toward equality "seems to have nearly reached its natural limits."[83] In direct contrast to aristocratic society, the laws of inheritance of the United States call for equal partition of property, which makes for a "constant tendency [for property] to diminish and . . . in the end be completely dispersed."[84] Tocqueville observed many wealthy individuals in the United States, but added that "wealth circulates with inconceivable rapidity, and experience shows that it is rare to find two succeeding generations in the full enjoyment of it."[85]

In their basic nature, then, aristocracies and democracies stand in fundamental opposition to one another, because they represent extremes in the structuring of equality. Yet in other respects they are similar. In both, the force of custom operates to mitigate the tendencies for despotism to arise. As a result, people enjoy a great degree of liberty in both types of society. And both enjoy relative political stability.[86]

If Tocqueville did not find the roots of despotism, tyranny, and instability in either aristocracy or democracy, where did he locate them? *In the transition between the two types of society.* If any single proposition dominates Tocqueville's interpretation of the causes of the French Revolution and its excesses, it is this: France had historical origins similar to those of many other Euro-

[82] Alexis de Tocqueville, *Democracy in America* (New York: Vintage, 1945), I:4.

[83] *Ibid.*, I:14.
[84] *Ibid.*, I:51.
[85] *Ibid.*, I:53.
[86] For a discussion of some of the mechanisms which diminish the probability of revolutions in America, see *ibid.*, vol. II, chap. 21. In 1848 Tocqueville described America as "not only the most prosperous, but the most stable, of all the nations of the earth." *Ibid.*, I, 10.

pean — and indeed American — societies. But in the eighteenth century France had experienced some social changes that *partially* destroyed aristocratic society and *partially* advanced the principle of equality. It was the unstable mixture of both principles — not the tendencies inherent in either of them — that made for the dissatisfaction, selfishness and self-seeking, conflict, despotism, and diminished national morale that culminated in the revolutionary convulsion in France late in the century.[87] One of the advantages that America possessed, moreover, was that it was able to start fresh, to establish a democracy without having to go through the process of destroying an aristocracy. "[America] is reaping the fruits of the democratic revolution which we [the French] are undergoing, without having had the revolution itself."[88] The comparison between eighteenth-century France and nineteenth-century America, then, becomes one of comparing a society that had proceeded part way along the transition from aristocratic to democratic, with one that had been born democratic and manifested, in relatively pure form, the characteristics of a democratic system.

Tocqueville's arguments concerning the impact of these changes on the various social estates in France are familiar. Through a process of decay of the customs of local aristocracy and the centralization of the government in the monarchy, local nobles still possessed their ranks and titles but were gradually losing their authority. Other groups experienced changes in their social condition, but unlike the aristocracy — which was being edged out of its former position of influence — they were enjoying partial advances. The bourgeoisie improved its situation with respect to wealth, education, and style of life, but failed to gain access to various feudal rights and to high society. The peasants owned more land than in times past and were freed from the harshness of government and landlords, but they were still subjected to some traditional duties and taxes.

Why should the changes in eighteenth-century France have been unsettling to so many groups? To answer this question Tocqueville invoked — although only implicitly — a version of the

[87] Alexis de Tocqueville, *The Old Regime and the French Revolution* (Garden City, N.Y.: Doubleday Anchor, 1955), pp. xii–xiv.
[88] Tocqueville, I:14.

psychological principle we now know as *relative deprivation.* The social changes yielded a number of groups that were losing in some respects while retaining or gaining in others, or gaining in some respects while not gaining or losing in others. For Tocqueville these inconsistencies were psychologically more unsettling than the social arrangements of aristocratic feudalism, because under that system people may have been worse off in some absolute sense, but their access to the good things in life was organized according to a consistent principle. On the basis of such an assumption, Tocqueville argued that the various groups — noblemen, middle classes, and peasants — were more dissatisfied with the changing state of affairs in France than they had been with the feudal past.

This complicated system of social inequities had the consequence of isolating these groups and setting them at odds with one another. Each group tried to clutch those privileges it had, to gain those it did not have, and to rid itself of burdens not shared by other groups.

As Tocqueville's analysis implies, one of two distinguishable reference points may be salient in the experience of relative deprivation. The first is that some group feels deprived so far as its experiences — performances, rewards, and so on — do not measure up to particular *values or normative standards.* The local nobles of eighteenth-century France, for example, felt that their position had deteriorated relative to the ideals of feudal aristocracy; the bourgeoisie felt that their position was unsatisfactory with respect to the ideals of democracy — that is, equal access to privileges and power. The second reference point is that some group feels deprived so far as its experiences do not measure up to those of some *other groups.* The bourgeoisie, for example, felt deprived because they did not have access to the same kinds of privileges as the nobility; the peasants felt deprived because they labored under traditional burdens, not experienced by other classes. In practice, of course, the experience of relative deprivation implies both these reference points, in that a group's position relative to another group is always measured by some notion of equity or justice in relation to a value or normative standard.

The essence of Tocqueville's insights, then, is that the partial institutionalization of two competing value or normative standards in a social system creates a greater potential for relative deprivation and conflict than the consistent institutionalization of either of them. First, the values themselves are in some important respects in conflict and call for different institutionalized solutions; most obviously, commitment to aristocratic ideals calls for a very different distribution of wealth, power, and privilege in society than a commitment to democratic ideals. Second, because of the side-by-side *partial* institutionalization of both sets of values, *any* social arrangements will be vulnerable to criticism. A royal court with numerous privileges may be attacked for not being democratic, but any attempts to "democratize" such a court are vulnerable to attack in the name of the ideals of feudalism and monarchy. And finally, group conflict is likely to be encouraged by the partial institutionalization of competing normative standards, because groups in conflict have competing sets of *legitimizing values* which they can relate to their claims to resources and rewards.

In a social system with a consistently institutionalized set of moral standards — for example, Tocqueville's model of an aristocratic society — conflicts are likely to be expressed by a given group not living up to expectations that are regarded by all as legitimate. When, however, competing normative standards are partially institutionalized, groups in conflict are able to criticize social arrangements on the ground that they are *illegitimate*, not simply inequitable. Thus, under the partial institutionalization of competing normative standards, conflicts are likely to take on a moralistic caste — that is, they become conflicts between competing moral principles.

A Source of Endemic Conflict: The Institutionalization of the Normative Standards of Competitive Excellence and Egalitarianism

Although both sets of values — those of competitive excellence and those of egalitarianism — act as general stimulants to growth, they also often stand in a relation of tension, if not contradiction. In any concrete case it appears impossible to maximize both sets of values at once. For a given campus, for example, the implementation of the values of competitive excellence would call for, among other things, highly selective admission policies. From the standpoint of the values of egalitarianism, however, such policies would be regarded as exclusivist. The maximization of egalitarian values would call for open admission policies, with equal access for all. But these policies would seem to undermine the values of excellence. The conflicts that can arise in an attempt to institutionalize both sets of values in the same educational institution are nowhere better illustrated than in the recent efforts to institute a policy of open admissions at the City University of New York.

One of the main features of the history of public higher education in California has been an attempt to institutionalize both sets of values and to mediate the tension between them. To express one of the guiding principles for growth, the regents of the university and the state Board of Education resolved the following just before the Master Plan was adopted:

> The expansion of existing institutions and the establishment of new ones should depend on the optimum use of the state's resources for higher education in relation to the *greatest relative need both geographically and functionally.* [89]

This principle called for the incorporation of both the values of competitive excellence and the values of egalitarianism. The emphasis on geography suggests serving the people and minimizing the geographical barriers to higher education, and the emphasis on function suggests that, despite the geographical criterion, the system of higher education should retain its ingredient of functional stratification.

By and large, the tension between the two sets of values has been resolved through the principle of functional differentiation. From the beginning of its existence the university has been the primary focus for the institutionalization of the values of competitive excellence and elitism, and it gains political and financial support by declaring that it must be as good as the best, if not the best. [90] The junior colleges have been the primary focus for the

----

[89] Holy, *Summary, op. cit.* (n. 18, above), p. 11. Emphasis added.

[90] This is not to say that other values do not come into contact with those of competitive excellence in the university. The university itself experiences considerable egalitarian pressure. One example is the pressure to honor transfer students from junior colleges and state colleges without penalty. Recently, the question of exceptions to qualified candidates for admission has illustrated the force of egalitarian values. In the Master Plan policies, it was stipulated that university campuses could recruit 2 percent of their entering classes from among students who did not fall above the top 12½ percent of the graduating high school class. At

institutionalization of the values of egalitarianism, by giving all young people with specific minimum prior educational experience access to the system of higher education. This is not to say that the values of competitive excellence are not relevant for the junior colleges. It is often claimed that California's is the best junior college system in the nation. Yet regarding the institutionalization of the junior college system *within* California, its primary legitimizing value is equality of opportunity.

In many respects the Master Plan of 1960 constituted an effort to provide for *both* the values of competitive excellence and egalitarianism.[91] The plan preserved the elite status of the university in several ways: the university retained a near monopoly over research, the virtually exclusive right to grant doctoral degrees, and an exclusive jurisdiction over training in some elite professions. Furthermore, the university was authorized to become slightly more exclusive in admitting high school graduates. Several of the plan's provisions stressed the values of egalitarianism. It envisioned that the junior college system would expand to the point that it would be able to admit *all* high school graduates. At the same time it envisioned that the junior colleges would continue to devote part of their instruction to collegiate courses — that qualified junior college students could transfer easily to four-year schools. The Master Plan, in short, compromised between the values of competitive excellence and the values of egalitarianism by institutionalizing a functionally stratified system that was open at the bottom and provided for a flow of qualified students from tier to tier.

Such an arrangement, although cushioning the system against internal value-conflict by creating separate types of educational institutions, could not resolve once and for all the tension between competitive excellence and egalitarianism. This tension, moreover, comes to the surface especially clearly in the competition among

---

the time it was adopted, it seemed to aim mainly at permitting campuses to recruit talented athletes whose academic records were not up to the usual standards of admission. Subsequently, however, under pressure to increase admissions of minority group members — an egalitarian pressure — the rule was relaxed into the "2 + 2" principle, mainly to permit the university to increase admissions of minority students whose academic qualifications fell below the usual criteria.

[91] Many of the ideas developed in the following paragraphs grew out of conversations with Clark Kerr.

the different segments for scarce resources. In discussing the problem of equity in the public higher education system, the Joint Committee on Higher Education of the California legislature produced figures in 1968 that indicated "a major discrepancy in the level of resource expenditures per student among the three segments," with the university spending the most, the state colleges an intermediate amount, and the junior colleges least.[92] Thus, the state's educational system reveals a "tacit acceptance of the notion that a disproportionate share of educational resources should be made available for the instruction of those judged to be the ablest students."[93] The committee assigned the responsibility for this undemocratic state of affairs to the values of competitive excellence, and it called for a shift in the populist direction, recommending that "all who are enrolled in similar curricula should get roughly the same expenditure of resources, or, perhaps, a greater percentage of available resources might be devoted to those who are found to rank lowest in previous achievement."[94] Whatever the merits of the committee's recommendation, its reasoning reflected the importance of the values of competitive excellence and egalitarianism, and the importance of the tension between them.

Conflict between the university and the state colleges. The situation of the state colleges can also be understood in the light of California's peculiar attempt to resolve the tensions between these two sets of values. Historically the legitimizing principle for the early normal schools (later state colleges) was that they provided training for a particular occupation — primary and secondary teaching. As the schools became colleges and began to offer collegiate courses, their programs began to overlap more with the university's undergraduate program. When, in the 1950s, the colleges began to develop a number of graduate programs, the overlap between the functions of the state colleges and the university increased. And when the Master Plan opened the crack in the door slightly wider by providing for the joint doctorate and a modest research program for the state colleges, the system moved even further toward functional overlapping with the university.

[92] Joint Committee on Higher Education, *The Challenge of Achievement, op. cit.* (n. 6, above), p. 51. The committee acknowledged the frailty of the data on which they based this conclusion.

[93] *Ibid.*, p. 52.

[94] *Ibid.*

This historical evolution of the state colleges placed them in a somewhat anomalous position with respect to the main legitimizing values of public higher education. They overlapped functionally in many respects with the university, but they were always prevented in various ways from striving to be as excellent. The Master Plan solidly institutionalized this status. It gave the state colleges semi-elite recognition with respect to standards of admission by granting them the privilege of admitting the top one-third of high school graduates, but it gave a more exclusive standard (the top one-eighth) to the university; it continued to exclude the state colleges from doctoral training, except for the little used joint doctorate; it continued to exclude the state colleges from establishing prestigious professional schools; and, despite some relaxations, it continued to limit the research function of the state colleges. On the other hand, because the state colleges were semi-elite, they could not effectively lay claim to legitimization on the values of egalitarianism. The junior colleges were solidly established as the agencies to provide an opportunity for higher education to "everyone" who had completed the prerequisite education. The state colleges, in short, found themselves in a classic Tocquevillian situation of an estate with partial access to the activities and rewards of another estate while facing rigid barriers to further access.[95]

This perspective also reveals much about the kinds of relative deprivation that were experienced throughout the system, and the kinds of competitive stance taken by each of the three segments. Throughout the several decades preceding the Master Plan, the junior colleges were defined institutionally as part of secondary

[95] See Tocqueville's characterization of the situations of the nobility and the bourgeoisie: "Education and a similar style of living had already obliterated many of the distinctions between the two classes. The bourgeois was as cultivated as the nobleman and his enlightenment came from the same source. Both had been educated on literary and philosophic lines, for Paris, now almost the sole fountainhead of knowledge for the whole of France, had cast the minds of all in the same mold and given them the same equipment. No doubt it was still possible at the close of the eighteenth century to detect shades of difference in the behavior of the aristocracy and that of the bourgeoisie; for nothing takes longer to acquire than the surface polish which is called good manners. But basically all who ranked above the common herd were of a muchness; they had the same ideas, the same habits, the same tastes, the same kinds of amusements; read the same books and spoke in the same way. They differed only in their rights." De Tocqueville, *The Old Regime and the French Revolution, op. cit.* (n. 87, above), pp. 80–81.

education. Many aspired to escape this status, and during those decades there were several social movements in which junior colleges pressed to achieve four-year status and inclusion in the system of higher education. In 1960, the Master Plan upgraded the entire system of junior colleges into higher education for the first time, while limiting them to two years of college instruction. At that time the Master Plan defined the junior colleges as the main bulwark of egalitarianism in the system and adopted policies that encouraged their vast expansion.[96] Since that time the major political stance of the junior college system has been to consolidate itself in the system of higher education: by seeking (and achieving in 1967) a governing body separate from the state Board of Education, which is now responsible only for secondary education; by consolidating new junior college districts different from the older high school districts in which many were located; and by attempting to assure unrestricted transfer of junior college students to the other segments.[97] Early in the 1960s, a survey of faculty sentiment by the Coordinating Council for Higher Education indicated that junior college faculty members wished to have a system of academic rank (like the other segments), and that they desired that junior colleges presently within high school districts or unified school districts be given separate districts. A typical respondent stated that "since there is no academic rank, and since some junior colleges are within unified school districts, the atmosphere of a 'glorified high school' prevails."[98]

The state colleges, however, were more restless than either the junior colleges or the university with respect to their position in the system. This restlessness was expressed in several ways — by a search for self-definition, by an attitude of hostility (or ambivalence) toward the university, by an incessant pressure to develop parity with the university, and by an equally incessant pressure toward quantitative growth and increased political influence. All these responses, moreover, reflect the position of the state

[96] Above, pp. 47–48.

[97] Coordinating Council for Higher Education, *Faculty Opinion toward Salary, Fringe Benefits and Working Conditions* (Report No. 1007), (Sacramento and San Francisco, August 1963), p. 36.

[98] See Coordinating Council for Higher Education, *A Consideration of Issues Affecting California Public Junior Colleges* (Report No. 1018), (Sacramento and San Francisco, April 1965); Medsker and Clark, *op. cit.* (n. 20, above); and Coons, *Crises in California Higher Education, op. cit.* (n. 68 above), pp. 177–181.

colleges as a semi-elite estate facing obstacles to mobility — obstacles that took the form of legislative restriction on their functions and university efforts to protect its traditional elite status.

In 1966, the California state colleges sponsored a conference on educational philosophy. The role of the state college with respect to general education, research, occupational training, and the like was explored by various speakers. On that occasion, Chancellor Glenn S. Dumke delivered an address in which he identified the primary goal of the California state colleges in the following way:

> Our major job is to turn out the people who will operate our society, who will run our civilization, who will head up our businesses so that our economy can support an ever-increasing bill for public education, who will manage our government agencies and our governments themselves, who will take the risks and bear the responsibilities and concern themselves with the moral values that . . . are the proper concern of leadership. Our mission is to train our students to face the discomforts and dangers of action, as opposed to the comfort and security of contemplation, while at the same time urging them to bring the benefits of contemplation to the decisions they must make in their leadership roles.[99]

To realize this goal Dumke urged the state colleges "to cling to the realization of their dual mission — to teach students how to live, as well as how to make a living," to expose their students to responsibility earlier, and "to remain proud of our teaching mission."[100] Valid as this purpose might intrinsically be, it still must be added that it does appear to be a struggle to define some kind of distinctive mission — a mission stressing roles of occupational placement and general education, both of which were shared in some degree by the universities and the state colleges.

Dumke's remarks were also salted with hostility toward the university and with denials that the state colleges wished to become like it. He noted that it had not been the major job of the state colleges to turn out scholars and experts; "we leave that," he added, "to the research institutions, those with elaborate graduate schools who have teaching assistants teaching the freshmen."[101] At the same conference, however, the president of Fresno State Col-

[99] Office of the Chancellor, California State Colleges, *Papers Presented at the Conference on Educational Philosophy* (Los Angeles, January 18, 1966), p. 3.
[100] *Ibid.*, pp. 4–5.
[101] *Ibid.*, p. 3.

lege, Frederic W. Ness, called for "increasing our emphasis on research in our system." Ness indicated that this would mean "adjusted teaching loads, travel money, clerical help, equipment, space, and so forth and so on."[102] In the same address, he asserted that the joint doctorate with the university "contains all the ambiguities of a mermaid, only with far less allure," and predicted that "our fellow citizens are ultimately going to require the state colleges to offer some form of doctorate."[103]

A survey by the Coordinating Council on Higher Education on the opinions of faculty about their conditions of employment indicated that faculty satisfaction was higher at both the university and the junior colleges than at the state colleges.[104] The recommendations by state college faculty members on how to improve their present position were summarized in the Coordinating Council report as follows:

> The faculty members of the state colleges who have tenure believe that travel expenses to attend conferences and professional meetings are inadequate and should be substantially increased. They state that it is very important for the faculty to be aware of all the latest developments in their fields, and that it is therefore necessary to attend conferences and professional meetings.
> All faculty groups in the state colleges strongly urge that teaching loads be reduced so that more time is made available for research. Closely related is the recommendation for an improvement in library facilities.[105]

[102] *Ibid.*, pp. 27–28.

[103] *Ibid.*, p. 25.

[104] When asked whether they were satisfied with their present appointment, 88 percent of junior college faculty members reported positively, 71 percent of university faculty, and 65 percent of state college faculty. Coordinating Council for Higher Education, *Faculty Opinion Toward Salary, Fringe Benefits and Working Conditions, op. cit.* (n. 97, above), p. 20.

[105] *Ibid.*, p. 36. One of the contributing factors to these faculty demands is the relative deprivation generated by the state college recruitment policies. In their own drive toward excellence, they attempted to recruit as high a proportion of faculty members with doctorates as possible. (Note Chancellor Glen Dumke's dismay at the decreasing proportion of doctorates in the middle 1960s, when the market for Ph.D.s was very tight. See the Fourth Annual Report of the Chancellor to the Trustees of the California State Colleges, 1965–1966 [Sacramento: California Office of State Printing, 1966]. Dumke used these figures to call for higher salaries and greater financial support for the state colleges, so that they could improve their recruitment. *Ibid.*, pp. 2–6.) Faculty members with doctorates, however, are trained mainly in universities which stress research, and it may be assumed that in their graduate years these faculty members absorb the attitude that re-

In general, the impetus to carve out a distinctive role, separate from the university, was much weaker than the drive to attain parity with the university. The political tensions generated by the drive for new state college campuses stimulated the legislature to commission the Master Plan Survey Team.[106] Also, in the late 1950s, the state colleges were exerting strong political pressure to gain the doctorate. In the gubernatorial campaign of 1958, Edmund G. Brown had promised to work for a status separate from the state Board of Education for the state colleges if he was elected.[107] Given these political forces, it is not surprising that many of the features of the Master Plan legislation appear as a political compromise between the ambition of the state colleges and the resistance of the university. On the one hand the Master Plan encouraged some expansion of the research function in the state colleges; it gave them token access to doctoral education; and the state colleges gained a separate Board of Trustees. On the other hand, the state colleges still were excluded effectively from many university functions and were unable to attain constitutional status. Thus the Master Plan, although it made some changes in the *status quo*, actually locked the state college system even more firmly into the institutional position that had given rise to its competitive striving in the first place.

After the enactment of the Master Plan legislation, the state colleges became, if anything, even more aggressive in their drive for parity with the university. Much of the competition between the two segments, moreover, was manifested in the new coordinating body created by the Master Plan, the Coordinating Council for Higher Education. The council was made up of three members each from the university Board of Regents, the state college Board of Trustees, the junior colleges, and the private sector of higher education, and three public members appointed by the governor. Its functions were advisory to each segment, to the legislature and to the governor, and it did not have binding authority.

In its early years the CCHE was a relatively harmonious

---

search is prestigious. To be recruited, after such training, into a state college whose policies discourage research creates feelings of more or less chronic dissatisfaction in faculty members, and pressure to increase the opportunities for research is to be expected.

[106] Above, pp. 43–46.

[107] Personal conversation with Clark Kerr.

group, and its minutes show little bickering over the rights and privileges of the universities and state colleges. On occasion, however, competition would flare. On December 19, 1962, for example, two issues occasioned a controversy between the representatives from the respective segments. The first had to do with the respective jurisdictions of the state colleges and universities over extension courses. The issue was whether state college extension courses should be limited to teacher training or improvement — with the university extension program responsible for courses in all other areas — or could offer a more general range of courses. The university representatives favored the narrower role for the state colleges, but Chancellor Dumke argued that

> this was an undue restriction upon the already limited activities of the state college extension services and further that this would not allow the individual colleges to serve their communities. He suggested that a better alternative would be to allow both systems to continue their functions but to allow future growth only on the basis of increases in full-time campus enrollments.[108]

In this instance the state college point of view prevailed, and a more permissive formulation of the state college role passed over the opposition of the university representatives.

At the same meeting, the director of the council presented a staff report which recommended an 8.8 percent increase in university faculty salaries and a 6 percent increase for the state college faculty. Again Chancellor Dumke spoke against the measure, urging "that the council not establish a differential salary increase between the university and the state colleges."[109] Dumke introduced a substitute motion calling for a 8 percent increase for the faculties of both segments, a motion which received the votes of only the state college representatives. The original motion was then passed, over the opposition of the state college representatives, with Regent Edwin Carter entering the diplomatic qualification that "adoption of the motion should not be considered as setting a precedent for future years."[110]

This kind of opposition was not chronic, however, and its

[108] *Minutes*, Coordinating Council for Higher Education, December 19, 1962, p. 8.
[109] *Ibid.*, p. 4.
[110] *Ibid.*

significance for the Coordinating Council's work should not be exaggerated. In a survey of the votes of the council in the first six years of its existence, James Paltridge calculated that 264 of the 271 voice votes of the council were unanimous, and that only 17 roll-call votes — which usually indicated sharp division — were necessary. On 12 of these 17 roll-call votes, however, the university and the state college segment voted, in bloc, against one another.[111] This suggests that when conflict reached the point of division, this division usually followed segmental lines between the university and the state colleges. It should be noted further that the move, in 1965, to add more public members to the Coordinating Council was advanced with the argument that it would diminish the effect of bloc voting on the council.[112]

Until 1967 the state colleges directed their energies mainly toward establishing new campuses, narrowing the salary differential between themselves and the university, seeking direct state support for research, reducing the teaching load, and expanding their graduate programs. In 1967, however, the chancellor and the Board of Trustees mounted a much more ambitious program of change. On March 23 the Board of Trustees passed a resolution calling for inclusion of the state college system into the constitution and for provision of doctoral programs approved by the Coordinating Council, urging that "no [constitutional] provision be included which prevents recognition and encouragement of instructionally related faculty research," and urging that "the constitution not prevent a change in name from 'state college' to 'state university,' both for the California state colleges and for such state colleges as the board may determine."[113]

In 1967 the Coordinating Council undertook to investigate the issue of a name change and sought statements from both state college and university officials. Chancellor Dumke's office argued that the name *university* was in fact proper for the present functions of the state colleges and that the change in name would help recruit faculty, would help secure federal and foundation funds,

[111] James G. Paltridge, *California's Coordinating Council for Higher Education* (Berkeley: Center for Research and Development in Higher Education, University of California, Berkeley, 1966), pp. 101–102.
[112] *Ibid.*, p. 100.
[113] *Minutes*, California State College Board of Trustees, March 23, 1967, pp. 1780–1782.

but would not change the basic mission of the colleges or call for any greater state support.[114] Vice-President Frank Kidner of the University of California voiced the university's opposition to the proposal by calling for the council's continued attention to the criterion of maintaining academic quality — that is, competitive excellence. Ultimately the staff report to the Coordinating Council recommended against the change in name,[115] but the council was persuaded to endorse the state college's proposal, with the proviso that the change in name would in no way entail any change in function of the state colleges under the Master Plan.[116] Despite this endorsement and despite the continuing pressure from the state colleges, the change-of-name issue remained stalemated for some time in the legislature. Early in 1972, however, the legislature authorized the use of the term *state university*, although insisting that no change in function would accompany the change in name.

To summarize: The university has traditionally been institutionalized in the name of competitive excellence, the junior colleges in the name of egalitarianism. Although the universities have been subjected to egalitarian pressures, and although the junior colleges have attempted to upgrade themselves to four-year institutions, both segments have continued to function predominately in the name of their respective legitimizing values. The state colleges, originating as a supplementary type of institution to supply recruits to the teaching profession, gradually evolved as a general educational segment which could not enjoy solid legitimization through either of the two principal values on which the system of higher education was built.

The political orientations of the several sectors also can be understood in this light. The university has taken the stance of a conservative elite, attempting to safeguard its custody over those functions — research, the doctorate, and training in the liberal professions — that guarantee its lead in realizing the values of competitive excellence. The state colleges have chosen aggressive

[114]*Ibid.* See also Coordinating Council for Higher Education, *A Study of the Implications of Changing the Name of the California State Colleges to the California State University* (Report 68–6), (Sacramento: March 19, 1968), pp. 4–6.
[115]*Ibid.*, p. 60.
[116]*Minutes*, Coordinating Council for Higher Education, May 6, 1969.

upward mobility, and most of their strategies have attempted to duplicate or assume the functions that have historically been monopolized by the university. Furthermore, each segment appeals to one of the two dominant values of the system in pressing its claims. The main complaint of the state college system, put oversimply, is: "Why are we prohibited from striving to be as excellent as the university?" — an appeal to the value of equal opportunity. The university's main defense is that to grant the same privileges to the state colleges would result in wasteful duplication and a decline in quality (an appeal to the value of competitive excellence). Finally, the junior colleges, enjoying solid legitimacy on the basis of egalitarian values, have mainly been content to secure an established place in the system of higher education.

Conflict among campuses of the university. As the university developed into a system of multiple general campuses, a pattern of competition similar to that between the state colleges and the university developed among the campuses. The establishment of the university's professional schools in the late nineteenth century and the establishment of several research stations around the turn of the century did not generate significant opposition from the Berkeley campus, because its exclusive jurisdiction as a general campus was not jeopardized. But when pressure began to grow for the development of a general university campus in the southern part of California early in the twentieth century, opposition from Berkeley was heated and substantial enough to delay the creation of a general university campus in Los Angeles for a number of years.[117] Competition between Berkeley and UCLA for funds and facilities has always been keen.

Intercampus rivalry became very intense in the late 1950s and continued into the 1960s. Just before the Master Plan was submitted by the Survey Team to the various governing bodies for approval, the chancellors from Berkeley, UCLA, and Davis expressed some opposition to the plan on the grounds that it would permit the development of several new campuses. In the early 1960s, moreover, some Berkeley faculty members opposed the decentralization of the graduate division and the decentralization of

[117] Stadtman, *op. cit.* (n. 10, above), chap. 15.

the Academic Senate into a system with a division on each campus and with substantial powers for the statewide senate.[118]

Few issues of academic policy escaped definition in terms of intercampus rivalry in the 1960s. When the policy of setting a maximum limitation of 27,500 students for the Berkeley and UCLA campuses was put in effect in the early 1960s, the question of the criteria by which applicants would be diverted from one campus to another arose. Representatives from the Santa Barbara and Davis campuses — which were regarded as upwardly mobile general campuses at the time — called for the principle of "random selection of students for redirection," and Riverside, also a "coming" general campus, called for "equal standards of quality on each campus." The statewide Committee on Educational Policy also called for a policy of random selection. Berkeley, however, dissented from this vote, "expressing itself in favor of academic qualifications and against random selection." Berkeley, as the campus in greatest demand by applicants at the time, wished to set up arrangements that would permit it to insist on academic qualifications and thereby perhaps keep the best students for itself; the newer, striving campuses argued for an arrangement based on equality.

The Berkeley campus, in short, struck a posture of opposition — varying in strength from issue to issue — to measures that would decentralize features in which Berkeley had always had a leading position, would standardize procedures for all campuses, and would centralize administrative and faculty authority in the university-wide system. (UCLA often took the same stance, except when the issue involved the possibility of gain over Berkeley.) Berkeley acted toward the remainder of the system in much the same way the university acted toward the state colleges — as a conservative elite resisting standardization and further overlapping of functions. One could speculate that the strong opposition on the part of many of the Berkeley faculty over the issue of the academic calender (expressed especially in the period 1963–1965) derived its heat less from the intrinsic merits of one academic calendar over another than from the symbolic character of that issue — forcing the Berkeley campus into the mold of centralization and standardi-

---

[118]The facts of this paragraph are based on a conversation with Clark Kerr and on a communication from Frank Newman.

zation that seemed to be accompanying the inevitable move toward a system of multiple general campuses.[119] Furthermore, this series of defeats in the early 1960s — over libraries, governance, graduate studies, and the calendar — may have increased the Berkeley faculty's displeasure with the university administration in these years and may have predisposed them to regard the 1964 student rebellion against the administration with more favor than they might have felt a half-dozen years earlier.[120]

On other occasions policy changes have brought cries of anguish from the newer, building campuses. In one vision of the Master Plan, all the campuses in the university (except the San Francisco campus) were gradually to be converted into large, general campuses. In 1971, however, revised demographic estimates and budgetary restrictions led university-wide officials to revise the growth estimates downward and to set much smaller ceilings for the newer campuses than those anticipated in the earlier plans. (The new ceiling for Riverside, for example, would be around

[119] Debates on the year-round conversion dotted the agenda of the Berkeley Division between 1963 and 1965. In a poll of the Berkeley Division on April 17, 1963, 420 respondents voted for the "status quo" calendar, and 349 voted for year-round operations (47 abstentions). On a separate question, which asked what form of year-round operations were preferable if they became necessary, 114 voted for a trimester system, 296 for a three-term calendar with a shorter summer session, and 362 voted for a four-term calendar (44 abstentions). (*Minutes*, Berkeley Division, April 29, 1963, p. ii.) In October, 1964, the Berkeley Committee on Educational Policy complained bitterly that "[early] in the year, the University-wide Committee was notified by the president that the calendar form for year-round operations was not a closed issue. The Berkeley CEP reviewed the matter in discussions and passed a resolution requesting university-wide CEP to reaffirm its earlier position to the effect that the quarter system 'is inferior to other calendars which had been suggested. The university-wide CEP took this action. Some time later it was announced that the quarter system was to be adopted." (*Minutes*, Berkeley Division, October 13, 1964.) In a subsequent poll in April, 1965, faculty members were again asked what form of year-round operation they would prefer. Three hundred nineteen voted for the quarter system and 497 for a semester system with a summer term supported by state funds. "Report of the Committee on Elections to the Berkeley Division, May 3, 1965." This committee's report also recorded a number of comments by respondents, pro and con. One faculty member's comment is typical: "I object to the way year-round operation and the quarter system have been forced on the faculty, with regents and administration ignoring the committee reports that opposed their desired ends and thereby making a mockery of faculty control of education." *Ibid.*, p. 10.
[120] If these speculations are correct, they provide a striking example of the interrelatedness of system-wide changes and a political situation on one campus.

12,000, and those for Irvine and San Diego about 10,000.) Berkeley and UCLA would retain their current maximum of 27,500. These revised plans drew negative reactions from administrators and faculty members at the Santa Cruz, Riverside, Irvine, San Diego, and Santa Barbara campuses. The new growth plans also called for greater specialization of campuses, which would require each campus to concentrate in some areas and to maintain no programs or very small ones in others. Berkeley and UCLA officials welcomed this revised plan, but it was strongly opposed on the newer campuses.[121]

The issues of the early 1960s are thus being raised again in the early 1970s, although in a somewhat different guise. In the earlier period of rapid growth, the hold of Berkeley and UCLA on the resources that would guarantee them a lead in competitive excellence seemed to be slipping, as the developing campuses were pressing for standardized policies that would afford equal treatment to all campuses. Furthermore, the arguments for standardization were, in the end, egalitarian ones — "Why shouldn't the new campuses be allowed to aim for excellence, too?" In the scenario for the 1970s, which calls for slower growth and more specialization of campuses, the large general campuses are relatively content, and the smaller campuses are complaining of inequities. Moreover, in California's system of higher education — and perhaps generally — it appears more difficult to resist the claims of aspirants to equal status under conditions of abundance and rapid growth than under conditions of scarcity and possible stagnation.

The Changing Fortunes of Several Academic Estates Within the University

The university experienced a number of distinct structural changes between 1950 and 1970, but several campuses experienced these changes in different degrees and at different times. In 1950, Berkeley and UCLA were already general campuses; for them the next two decades brought some expansion of their undergraduate teaching, greater expansion of their graduate teaching, and an enormous expansion of their research activities. Berkeley led the way in these trends, with UCLA following close behind.

[121]*Los Angeles Times*, July 11, 1971.

Davis, Santa Barbara, and Riverside became general campuses only in the late 1950s, and did not begin expansion of graduate training and research until the early 1960s. Finally, the new campuses of San Diego, Irvine, and Santa Cruz, although at first charged with very different respective missions, were, in 1970, only beginning to establish themselves as general campuses committed to undergraduate education, graduate education, and research.

In this section I trace the implications of the broad pattern of structural responses for some of the different academic estates — especially faculty, graduate students, undergraduate students, and research personnel. Relying again on Tocqueville's perspective, I try to demonstrate that many of these structural responses created relative deprivation, disaffection, and diminished institutional loyalty in many of the estates.

The changing composition of student enrollments. Table 8 shows the changes in different categories of students, for the university as a whole and for three selected campuses — Berkeley, Davis, and Santa Barbara — in four-year periods between 1952 and 1968. The university showed a considerable increase in rate of total growth in the 1960s over the 1950s (approximately 40 percent growth in four-year periods during the 1960s, 20 percent during the 1950s). The proportion of lower division students remained approximately one-third of the total throughout the 1950s, while the upper division proportion declined slightly, mainly because of the substantial increase in graduate students. In the 1960s, the lower division and graduate proportions began to decline slightly and the upper division proportion to rise again, largely as a result of the partial implementation of the Master Plan, which called for a diversion of lower division students to the junior colleges and for increased transfers at the upper division level.

The several campuses of the university experienced these trends very differently, however. Berkeley led the way and went further than the other campuses in increasing the proportion of graduate students and decreasing the proportion of lower division students. The Davis campus, beginning the 1950s primarily as an agricultural research and graduate training center and becoming a general campus only late in the decade, showed more continuity in the proportion of lower division, upper division, and graduate stu-

Table 8
RATES OF GROWTH AND CHANGING COMPOSITION OF LOWER-DIVISION, UPPER-DIVISION AND GRADUATE STUDENTS, UNIVERSITY OF CALIFORNIA AS A WHOLE, AND BERKELEY, DAVIS, AND SANTA BARBARA CAMPUSES, 1952–1968

Campus	Year	Total students	Four-year percent growth	Lower-division	Percent of total students	Four-year percent growth	Upper-division	Percent of total students	Four-year percent growth	Graduate students	Percent of total students	Four-year percent growth
Total UC	1952	31,557	—	10,902	35	—	13,187	41	—	7,468	24	—
	1956	37,805	20	13,170	35	21	16,119	43	22	8,516	22	14
	1960	46,057	22	16,282	35	24	16,383	35	2	13,412	30	57
	1964	66,728	45	22,835	34	40	23,987	36	46	19,906	20	49
	1968	91,035	42	29,725	32	30	36,364	40	52	24,946	27	25
Berkeley	1952	15,630	—	5,380	34	—	6,288	40	—	3,972	26	—
	1956	17,425	11	6,035	35	12	6,945	40	10	4,445	25	12
	1960	20,825	20	7,166	34	12	6,832	33	1	6,827	33	54
	1964	27,039	30	7,232	27	1	10,145	38	49	9,562	35	39
	1968	27,319	0	6,773	25	6	11,006	40	8	9,540	35	0
Davis	1952	1,398	—	709	50	—	371	27	—	318	23	—
	1956	2,103	58	1,035	49	46	622	30	68	446	21	40
	1960	2,882	32	1,276	44	23	887	31	43	719	25	61
	1964	6,331	124	2,853	45	124	2,016	32	127	1,462	23	103
	1968	10,624	68	4,172	49	46	4,156	39	106	2,296	22	57
Santa Barbara	1952	1,466	—	630	43	—	835	57	—	1	0	—
	1956	2,148	47	1,095	51	74	993	46	20	60	3	20
	1960	3,397	58	1,926	56	76	1,342	40	35	129	4	115
	1964	7,728	127	4,207	55	118	2,872	37	114	649	8	403
	1968	12,220	55	5,182	42	23	5,305	43	85	1,733	14	167

dents than either Berkeley or Santa Barbara. Although the late 1950s and early 1960s brought a substantial expansion of graduate students to Davis, the proportion of *graduate* students remained consistently between 20 and 25 percent of the total, largely because the undergraduate student body was also expanding rapidly as the Davis campus began to develop its new program of undergraduate education in the arts and sciences. In the 1960s, the proportion of lower division students began to decline and the proportion of upper division students began to increase; these changes were associated with the Master Plan policies of diversion and transfer. Davis, however, consistently maintained a higher proportion of lower division students than did the system as a whole.

The Santa Barbara campus, almost exclusively an undergraduate college in the 1950s, experienced an extraordinary takeoff into graduate education in the late 1950s and early 1960s; like the other smaller campuses, it maintained this rapid growth while Berkeley and UCLA ceased to grow and consolidated their positions as large general campuses in the middle and late 1960s. Yet Santa Barbara still kept its undergraduate emphasis. By 1968 only 14 percent of Santa Barbara's students were graduates, and its proportion of lower division students was still higher than either Berkeley or the university as a whole.

Table 8 also reflects the decline in Berkeley's relative contribution to the educational enterprise as a whole. In 1952 Berkeley had about half of the total students in the university, and more than half the graduate students. By 1968 its share was closer to one-third in most categories, and it had less than one-quarter of the lower division students. UCLA experienced a similar relative decline. Each of the university campuses was thus moving in the direction of a fully general campus, although the takeoff points and the rates of change for the different campuses differed considerably. Moreover, as the general movement proceeded, the campuses tended to become equal with respect to performance of the university's various functions.

One further point concerning the composition of student enrollment in the university must be mentioned — a datum dealing with student turnover. A central feature of the Master Plan was that students in one segment should be able to transfer to other segments if they were academically qualified. In particular the plan stressed the transfer of junior college students to other segments. The Coordinating Council on Higher Education also pressed for institutionalizing procedures — such as easy transfer of course credits — that would facilitate transfer.[122] One procedure is revealed in Table 9, which shows the immediate educational origins of university students for the years 1961–1969.[123] For the university as a whole, in any given year, more than one-third — and sometimes more than 40 percent — of the enrolled students had not been at the university in the previous year. This percentage was higher (usually more than 50 percent) for lower division students because of the many new freshmen, but between one-fifth and one-fourth of the upper division students were also new or returning in most of these years. Actually, the figures in Table 9 are underestimated, because they do not include interuniversity transfers from one campus to another. These turnover data suggest that it is difficult to conceive of a University of California campus in those years as a campus community in the traditional sense — in which a student is continuously involved for four years before graduating. The figures also suggest the magnitude of individual student adjustment to a new campus setting, one which is difficult to adjust to because of its shifting and transient population.

The changing composition of the faculty and the changing pattern of its activities. Between 1952 and 1968, the regular faculty of the entire univerity (professors, associate professors, assistant professors) grew from 1,987 to 4,954, a 105 percent increase. During the same period the number of students increased from 31,557 to 91,035, a 189 percent increase. Overall, then, the ratio between faculty and students declined somewhat. This trend, combined with several others, altered the pattern of teaching activities in the system, with a decline in undergraduate teaching — especially lower division teaching — by regular faculty members. What were these trends?

Consider first the changes in different categories of faculty personnel. As Table 10 indicates, the system as a whole experienced a slight increase in the proportion of full and associate pro-

---

[122]The legitimizing value for these arrangements is, of course, the value of equality of opportunity. Above, pp. 00–00.

[123]Table 9 does not reflect *only* the transfer phenomenon. Induction into selective service, or dropping out and subsequently returning, also contributed to turnover.

Table 9
FLOW OF UNDERGRADUATE STUDENTS TO THE UNIVERSITY OF CALIFORNIA, 1961–1969

Year	New students	Continuing students	Returning students	New students from:					Percent new or returning students	Percent new or returning lower-division	Percent new or returning upper-division
				State colleges	Junior colleges	Private colleges	No colleges[a]	California high schools			
1961	13,030	21,336	1,851	368	2,176	1,604	1,504	7,378	41	58	22
1962	13,741	23,092	2,053	447	2,260	1,509	1,752	7,713	41	56	24
1963	15,514	22,955	2,361	495	2,049	1,906	2,051	8,752	44	58	24
1964	17,664	27,496	2,382	515	2,660	2,049	1,969	10,471	42	59	24
1965	19,176	31,508	2,424	700	2,901	1,728	2,098	11,749	41	57	22
1966	20,757	34,881	2,158	788	3,073	1,964	3,211	12,341	40	56	23
1967	22,623	39,218	2,406	857	3,685	2,213	2,796	13,072	39	56	22
1968	20,079	44,666	2,185	811	3,768	596	3,264	11,640	31	49	18
1969	20,476	47,791	2,518	909	4,438	494	2,569	12,066	32	49	18

Source: Kenneth E. Golden, "Optimal Diversion Policies for Enrollment Planning" (Master's Essay, Graduate School of Business Administration, University of California, Berkeley), Appendix, Table A1.

[a]A miscellaneous category referring mainly to students coming from colleges and high schools outside of California.

Table 10

RATE OF GROWTH, PERCENTAGE OF TOTAL FACULTY OF DIFFERENT CATEGORIES OF FACULTY MEMBERS FOR THE UNIVERSITY OF CALIFORNIA AS A WHOLE, AND FOR THE BERKELEY, DAVIS, AND SANTA BARBARA CAMPUSES, 1952–1968

Campus	Year	Professors	Percent of faculty	Four-year percent growth	Associate professors	Percent of faculty	Four-year percent growth	Assistant professors	Percent of faculty	Four-year percent growth	Lecturers and instructors	Percent of faculty	Four-year percent growth
Total UC	1952	779	29	—	525	19	—	683	25	—	738	27	—
	1956	1,012	29	30	750	21	43	939	26	37	870	24	18
	1960	1,225	35	21	787	22	5	862	24	-8	685	19	-21
	1964	1,379	33	13	738	18	-7	1,181	28	37	855	21	23
	1968	2,026	33	46	1,045	17	42	1,883	31	59	1,202	19	41
Berkeley	1952	431	35	—	216	18	—	248	20	—	332	27	—
	1956	507	37	18	282	21	31	237	17	-4	335	25	1
	1960	542	39	7	280	20	-1	249	18	5	323	23	-4
	1964	613	38	13	247	16	-12	383	24	54	353	22	9
	1968	729	40	19	284	15	15	428	23	12	398	22	12
Davis	1952	64	24	—	55	20	—	73	27	—	78	29	—
	1956	84	27	31	82	26	49	93	30	27	55	17	-29
	1960	147	30	75	114	23	39	148	30	59	82	17	49
	1964	79[a]	22	-46	76[a]	21	-42	142[a]	39	-4	70[a]	19	-15
	1968	189	29	119	129	20	70	222	34	56	109	17	56
Santa Barbara	1952	26	15	—	41	24	—	74	44	—	27	16	—
	1956	34	17	31	56	28	12	76	37	3	34	17	22
	1960	49	20	44	68	28	21	91	37	20	37	15	9
	1964	93	25	90	81	21	19	128	34	41	74	20	100
	1968	181	27	95	123	19	52	230	35	90	121	18	64

[a]The decline in numbers of all categories of faculty members on the Davis campus between 1960 and 1964 has to do with the re-classification of many research personnel from academic to nonacademic when the Davis campus was converted to a general campus.

fessors in the 1950s, and a slight decrease in the proportion of assistant professors and nonregular faculty (lecturers and instructors). This trend probably reflected the brisk national competition for highly qualified academic personnel during this decade. These gentle trends were reversed in the 1960s, and the proportion of assistant professors in particular began to rise noticeably. This trend is perhaps associated with the tendency of the new, teaching-oriented institutions to recruit young personnel. In 1967, for example, assistant professors at the Santa Cruz campus (69 in number) made up almost half of the entire regular and nonregular faculty (142); in the same year assistant professors at Irvine campus (117) outnumbered all other categories of faculty combined.

As Table 10 also indicates, the several campuses experienced very different changes in the composition of their instructional staffs. Throughout the period, Berkeley consistently had a larger proportion of full professors and a lower proportion of assistant professors than the system as a whole, whereas Davis and Santa Barbara generally had a lower proportion of full professors and a higher proportion of assistant professors. This can be attributed to the fact that Berkeley was more involved in intense national competition for distinguished faculty personnel than the other campuses, and as a result was forced to rely more on high-level offers and accelerated promotions to secure and retain its faculty.[124] The distribution of "special salaries, individually determined and above the top of the regular scale," reflected the same situation. Of the 267 above-scale appointees in the entire system in 1968–1969, Berkeley had 131, or 49 percent. Berkeley and the three new campuses of Irvine, San Diego, and Santa Cruz have age-graded salary levels above the average for the system as a whole, with the four campuses of Los Angeles, Riverside, Davis, and Santa Barbara falling below the average.[125] These differentials undoubtedly also

[124] Between 1960–1961 and 1967–1968, a grand total of 141 professors and associate professors resigned from the Berkeley and Los Angeles campuses to take positions at other American universities and colleges. Of these, 49, or 35 percent, went to nine "high-ranking universities (with "distinguished" graduate faculties in two or more general areas of study, according to the American Council of Education Study of 1967) — Harvard, Stanford, Yale, Wisconsin, Michigan, Princeton, Columbia, Illinois, and Chicago. A total of 74 professors and associate professors resigned from all the other campuses, with only 11, or 15 percent, moving to these nine universities. Office of the President, University of California, *Academic Personnel Report, 1968–69*, Table XX.

[125] *Ibid.*, p. 10.

reflect Berkeley's competitive situation, as well as the efforts of the new campuses to gain a secure foothold in their early years by bidding competitively at all levels for scarce talent.[126]

The implications of these trends are considerable. In general, the national competition for the most distinguished talent was a competition for distinguished *research* talent, with teaching ability playing a less salient role. Those campuses most involved in national bidding for talent (Berkeley and UCLA) tended to recruit persons committed more to research and to graduate students — who are more involved in research — than to undergraduates. Furthermore, the senior faculty tended to supervise graduate instruction more than junior faculty and nonregular faculty did, and assistant professors and nonregular faculty tended to offer undergraduate courses more than senior faculty (although the entire faculty was to some degree involved in both kinds of instruction). So far as a campus defined its mission as securing a distinguished faculty, and so far as it recruited and promoted to secure this faculty, it tended to place greater stress on research and graduate education than on undergraduate education.

Although the foregoing analyses reveal some university-wide trends between 1950 and 1970, some campuses experienced them more than others. In 1950, Berkeley emphasized research and graduate training more than the other campuses, and it pushed this preference farther than any of the other campuses in the twenty years that ensued. Several kinds of indirect evidence point to the same decreased emphasis on undergraduate teaching on other campuses of the university. In 1970, the Office of the President released a report — based on surveys of faculty members in 1960 and 1969 — on faculty effort and output. Although faculty reports of time spent in various kinds of activities are likely to be unreli-

---

[126] Of initial appointments made in 1968–1969 Berkeley offered tenure to 34 percent, San Diego to 31 percent, Irvine to 42 percent and Santa Cruz to 36 percent. The Office of the President described the high percentages at the new campuses as reflecting the recruitment of "initial cadres of mature scholars . . . to start new departments and programs." *Ibid.*, p. 5. San Diego from the beginning tended to be heavily represented at the higher ranks, but the recruitment policies of Santa Cruz and Irvine apparently represented a change from their very early years in the early and middle 1960s, when they recruited mainly assistant professors. The average percentage of initial appointees receiving tenure for the Los Angeles, Santa Barbara, Davis, and Riverside campuses was 24 percent.

able, the comparisons between the two years are in the expected directions. Throughout the university, the proportion of faculty time spent on regular courses dropped from 24 percent in 1960 to 21 percent in 1969, whereas time spent in supervising independent study (a typical mode of graduate instruction) and time spent on research showed slight increases.[127] More impressive, however, is the direct evidence of a significant shift of regular-faculty instruction away from undergraduate — especially lower division — teaching, toward graduate instruction. Table 11 shows this shift in a dramatic way. Several other surveys, shown in Chart 3, also reveal a changing pattern of contact between regular faculty[128] and students. All the campuses except Davis[129] showed a decline in weekly class hours between 1954 and 1962, and a steady downward trend between 1962 and 1966. Berkeley and UCLA seem to have led the way in this trend, although by 1966 there is little difference in weekly class hours among the campuses. Also, the time spent in individual supervision of study also increased steadily between 1962 and 1966, with Berkeley and UCLA showing consistently higher figures on this count as well.

Data relating to the increasing emphasis on research are even more unsatisfactory. Certainly the fact that for each year between 1954 and 1964 one-fourth of the tenured faculty was on leave for at least half the year suggests a research commitment of considerable magnitude.[130] Two surveys were made of faculty workload, one in 1954–1955,[131] and one in 1963.[132] Unfortunately, these surveys are scarcely comparable because of one important difference in

[127] Memorandum from the president to the Statewide Committee on Educational Policy, January 9, 1970, p. 11. The publication of these results coincided with President Hitch's call for a renewed emphasis on undergraduate teaching in the university.

[128] Chart 3 includes "instructors" as regular faculty; Table 9 does not.

[129] Classroom instruction increased at Davis because, between 1954 and 1962, the campus was converted from a primarily research and graduate training center in the agricultural sciences to a general instructional campus.

[130] Heirich, *op. cit.* (n. 8, above), p. 57. Heirich's figures refer only to the large social science and humanities departments. For the physical and life sciences, where research funds were more plentiful, the figures would undoubtedly be higher.

[131] General Survey Committee 1954–1964, *Western Conference Cost and Statistical Study* (November, 1957).

[132] Coordinating Council on Higher Education, *California Public Higher Education Cost and Statistical Analysis* (June, 1965).

Table 11
DISTRIBUTION OF FACULTY EFFORT BY LEVEL OF STUDENT IN 1960 AND 1968, AND ENROLLMENT ALL FACULTY APPOINTMENTS, UNIVERSITY OF CALIFORNIA

Level of student	Percent of total enrollment		Weekly hours spent in course and tutorial activities		Percent of weekly hours in course and tutorial activities		Faculty hours per student per week	
	1960	1968	1960	1968	1960	1968	1960	1968
(1)	(2)	(3)	(4)	(5)	(6)	(7)	(8)	(9)
Lower division	36	33	6.95	4.14	22.1	15.1	1.18	.69
Upper division	37	40	12.82	9.30	40.8	33.9	2.11	1.26
Graduate	27	27	11.65	14.00	37.1	51.0	2.62	2.88
TOTAL	100	100	31.42	27.44	100	100		

Source: The University of California, Office of the Vice President — Planning and Analysis, based on 1960 Faculty Time Study and 1968 Faculty Effort and Output Study.

Chart 3
WEEKLY CONTACT HOURS PER FTE REGULAR FACULTY OF THE UNIVERSITY

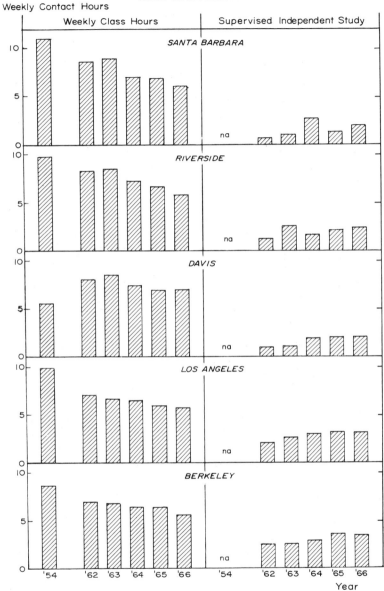

NOTE: Regular Faculty: Professor, Associate Professor, Assistant Professor, Instructor

SOURCES: *California and Western Conference Cost and Statistical Study*, General Survey Committee 1954–1955 (published November 27, 1956), *California Public Higher Education Cost and Statistical Analysis*, CCHE, Fall 1963 (Summary published June 1965), and *University of California Summary Analysis of Basic Data, Fall Terms 1962, 1963, 1964, 1965, 1966*, Office of Analytical Studies.

method: in the 1954–1955 study, time spent in organized research was independently reported, while the 1963 survey excluded all faculty time spent in organized research regardless of the source of salary payment. This discrepancy is particularly serious, because organized research was increasing rapidly in the decade between the two surveys. Notwithstanding this deficiency in data, some interesting general contrasts among the several campuses can be seen in Chart 4. The balance between teaching and departmental research at Berkeley and UCLA appears to remain largely unchanged — although again there may have been significant changes in time spent in organized research which is absent from Chart 4. As the Davis campus changed from a largely agricultural program in its teaching-research, balance moved closer to that of the larger campuses. Similarly, as Santa Barbara and Riverside were changing from primarily undergraduate institutions to general campuses, the proportion of time devoted by faculty to research rose almost to the levels of Berkeley and UCLA. These trends corroborate the point that, in the late 1950s and early 1960s, the shifts of growth and function in the smaller campuses were moving them toward the Berkeley-UCLA pattern.

The size and structure of courses were also changing. I define *class* here as the unit assembled for instruction; *course* as a fixed program of instruction for credit for which the students may or may not ever assemble, or for which they may sometimes assemble for course-wide lectures and sometimes be subdivided into smaller classes. Chart 5 compares the mean class size for five campuses in 1954 and 1963. The two largest campuses did not change significantly in this period. But Davis, Santa Barbara, and Riverside, all of which took off in the late 1950s, increased class size notably.[133] The changes in course size were more dramatic, especially at the lower division level. Chart 6 compares the number of courses offered per 100 students in lower division mathematics, physical science, and engineering-science between 1954 and 1963. Chart 7 makes the same comparison for lower division social science courses. At Berkeley and UCLA, course size rather than class size was expanding, largely because lecture courses were supplemented by smaller classroom meetings with teaching assistants.

[133]The one exception is graduate instruction at Davis, which declined because much of this instruction was converted to professional research activity.

Chart 4

CHANGES IN FUNCTIONAL EMPHASIS FROM 1954–1955 TO FALL UNIVERSITY OF CALIFORNIA

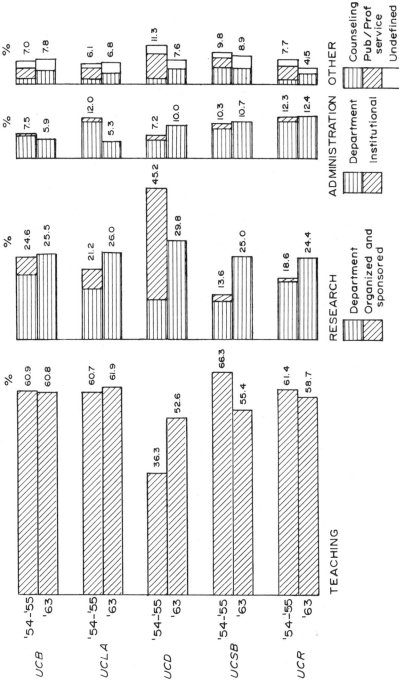

SOURCES: *California Public Higher Education Cost and Statistical Analysis*, CCHE, Fall 1963 (Summary published June 1965) and *California and Western Conference Cost and Statistical Study*, General Survey Committee 1954–55 (published November 27, 1956).

Chart 5
MEAN CLASS SIZE (TOTAL) COMPARISONS, 1954–1955 AND FALL, 1963 UNIVERSITY OF CALIFORNIA

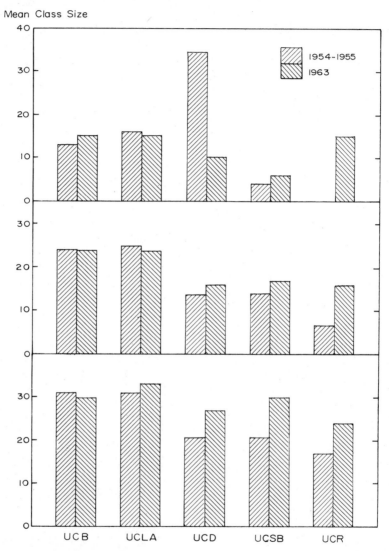

NOTE: 1954–1955 data are an average of the two semesters for the academic year.

SOURCE: *California Western Conference Cost and Statistical Study*, General Survey Committee 1954–1955 (published November 27, 1956) and *California Public Higher Education Cost and Statistical Analysis*, CCHE, Fall 1963 (Summary published June 1965).

Chart 6

UNIVERSITY COMPARISON OF NUMBER OF COURSES OF-
FERED PER 100 STUDENTS ENROLLED IN LOWER DIVISION
MATHEMATICAL, PHYSICAL AND ENGINEERING SCIENCES

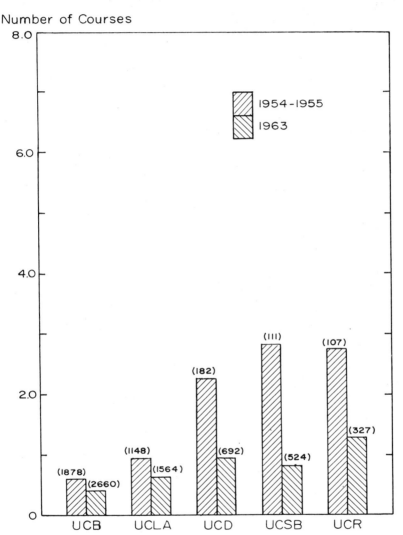

NOTE: Number in parenthesis is FTE enrollment. The
1954–1955 FTE is semester average.

SOURCES: *California Western Conference Cost and Statistical
Study*, General Survey Committee 1954–1955 (published November
27, 1956) and *California Public Higher Education Cost and Statistical
Analysis*, CCHE, Fall 1963 (Summary published June 1965).

Chart 7

UNIVERSITY COMPARISON OF NUMBER OF COURSES OF-
FERED PER 100 STUDENTS ENROLLED IN LOWER DIVISION
SOCIAL SCIENCE COURSES

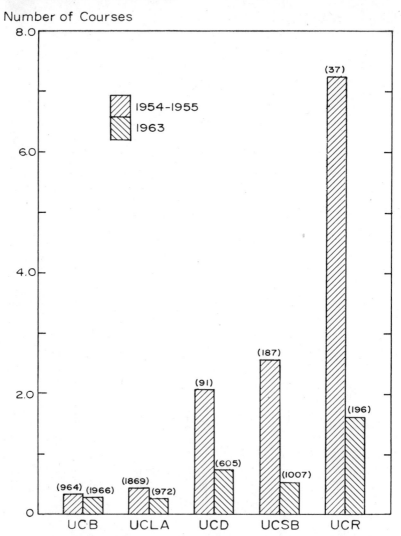

NOTE: Number in parenthesis is FTE enrollment. The
1954–1955 FTE is semester average.

SOURCES: *California Western Conference Cost and Statistical
Study*, General Survey Committee 1954–1955 (published November
27, 1956) and *California Public Higher Education Cost and Statistical
Analysis*, CCHE, Fall 1963 (Summary published June 1965).

In any event, contact between regular faculty and undergraduate students was declining, either because of larger classes for regular faculty members or because of increased subdivision of courses into classes taught by graduate students.

The growth of ancillary personnel: teaching assistants and research personnel. I have reviewed a number of trends that affected university teaching between 1950 and 1970. Among these were the slowly declining ratio between regular faculty and students; a tendency for regular faculty to become more involved in research, and for some campuses to become top-heavy with senior faculty; a decline in proportion of faculty time spent in undergraduate teaching, especially in the lower division; and increasingly superficial contact between regular faculty and undergraduates, owing either to larger classes or the sectioning of large lecture courses. These trends, combined with a high turnover rate at the undergraduate level, all pointed toward less intense and continuous contact between regular faculty and students in the university. Most of these trends were greater on the Berkeley campus, with UCLA following close behind; they began to appear in the late 1950s at Santa Barbara, Riverside, and Davis; and they were only beginning to appear in the late 1960s on the newer, smaller campuses.

The increasing size of the campuses, then, along with the functional shift toward research, suggests that a teaching gap had developed. Faculty members were placing greater emphasis on some aspects of their role — research and its administration, administration associated with increasing scale, and involvement in national and international affairs — and had meanwhile reduced their undergraduate teaching commitments without actually abandoning their teaching responsibilities. Just as the university campuses had in varying degrees become functionally overloaded in response to the opportunities and demands of the 1950s and 1960s,[134] so had the roles of many faculty members become over-extended.

The university tended to fill this teaching gap by greater use of graduate students as teaching assistants and readers. The teaching assistant was a graduate student, hired usually on a half-time basis, at a pay scale somewhat lower than that of a junior faculty

[134] Above, pp. 51–56.

member. He might be given exclusive responsibility for instruction of a class (for example, in introductory languages), or closely or loosely supervised conduct of a subdivided section of a large lecture course; he might assist the professor in preparing reading lists, drawing up and grading examinations, conferring with students, and so on; or he might assist the professor in supervising laboratory experiments.[135] A reader did not, as a rule, instruct students but assisted faculty members in administering the class, grading exercises and examinations, and the like.

Table 12 shows that the growth in the number of teaching assistants in the university as a whole was considerably more rapid than the growth in the number of regular faculty between 1952 and 1964, with exceptional increases in the years 1960–1964. Beginning in 1965, the proliferation of teaching assistants was halted by legislative action, and although the number of teaching assistants increased slightly over the next few years, the percentage of total faculty who were teaching assistants decreased. Interestingly, though, the legislative action did little to affect the use of graduate students and nonregular faculty for instruction. On the Berkeley campus, for example, when the number of teaching assistants was reduced from 1,543 in 1965 to 1,518 in 1966, the number of teaching associates (a job category that usually pays a bit more and has more responsibility than the teaching assistant) jumped from 82 to 233; and the number of instructors (one-year junior appointments) went from 61 to 140. At UCLA, the number of teaching assistants dropped from 1,030 in 1965 to 582 in 1969; during the same period, however, the number of teaching associates grew from 66 to 454.

The ratio of teaching assistants to faculty varied greatly among the campuses. Throughout the two decades Berkeley, with its large undergraduate student body and its large supply of graduate students, had a higher ratio of teaching assistants to faculty than the other campuses and the system as a whole; by the peak year of 1964 the teaching assistants outnumbered the regular faculty. The Davis campus showed a rapid increase of teaching assistants in the 1960s, although they never became more than two-thirds of the faculty. Santa Barbara, almost exclusively an undergraduate institution in the 1950s, experienced an extraordinary increase in numbers of

---

[135] Office of the President, "Teaching Assistant System in the University of California," November 11, 1966, p. 2.

Table 12

GROWTH OF TEACHING ASSISTANTS, AND PERCENT OF REGULAR
FACULTY, FOR THE UNIVERSITY OF CALIFORNIA AS A WHOLE, AND
FOR THE BERKELEY, DAVIS, AND SANTA BARBARA CAMPUSES,
1952–1968

Campus	Year	Number of teaching assistants	Number of regular faculty	Teaching assistants as percent of regular faculty
UC Total	1952	989	1,992	50%
	1956	1,140	2,721	42
	1960	1,480	2,874	52
	1964	2,975	3,298	90
	1968	3,016	5,044	60
Berkeley	1952	560	895	63
	1956	660	1,026	64
	1960	882	1,071	83
	1964	1,430	1,243	114
	1968	1,162	1,531	76
Davis	1952	24	192	12
	1956	30	279	11
	1960	57	409	14
	1964	198	297	66
	1968	329	540	61
Santa Barbara	1952	1	146	1
	1956	0	166	0
	1960	7	208	3
	1964	243	302	80
	1968	408	534	76

teaching assistants in the early 1960s, which was also its period of
phenomenal increase in graduate and undergraduate students (see
Table 8).

The extent of the involvement of teaching assistants in undergraduate education is shown in the results of a poll of the 1965
graduating class at Berkeley, where

> thirty-one percent of the number of all undergraduate classes taken
> during the four years of undergraduate work were regularly taught

by teaching assistants, or were laboratory sessions supervised by assistants. The proportion of the number of all classes taught by teaching assistants was even greater (41 percent) for lower division courses taken by the 1965 graduating class. The traditional picture of the professor reserving to himself the opportunity to meet with smaller groups of students in seminar-like sessions is also inaccurate. In the undergraduate classes of 15 or fewer students, fully 65 percent were instructed by assistants at Berkeley.[136]

Berkeley's situation was most extreme, given its high proportions of full professors and teaching assistants; but so far as the other campuses gave greater emphasis to graduate education and research, they, too, moved toward greater reliance on graduate students to teach undergraduates. In 1966, the Office of the President submitted to the Board of Regents a report on teaching assistants. The report included the percentage of instructional time the teaching assistants carried on the various campuses in the fall of 1964 and the fall of 1965. The results are shown in Table 13.

Table 13
HOURS SPENT WITH TAs AS A PERCENTAGE OF TOTAL
STUDENT-CLASSROOM HOURS BY LEVEL OF INSTRUCTION

Campus	Fall 1964		Fall 1965	
	Lower-division instruction	Upper-division instruction	Lower-division instruction	Upper-division instruction
Berkeley	38.6	11.1	39.7	11.2
Los Angeles	36.1	8.5	36.9	8.2
Davis	24.8	7.7	28.0	9.4
Riverside	22.9	7.3	22.3	6.0
Santa Barbara	24.4	5.5	25.7	5.9
San Diego	33.2	—[a]	44.7	17.3

[a]The San Diego campus had only one upper-division student in 1964.

Source: Office of the President, University of California, "Teaching Assistant System in the University of California," p. 3.

I noted earlier the rapid growth of research funds — especially extramural funds — and the corresponding growth in research units between 1950 and 1970.[137] Many faculty members had part-time appointments at these research facilities, and others used

---

[136] Robert Dubin and Frederic Beisse, "The Assistant: Academic Subaltern," *Administrative Science Quarterly*, 20 (March 1967) 4:529.

[137] Above, pp. 54–58.

them to administer extramurally financed research projects. In addition, the organized research units employed a large number of nonfaculty research appointees, with such titles as "professional research employee" and "research assistant." The full-time professional research employee is nontenured, without formal teaching rights and responsibilities (although many do supervise graduate-student research and teach in other ways); the research assistant is normally a graduate student employed on a short-term basis to assist the faculty member handling a research project. The duties of the research assistant range from full collaboration in research to menial tasks (getting library books, proofreading). Like a teaching assistant, he is paid less than a junior faculty member.

Table 14 shows the growth trend of nonfaculty research personnel between 1952 and 1968, for selected campuses and for the university as a whole. Growth was relatively modest in the early 1950s, but during the boom years of research support in the late 1950s and early 1960s, it rocketed. By 1964 the number of research personnel equalled that of regular faculty. After the retrenchments in extramural research support that began in 1966, the growth rate of research personnel declined, and their numbers fell in proportion to the faculty. Again, the different campuses showed characteristic patterns of growth.

By the peak year of 1964, then, the university had so expanded its ancillary personnel that the teaching-assistant population was virtually as large as the regular faculty, and the university had an equally large population of research personnel.[138] Further-

---

[138] Such phenomena led Burton Clark to observe, with some despair: "The new university has 1,500 or 2,000 men in the various clusters of faculty who have the rights and full citizenship. . . . This already massive core aggregation is surrounded by ever larger aggregations of educational workers who do have an ever larger share of the teaching and the research who do not have full rights. In the research centers, there are two nonfaculties, one composed of postdoctoral researchers and the other of predoctoral research assistants. Back in the departments, there is an army of teaching assistants, an aggregation whose use and abuse has become a scandal on more than one campus; and in the new university, with its metropolitan location, one increasingly finds a fourth-fringe faculty in the person of the lecturer — an elastic category that insures there will be someone at the podium in each classroom. One now finds departments, and indeed campuses, where half of the undergraduate day session classroom instruction is offered by persons who are on the books as full-time and part-time lecturers and hence do not have a regular faculty position." Burton R. Clark, "The New University," in *The State of the University: Authority and Change* ed. Carlos E. Kruytbosch and Sheldon L. Messinger (Beverly Hills, Calif.: Sage Publications, 1968), p. 22.

Table 14
GROWTH OF RESEARCH PERSONNEL AND FACULTY FOR THE
UNIVERSITY OF CALIFORNIA AS A WHOLE, AND FOR THE BERKELEY,
DAVIS, AND SANTA BARBARA CAMPUSES, 1952–1968

Campus	Year	Number of research personnel	Number of total faculty	Research personnel as percent of faculty
UC				
Total	1952	305	1,992	15
	1956	399	2,721	15
	1960	2,321	2,784	83
	1964	3,305	3,298	100
	1968	4,054	5,044	80
Berkeley	1952	220	895	25
	1956	295	1,026	29
	1960	1,177	1,071	110
	1964	1,424	1,243	115
	1968	1,486	1,531	96
Davis	1952	46	192	24
	1956	50	279	17
	1960	208	409	51
	1964	318	297	107
	1968	426	540	79
Santa Barbara	1952	1	146	1
	1956	1	166	0
	1960	5	208	2
	1964	40	302	13
	1968	184	534	34

more, by comparing Tables 12 and 14, one can observe that these
two ancillary job categories were more volatile in their growth and
contraction than was the faculty. Teaching assistants, employable
without elaborate formal review, could be hired more readily to
accommodate growing and shifting numbers of students; because
they are nontenured, their numbers could also be more readily
reduced on a year-by-year basis than those of the faculty. Similarly,
research personnel could be hired freely as research funds became
available; and because they were also nontenured, they could be
let go as research projects came to an end. In sum, the use of these

two types of ancillary personnel — as well as the use of temporary faculty — was a principal means by which the university could adapt to changing demands for teaching and changing opportunities for research.

The implications of the changing fortunes of academic estates for relative deprivation and conflict. Let us return for a moment to Tocqueville's basic themes in his analysis of the estates in eighteenth-century France. Owing to a variety of historical trends, the different classes had experienced different fortunes with respect to the stratification system and its rewards. The lesser nobles retained title and position, but the authority and responsibilities traditionally associated with these positions had gradually been usurped by the central administration of the state. The bourgeoisie moved ahead of the nobility in education and wealth but was systematically excluded from some privileges and from access to high society. The peasants had gained some property rights and ownership but were still rankling under traditional duties and obligations, especially taxes. All classes felt to some extent excluded from the stratification system and developed feelings of relative deprivation and antagonism toward other groups as well as toward the government.

In my view, a similar situation emerged at the University of California during its period of rapid growth between 1950 and 1970. This is not to belabor the historical analogy between two social systems — a society and a system of public higher education — whose circumstances were different in many respects. I do argue, however, that the two cases are similar in that both systems had a pattern of stratification, and, because of various structural changes, different academic estates felt deprived in the distribution of rewards associated with that pattern of stratification. I will first consider the principal bases of the university's stratification system and then trace the fortunes of the several estates in relation to this system.

As we have seen, two of the university's central functions are to generate knowledge through research and scholarship and to impart knowledge through teaching. (This distinction is, of course, oversimple, because new knowledge can be created not only by research and scholarship but also as a result of teaching. Nevertheless, the distinction has merit, and it is certainly meaningful to university administrators and faculty.) The university's official criteria for rewarding faculty members — the basis for recruitment and promotion by faculty review committees and administrative officers — emphasized excellence in research and teaching, as well as contribution to the university community, to the general public, and professional service.

But in fact these criteria for such rewards as rank, salary, prestige, and esteem did not weigh equally in the university in the 1950s and 1960s.[139] Creative contribution to knowledge stood far above the other activities. In the postwar period, the main basis for promoting a faculty member was his national reputation for scientific and scholarly distinction, attested by competitive offers from other prestige institutions and by such honors as Guggenheim fellowships, nomination to prestigious organizations, and election to office in professional societies. This was true of Berkeley and UCLA in particular, but as the other campuses moved into the same national arena — as they developed into general campuses with substantial research and graduate training — they, too, began to draw these lines of stratification.

During the 1950s and 1960s, the tremendous expansion of research opportunities for faculty meant increased opportunities for faculty to enhance their prestige according to the dominant values of the system — by publishing important and influential results of research. This increasing emphasis on and involvement in research had a number of profound effects on group life in the university.

Most generally, the encouragement of research increased the premium on contributions to knowledge and decreased the premium on the transmission of knowledge. Joseph Tussman has described this impact eloquently as a conflict between the "university" and the "college":

> The most significant conflict on the modern campus is not the most dramatic one. It is not between students and administration, or faculty and administration, or faculty and students; it is the subtle conflict between the university and the college. It is a peculiarly internal conflict between two tendencies within the same company of men, two purposes, two functions.

[139] They still do not weigh evenly, research being given greater stress than teaching. But in the past few years the university has made efforts to upgrade teaching as a criterion for recruitment and promotion.

The university is the academic community organized for the pursuit of knowledge. It is arrayed under the familiar departmental banners and moves against the unknown on all fronts. Its victories have transformed the world.

The university is a collection of highly trained specialists who work with skill, persistence, and devotion. Its success is beyond question, but it pays the price of its success. The price *is* specialization, and it supports two unsympathetic jibes: the individual specialized scholar may find that, with Oedipus, the pursuit of knowledge leads to impairment of vision; and, the community of scholars, speaking its special tongues, has suffered the fate of Babel.

The men who are the university are also, however, the men who are the college. But the liberal arts college is a different enterprise. It does not assault or extend the frontiers of knowledge. It has a different mission. It cultivates human understanding. The mind of the person, not the body of knowledge, is its central concern. This, I am sure, is the heart of the matter. . . . The university for multiplicity and knowledge; the college for unity and understanding.

The college is everywhere in retreat, fighting a dispirited rearguard action against the triumphant university. The upper division, dominated by departmental cognitive interests, has become, in spirit, the preparatory run at the graduate school, increasingly professional. Only the lower division remains outside the departmental fold — invaded, neglected, exploited, misused.[140]

Tussman might have added that the lower division general education functions have recently been nibbled away by other teeth. As high-level general education courses increase, as well as high school courses introducing the student to academic disciplines, the undergraduate years are threatened from above by the tendency to professionalize and from below with the tendency to upgrade secondary education.

Yet the conflict goes beyond the emphasis on the specialized academic disciplines versus the emphasis on liberal education. Faculty members have always been ranked by excellence, and invidious comparisons among them are not new. Yet the differential increase in research opportunities during the 1950s and 1960s exacerbated such status conflicts among colleagues. Three examples come to mind: (1) Widely available opportunities for research entrepreneurs — either in external agencies or in organized research institutes on the campus — created a centrifugal force in academic

[140] Joseph Tussman, *Experiment at Berkeley* (New York: Oxford University Press, 1969), pp. xiii–xiv.

departments. Some faculty members were able to cut down their departmental responsibilities considerably, making a research institute or research project their intellectual home — and thereby arousing the resentment of those faculty members who were minding the departmental store (departmental teaching and administration have less prestige than successful research). (2) Research opportunities were differentially distributed throughout the university, with the natural and life sciences receiving the lion's share, the social sciences somewhat less, the humanities almost nothing. This differential support inevitably gave rise to feelings of inequity and injustice among language teachers, philosophers, musicologists, and historians who were excluded from the seeming cornucopia of research opportunities in those boom years. (3) The conflict between senior and junior faculty was exacerbated. The majority of research opportunities came to known scholars with established reputations, because the granting agencies considered them the best bets. Thus senior faculty members were likely to receive more leave for research grants and lighter teaching loads. Junior faculty members, especially assistant professors, did not yet have the reputations to attract such grants. As a result they had, in fact if not in principle, heavier teaching loads, but they were aware that their advancement depended largely on their seniors' judgments of their scholarly productivity.

I noted earlier that, although the university experienced a functional shift in the direction of research and professional training (especially of graduate students in the academic departments), it responded to this shift mainly with structural additions (research units) rather than structural differentiation. Nor did university campuses become more specialized; if anything, the main pressure under the Master Plan was for every campus to become a general campus. Nor did the faculty member's role become more specialized. It, too, was functionally overloaded, or overextended. More heavily involved in research and its ancillary activities (travel, applying for research funds, serving on the review panels of granting agencies, and the like), the faculty member's role nevertheless retained all the traditional educational functions associated with it. Even though he was engaged more and more in research, he did not relinquish his teaching appointment, and usually he was still responsible for both graduate and undergraduate courses. Nonetheless, the regular faculty tended to do less under-graduate teaching.

As we have seen, the undergraduate teaching functions fell more and more into the hands of graduate assistants in the late 1950s and 1960s. The relations between faculty and graduate students are often strained by the fundamental fact that the professor is educating the graduate student to be "someone like himself." At the same time this tendency toward professional solidarity is jeopardized by the fact that the faculty member continuously exercises authority — through assessments which determine the fate of the graduate student's career — that underscores the faculty member's superordinate position. The role of teaching assistant, which advances the student toward the rank of colleague but simultaneously keeps him in a subordinate status, exacerbates these general sources of tension.

There is evidence that the role of teaching assistant is particularly fraught with anomalies and strains. In a remarkably frank survey made in 1964–1965, a UCLA committee enumerated some problems associated with the role. The first complaint concerned inequitable working conditions — "[individuals] paid on exactly the same scale work from nine hours a week in some departments to thirty-four and more hours a week in others."[141] Similarly, teaching assistants with full responsibility for sections were classed with — and paid the same as — those doing menial work.[142] As for the role itself, although it obviously prepared the student for his own future independent teaching, it was certainly not oriented toward the major work of graduate school — creative research; the teaching assistant is "constantly faced with the choice of whether to be a good teacher or to concentrate on getting his degree."[143] Graduate students generally preferred the financial support of scholarships or fellowships to teaching assistantships, because the former afforded more freedom; they also preferred the research assistantship to the teaching assistantship, because the former received "comparable salary for performing research toward his own degree, without extraneous duties that have virtually nothing to do

---

[141] "Report of the Chancellor's Coordinating Committee on the Teaching Assistant at UCLA," p. 3.

[142] *Ibid.*, p. 4.

[143] *Ibid.*, p. 3.

with his immediate progress."[144] As more research assistantships became available during the boom years of extramural research support, the abler graduate students — especially in the sciences — tended to become research assistants rather than teaching assistants.[145] The survey also revealed complaints about lack of faculty supervision, arbitrary exercise of faculty authority, crash hiring immediately before duties were to be assumed, and financial inequities.[146]

But the most fundamental source of strain in the teaching assistant's role, in my view, was its relation to the regular faculty. Called upon to perform many of the university's instructional activities, the teaching assistant was nevertheless often reminded that he did not have the faculty's privileges and prerogatives. He did not have tenure, was not a member of an academic department, was not normally permitted to teach other graduate students, and was not part of the faculty senate. Indeed, as a rule he was not *formally* responsible for undergraduate instruction, in that the faculty member "giving" the course was required to authorize final grades, even though his assistant actually taught and evaluated the students much more than the professor. Finally, the graduate student as teaching assistant was not involved in the reward structure of research, but rather in a kind of activity — undergraduate teaching — that the faculty considered less important. As the UCLA survey bluntly remarked, "in part the teaching assistant has allowed the professor to be concerned with nonteaching activities to a greater extent [for example, research or consultation] and this free time has contributed to a compounding of nonteaching interests."[147]

The teaching assistant, in short, was both in the system, in the sense that he performed one of its vital functions, and out of the system, in that he was denied the rewards associated with full citizenship in the faculty. This is a classic case of relative depriva-

---

[144] *Ibid.*, p. 5.

[145] Coordinating Council for Higher Education, *Feasibility and Desirability of Eliminating Lower Division Programs, op. cit.* (n. 47, above), p. 100.

[146] For UCLA, see "Report of the Chancellor's Coordinating Committee on the Teaching Assistant at UCLA," *op. cit.*, (n. 141 above), p. 19; for Berkeley, cf. Office of the President, "Teaching Assistant System in the University of California," *op. cit.*, (n. 135, above), Report on the Berkeley Campus, p. 5.

[147] Coordinating Council for Higher Education, *Feasibility and Desirability of Eliminating Lower Division Programs, op. cit.*, (n. 47, above), p. 100.

tion and parallels Tocqueville's analysis of the various estates in eighteenth-century France.[148]

It stands to reason, then, that the teaching assistant would be likely to protest, among other things, "not being accorded professional treatment, when he is under obligation to perform a professional function."[149] The union of teaching assistants on the Berkeley campus devoted much of its energy to "seeking those prerogatives and prerequisites that would accord their position a measure of status."[150] They were concerned about such matters as the firing of TAs when they ceased being students — the necessary status for becoming teaching assistants — as a result of disciplinary action; procedures for appointment and reappointment; increased participation in the design and content of the courses they taught; standardization of workload; and such office amenities as desks and telephones.[151] Teaching assistants took conspicuous part in the general political protests that afflicted the Berkeley campus in the 1960s — the Free Speech Movement, the Navy Table Strike in December of 1966, and the Third World Liberation Front Strike in the early months of 1969. This participation did not stem from their teaching-assistant status only. Many other factors in the university's complex political situation moved them to political protest. But their academic situation may have been one source of disaffection that contributed to their taking part in protest movements — and invariably on the side of the underdog.

The situation of the professional research personnel, although not as widely publicized as the teaching assistant's, was quite parallel. A survey of professional researchers (excluding teaching assistants) at Berkeley in 1966 pointed out that

> they are academic people in terms of background, qualifications, scholarly accomplishments, and aspirations. A substantial number have been at Berkeley for years, and many more plan to stay. They are heavily involved in the full range of university activities. Besides participating in programs of advanced research, many are or have been lecturers, offering undergraduate courses. Most act as mentors and guides to graduate students in the research process. Many help

[148] Above, pp. 61–62.
[149] Dubin and Beisse, *op. cit.* (n. 135, above), p. 531.
[150] *Ibid.*, p. 539.
[151] *Ibid.*, pp. 537–539; see also Sidney Ingerman, "Employed Graduate Students Organize at Berkeley," *Industrial Relations* 5 (October 1965) 1:146–147.

administer research organizations. In their latter capacity, many are de facto policy makers, helping give direction to the university's research programs, hiring graduate and other personnel, and developing funding sources.[152]

Yet as a rule they were excluded from full membership in academic departments; excluded from the right to be principal investigator on a research project — giving rise to some faculty fronting for a professional research person who could not formally be the head — and excluded from sabbatical leave, parking, library, and other rights of faculty members.

The survey of professional research personnel at Berkeley showed considerable dissatisfaction with their formal status.[153] Around 1964 the Academic Research and Professional Association was formed on the Berkeley campus, and this organization exerted periodic pressure on the administration and faculty to equalize, to some degree, the rights and privileges of the professional research personnel.

Finally, what implications do the structural changes and changes in groups have for the undergraduate? It is difficult to generalize about the undergraduate experience throughout the university, because the thrust toward excellence in research and graduate training took hold on the various campuses at very different rates and in different ways, with the result that conditions affecting undergraduates were not all the same throughout the university. Yet a few comments may be made about the Berkeley campus — where the trends I have analyzed were most extreme, and where there is some evidence on student attitudes.

In the eyes of many students, Berkeley was a prestigious institution and was upgrading itself in several ways. It was becoming increasingly professionalized as a leading national center of graduate education; the quality of its students appeared to improve during the 1950s and early 1960s;[154] and, in connection with the Master Plan of 1960, the university reduced the number of admissible California high school graduates from the top 15 to the top

[152] Carlos E. Kruytbosch and Sheldon L. Messinger, "Unequal Peers: The Situation of Researchers at Berkeley," in Kruytbosch and Messinger (eds.), *op. cit.* (n. 138, above), p. 263.

[153] *Ibid.*, pp. 258 ff.

[154] Select Committee on Education, *Education at Berkeley* (Berkeley: Academic Senate, Berkeley Division, 1966), pp. 16–17.

12.5 percent of the graduating class and began taking the cream of junior college and state college students as transfers. In the late 1950s, moreover, very likely as a result of the post-Sputnik concern with standards and rigor, the Berkeley campus tightened some major requirements and reduced elective freedom. Individual majors were discouraged and group majors phased out, students were encouraged to select majors early, and departments were permitted to raise the number of units required of their majors.[155] And although in the late 1960s the pendulum swung away from specialization, it is clear that the general curricular trends in the late 1950s and early 1960s were toward more specialization and more regimentation of the undergraduates' educational programs.

Such university policies and practices gave the undergraduate every indication that the university was expecting *more* of him, but the realities of undergraduate life seemed to indicate that the university was giving *less*. Various cues revealed that the most important feature of the university was its eminence, and that its eminence rested on the reputations of faculty members who had distinguished themselves nationally and internationally by their contributions to science and scholarship. The undergraduate, especially in the lower division, found himself increasingly remote from the most senior and prestigious faculty — who were teaching undergraduates less, teaching graduates more, and doing more research. More and more, these students were being taught by junior faculty, temporary faculty, and semi-faculty. Some students might well have felt that they had been invited to an elite institution only to be educated mainly by its second-class citizens in a large, impersonal setting.

Data on student satisfaction with their college experience are scarce. Two surveys of Berkeley students taken in 1964–1965 show a high level of general satisfaction with courses, professors, examinations, and being a student at Berkeley. But another survey of about 2,500 students in 1965 revealed great dissatisfaction with *specific* items:

> . . . one-third of the students said that classes were too large to learn very much in them; 47 percent thought the grading system inadequate to measure knowledge and understanding of course content;

[155] Lawrence Veysey, "Stability and Experiment in American Undergraduate Curriculum," mimeographed manuscript, pp. 53–55.

46 mentioned that student–faculty contact was unsatisfactory; 42 percent mentioned that most professors were more interested in research than in teaching; and one-half suggested that undergraduates should have a great voice in the formulation of educational policies. Furthermore, almost 80 percent said that the university operated as a factory.[156]

The image of the university experience as taking place in an impersonal, standardized bureaucracy also figured significantly in the rhetoric of student protest leaders in the 1960s.

Conclusion. The main structural responses to the pressures to grow and to the increased research opportunities were (1) increases in scale, which meant the significant growth of existing campuses; (2) segmentation, or the creation of new campuses which gradually moved toward the similar form of general campuses with undergraduate, graduate, and professional education, as well as a significant commitment to research; (3) shifts in emphasis, and the increased importance of graduate teaching and research. Furthermore, these responses were felt with different intensity on the various campuses.

Yet the faculty — the traditional intellectual elite — did not expand rapidly enough to meet all these demands or to take advantage of all these opportunities. Faculty growth did not keep pace with that of the students, and the faculty could not alone carry out all the research for which the university contracted. In these circumstances the university adapted by rapidly expanding the numbers of ancillary personnel, especially teaching assistants and research personnel. This adaptation, however, created some groups of second-class citizens who did crucial work on the campus but did not receive the commensurate rewards of full citizenship. The faculty was an elite which retained control over all its traditional teaching and research functions but threw some of the less prestigious tasks to junior faculty, nonregular faculty, teaching assistants, and research personnel. Moreover, the use of ancillary personnel in undergraduate teaching, and the faculty's partial withdrawal from such teaching, produced a strong sense of relative deprivation among many undergraduates.

One of the costs incurred by the university's enormous expansion and structural change, then, appears to have been a great

[156] Cited in Dubin and Beisse, *op. cit.* (n. 135, above), pp. 284–285.

increase in potential feelings of relative deprivation, generalized dissatisfaction, diminished loyalty, and proneness to attack the university administration and one another. Although the situation of each group was different, the various groups were similar in that they all felt in some sense isolated from the central and most rewarding aspects of university life, and correspondingly shortchanged by the university. The university, in its period of astounding expansion, had grown around the traditional core of faculty by adding new structures and new roles, but without fundamentally altering the faculty's positions and privileges. There were a number of splits within the faculty, and the development of some disgruntled estates of second-class citizens, disposed to come into conflict with the established authorities in the stormy years of the 1960s.

This diagnosis of the changing fortunes of the major academic estates by no means completely explains the kinds of conflict that developed in the 1960s. Clearly the changing political mood of the larger society, as well as the changing attitudes of students in the 1960s, were decisive. The specific behavior of university administrators — especially in their discipline of students — also played a salient role. Furthermore, many determinants of conflict were found in the dynamics of conflict itself — the waves of reaction and counterreaction, the backlash and boomerang of tactics, the mass media treatment of conflict, and the like. I have tried to demonstrate how, through an interrelated series of growth processes, structural changes, and changing fortunes of estates, the university system became ripe for conflict, because its structure was producing some significant groups with intense feelings of deprivation and disaffection. In short, I have concentrated on the processes that contribute to a situation of potential conflict in a social system.

GROWTH AND THE ABILITY OF THE SYSTEM TO ABSORB COMPETITION AND CONFLICT

I have dealt mainly with the *sources* of competition and conflict in California's system of public higher education. But the potential for conflict in a social system is a function not only of the sources of conflict but also of the ability of the system's apparatus of authority and coordination to prevent, contain, handle, and resolve conflicts as they flare up. In this final section I deal with the management of conflict. First, I outline some general theoretical principles and draw a general model of the processes involved in restructuring authority. This model has, I think, considerable general validity, but it will shed particular light on the recent history of California's statewide coordination and on some aspects in the history of one of its segments, the university.

The Fate of Authority and Coordination in Growing Social Systems

What most obviously happens in a growing system is an increase of things over which authority and coordination must be exercised. As a nation-state grows in population, resources, wealth, and institutions, the exigencies of integrating and coordinating them within a single political apparatus grow accordingly.[157] As a family grows in size, so do the problems of coordinating its activities. And as an educational system increases its resources, organizations, and population, its need for coordination and authority grows.[158] For example, although the university's Board of Regents has always been delegated authority in the same way by the state of California, it has experienced a de facto enlarging of authority as the university has grown, because more resources and more people have come under the scope of its authority. In this sense the growth of the system also means an *augmentation* of authority in the system.

At the same time, as the system grows in size and in the complexity of its units, ultimate authority must become more *centralized*, if the system is to remain an integral political unit. That is to say, with increasing size and complexity, more of the system's problems become system problems (rather than unit problems) because the units are increasingly more involved in relations with other units than they would be in small, simple systems. Of course, if the political unit splits into two or more separate political units, authority can be decentralized.

Simultaneously, though — and in seeming paradox — centralization of authority in a growing system leads to a process of increasing *differentiation* and *specialization* of authority. The recent history of the American federal government exemplifies these

---

[157] The social theorist who has most convincingly demonstrated this relationship between growth and integration is Emile Durkheim, in his *The Division of Labor in Society* (New York: Free Press, 1949). First published in 1893.

[158] Above, p. 38.

dual tendencies. As the government has taken over centralized responsibility for more and more system problems that cannot be regulated at the unit level — regulation of business practices and labor-management relations, for example — it has simultaneously developed a network of civil service bureaucracies to cope with the day-by-day activities. Similarly, as a giant corporation expands, it proliferates specialized branch offices that assume some portion of managerial responsibility, even though ultimate control of the business remains at the center. As a system grows in size and complexity, it becomes increasingly difficult for the central authority to administer the system on a day-by-day basis, so there is an increased delegation of authority through and into various sectors of the system. This principle, applied to a system of higher education, was formulated explicitly by the Restudy Team in its 1955 report:

> The magnitude and complexity of the problems facing California's institutions of public higher education in the immediate future, and the necessity of treating the state colleges and the University of California as integrated systems, make it necessary that the functions and relationships of governing boards and administrative officers be clearly defined . . .
>
> The final responsibility for system-wide policy formulation should be centralized, but in order to preserve the greatest possible degree of local administrative and educational vitality, the execution of policy should be decentralized as fully as may be possible consistent with the principle of unity. This should be interpreted to refer, not to one inclusive system, but to the state colleges as one system and to the university as another.[159]

Finally, in conditions of increasing size and complexity, authority tends to become increasingly *standardized* and *bureaucratized.* The clearest historical examples of this principle are found in the legal codes of large and complex political systems, but the principle extends to other types of systems as well. As more and more classes of individuals come under a system's authority, rules proliferate, and they tend to be administered in more standardized ways. In systems of higher education, we should expect growth to be accompanied by increasingly standardized procedures for budgeting, admissions, space allocations, and so on. As we shall see

[159] T. R. McConnell et al., for the Liaison Committee of the Regents of the University of California and the State Board of Education, *Digest of a Restudy of the Needs of California in Higher Education* (Berkeley: University of California Printing Department, 1955), p. 47.

later, however, standardization and bureaucratization create particularly difficult problems for institutions of higher education, which are in many ways institutionalized to keep organizational constraints on students and faculty at a minimum.

In the long run, growing systems produce authority structures that are at the same time more centralized, more specialized and differentiated, and more bureaucratized. Yet this statement tells us little about the dynamics of change in systems of authority and coordination. The growth of a social system is very imperfectly correlated with the changes in its system of authority; the process is uneven and irregular, with complex patterns of leads and lags. One part of the system may change faster than others, creating new problems of uncoordination, miscommunication, and conflict. In fact, rapidly growing social systems are forever threatening to outgrow the very structures designed to regulate their functioning, thus rendering these structures archaic and in need of reorganization.

As a rapidly growing system, California's public higher education system has certainly not been immune from the process of outgrowing the capacity of its regulatory structures to regulate. Moreover, one can identify an ideal-typical process of restructuring the regulatory system — that is, the system of authority and coordination. This process goes through the following stages:

(1) At any given moment in the system's history, there exists a regulatory mechanism (for example, a board of regents with a given range of jurisdictions) that has a given degree of centralization.

(2) The system experiences a season of growth under this regulatory apparatus, and as it increases in scale, it undergoes processes of segmentation and shifts in function.

(3) When conflict breaks out, there is crisis of governance that cannot be resolved by the existing apparatus of authority and coordination.

(4) In the heat of turmoil, authority is temporarily recentralized — that is to say, when conflict resists one level of authority, a higher level either is summoned or intervenes.

(5) After a period of cooling off and investigation, a new authority structure is devised with the hope of updating the regulative machinery and bringing it into line with the new realities of growth.

Needless to say, this sequence is only an ideal-typical one, because history rarely unfolds in such neat phases. Consider the following exceptions: (1) New regulative machinery is sometimes invented without a full-scale crisis of governance — for example, the separate Board of Governors established for the junior colleges in 1967. At the time, it was widely recognized that coordinating the relations among the junior colleges posed many difficult problems,[160] but the machinery was invented and implemented before any of these problems reached critical proportions. (2) Sometimes a suggested innovation is never carried out, and the period of crisis continues. For example, in 1955 the Restudy Team recommended reorganization of the structure of the Liaison Committee of the Board of Regents and the state Board of Education, a reorganization that called for the creation of a State College Board (separate from the Board of Education) and a nine-member Liaison Committee composed of three members each from the Board of Regents, the state Board of Education, and the proposed State College Board. The proposal was never implemented, because the legislature failed to create a state College Board. It is hard to predict how such a reorganized committee would have functioned in the late 1950s. The existing arrangements continued and "by 1959, it became apparent that the existing structure of coordination had not been able to contain the ambitions for expansion of facilities and new programs on the part of the public institutions."[161] (3) In periods of continuous and extreme crises, the higher-level authority may simply assert itself periodically without actually creating significant new regulatory machinery to deal with the crises at hand — for example, some interventions of the governor, legislature, and Board of Regents in the affairs of the University of California during the most dramatic upheavals of the 1960s. Despite these important qualifications, the ideal-typical sequence — and its exceptions — nevertheless lay out a series of important connections between the conflict, the crises of regulation, and the changing structure of authority.

Crisis and Change in the Coordination of the Entire System of Public Higher Education

In the 1920s, California's educational system was on the eve of

---

[160] For a discussion of these problems, see Medsker and Clark, *op. cit.* (n. 20, above).

[161] Paltridge, *op. cit.* (n. 111, above), pp. 23–26.

an integrative crisis of serious proportions. The state teachers' colleges were coming into their own, and the junior college system was developing rapidly; in that same decade California's population increased by almost two-thirds. The combined pressures of increased population and opportunity to grow produced a brisk regional college movement as well as an attempt to convert some junior colleges into four-year colleges. This provoked sharp opposition from university officials, who feared that an unrestricted number of four-year general colleges would undermine the university's traditional dominance of undergraduate education.[162] President Sproul persuaded the legislature to finance a study by the Carnegie Foundation for the Advancement of Teaching. (This marked a temporary recentralization of authority — that is, a temporary shift of the responsibility for coordination to the legislature.)

The report of the Carnegie Foundation — known as the Suzzalo report — recommended that the state not authorize any more four-year colleges until the Berkeley and Los Angeles campuses had reached their saturation points. The legislature accepted this, as well as some other recommendations. The Suzzalo report also called for the creation of a coordinating agency, the state Council for Educational Planning and Coordination, which the legislature established in 1933. (This marked the invention of a coordinating apparatus that was less centralized than the legislature, where the competitive battle for new and different institutions of higher education had previously been coordinated by legislative pressure and compromise.) President Sproul tried to use this coordinating body to stall the drive for an expanded system of state colleges. Yet because the state council was only advisory, it could not act decisively, and in the end it proved ineffective as a coordinating device. In these circumstances the conflict returned to the legislature, with the university holding firm to a conservative position against the communities and regions seeking authorizations for new four-year colleges.[163] The state council made some studies and issued some reports, but they had little effect and the council became inactive in 1941.

The next major instrument of coordination, the Liaison

[162] Stadtman, *op. cit.* (n. 10, above), pp. 261.

[163] For an account of President Sproul's activities during these years, see George A. Pettitt, *Twenty-Eight Years in the Life of a University President* (Berkeley and Los Angeles: University of California Press, 1966), pp. 42–48.

Committee of the Board of Regents and the state Board of Education, was created in 1945. The committee was soon confronted with a situation not unlike that of the late 1920s: a vigorous drive by communities to establish new colleges, and vigorous resistance to this by the university. This committee also persuaded the legislature to authorize and finance a thorough study of the needs of higher education, and this became known as the Strayer report.[164] Among other things, this report recommended that the Liaison Committee — also a purely advisory body to the regents and the state Board of Education — continue as the coordinating agency for higher education.

In 1955, the Restudy Team recommended that the coordinating machinery be expanded and consolidated, with a more prominent place for the state colleges. This recommendation was not implemented. By 1959, after several years of strong political pressure, the Liaison Committee found itself unable to function effectively, and the legislature was flooded each year with proposals for new state colleges that threatened to drive the system into totally unregulated growth. It was out of this situation that the Master Plan Survey Team was commissioned, and a quite new instrument of coordination was fashioned — the Coordinating Council for Higher Education. Up to 1960, however, the system was coordinated by the political processes in the legislature, which occasionally established a study commission and an advisory coordinating body for its own guidance.

I have already outlined the main features of the Master Plan legislation pertaining to the differentiation of functions and the growth of the various segments.[165] Before the adoption of the Master Plan, a number of different schemes for coordination had been discussed, including a super-board of governors, with constitutional status similar to that of the university's Board of Regents, but with binding authority over the entire system. What emerged in the Master Plan legislation was a compromise between a super-board and the old system of legislative coordination helped along by study commissions and the Liaison Committee. In some respects the Coordinating Council for Higher Education was stronger than earlier coordinating bodies. First, it was statutory

[164] Above, pp. 26–27.
[165] Above, pp. 28–30.

rather than voluntary, and was given specific responsibility by the legislature to coordinate the system of higher education. Second, it was more comprehensive than earlier bodies, bringing in representatives from private higher education for the first time, and also incorporating the junior colleges as an autonomous sector of higher education for the first time. Third, it had a director and staff in addition to the council itself. Fourth, it was given wide advisory scope, including the governor, the legislature, the superintendent of public instruction, and the four segments of higher education. And, finally, it was given a set of definite functions in its charter: to review the annual budget and comment on the general level of support being sought, to review plans for growth and development — including new campuses, and to advise on new and existing programs with respect to the differentiation of functions among the segments.[166] All this promised a stronger and more independent coordinating agency.

Yet there were two additional characteristics of the new Coordinating Council that were to affect its subsequent fate. First, the Master Plan Survey Team had recommended twelve members for the council, three from each of the four segments. The state legislature, however, added three public members, identified with none of the segments and appointed by the governor. This amendment marked a slight move toward a more centralized system, because it meant input into the coordinating machinery from the state's central political apparatus. Second, because of the unwillingness of each segment to sacrifice too much of its own autonomy, the council was given only advisory powers and no binding authority. Nevertheless, in its early years the council was seen as an attempt to decentralize the coordinating machinery:

> [The actions creating the Coordinating Council] had the effect of passing to the new Coordinating Council the task of mediation. On the one hand, the council represents a compact among the segments of higher education in the state *to self-police Master Plan agreements so as to remove tendencies for legislative interposition.* On the other hand, the legislature has looked to the council to interpret the needs of higher education, promote its orderly growth, and assure optimum utilization of facilities with maximum quality at minimum cost. Thus the council must reinforce political independ-

[166]*California Educational Code*, Division 16.5, Sections 22700–22704.

ence — and at the same time help prevent political isolation — of the higher education community.[167]

In 1963 the director of the state Department of Finance — traditionally responsible for formulating budgets for higher education at the state level — expressed "his understanding of the Donahue Act [Master Plan legislation] that the council should become a 'successor' to the Department of Finance in making certain higher educational judgments," and that "the Department of Finance is willing to pull back to allow the council to assume the function of determining appropriate priorities within higher education."[168]

Because of the council's ambiguous position between the system of higher education and the state government and because of its advisory status, the council's future was somewhat in doubt even when it began its work in 1960. It had the option of simply transmitting the various requests of the individual segments — for budgets, new campuses, and so on; or of attempting to fashion a position independent from any of the individual segments and from the state government; or the option of becoming subordinate to the politics of the state. In fact the brief history of the council showed some evidence of all three approaches; but in the end it was subordinated quite completely to state politics and may in fact be on its last legs.

Most of the council's activities can be described as independent of the special interests of each segment. Significantly, however, these activities were noncontroversial. For example, the council did much to eliminate barriers to the transfer of students from junior colleges to the other segments; it took administrative responsibility for the allocation of considerable sums of federal money to the various segments; it did much to increase the opportunities for poor young people in higher education.[169]

It will be recalled that one of the controversies leading to the Master Plan was the unquenchable competition for new state col-

[167] Coordinating Council for Higher Education, *The Budget Review Role of the Coordinating Council for Higher Education* (Report 67–10) (Sacramento: May 23, 1967), p. 1. Emphasis added.

[168] Coordinating Council for Higher Education, *Minutes*, September 24, 1963, p. 6.

[169] Memorandum from Owen Albert Knorr, Director, Coordinating Council for Higher Education to Members of the Conference Committee on the Budget, California State Legislature, June 18, 1970.

leges. It should come as no surprise, then, that the first critical test for the Coordinating Council concerned the establishment of new campuses. Under the Master Plan, new campuses were prohibited unless recommended by the Coordinating Council for Higher Education.[170] During the 1963 session of the legislature, however, political pressure began to mount. The old pattern of legislative politics seemed to reappear just after the Master Plan was established to prevent it. The council, however, resisted the pressure for immediate action and promised to issue a comprehensive report in 1965. But there was heated debate at council meetings, and ultimately the council compromised by calling for a delay in authorizing any new campuses. In a critical vote, the 1965 legislature honored the recommendation, and the council seemed to have attained a new position of influence in the eyes of many legislators.[171] The action also removed the council temporarily from the influence of the individual segments and of legislative politics.

The council's record with respect to the budgetary review process stands in striking contrast to its role in the development of new campuses. The early budget reports to the legislature tended to endorse the requests made by the individual segments (although the council did repeatedly request increases for the junior colleges).[172] The council's budget review role came under some criticism, and in 1965, the legislative analyst commented:

> As regards its three main statutory functions, the council has a mixed record of accomplishment. It has contributed very little through its annual review of university and state college budget requests, largely because of a failure to adopt a viewpoint which is significantly broader than that of any one of the individual segments.[173]

[170]*Education Code*, Section 22501, chap. i.

[171] Coordinating Council for Higher Education, *The Budget Review Role of the Coordinating Council for Higher Education, op. cit.* (n. 167, above), pp. 59–60.

[172] See, for example, Coordinating Council for Higher Education, *Minutes*, November 28, 1962, pp. 9–13; see also Coordinating Council for Higher Education, *Budget Report to the Legislature, 1963: Level of Support, Faculty Salaries, Admissions Standards, Student Fees* (Sacramento and San Francisco: February, 1963), pp. 11–31.

[173] Quoted in Coordinating Council for Higher Education, *The Budget Review Role of the Coordinating Council for Higher Education, op. cit.* (n. 167, above), p. 18.

This assessment was accepted by the chairman of the Coordinating Council, Arthur Coons, at least as it applied to the council's early years.[174] In 1968 the director of the council commented acidly that "it appears that 'orderly growth' has been going forward on three fronts rather than one, permitting certain undesirable situations to develop."[175]

With respect to annual budget reviews, then, the Coordinating Council did not carve out an independent role as it did in other areas. In addition, the effectiveness of the council's comments was severely constrained by the established budgeting procedures. Although the state Department of Finance and the Office of the Legislative Analyst expressed a willingness in principle to relinquish some kinds of educational judgments to the Coordinating Council, these agencies continued to exercise their detailed line-item scrutiny of the budgetary requests. The council did not have the staff to undertake such scrutiny, and it also lacked the information needed to make any kind of cost-benefit analyses of budget requests. Moreover, the budget preparation cycle was such that the council could not offer effective advice at any stage:

> The present budget preparation cycle is geared to the review and budget preparation processes of the Department of Finance and legislature. Thus the present time schedule does not allow an interval of time for the council to review the segments' entire requests and to develop advice to state government prior to the commencement of the state government review. The schedule also precludes the council from offering any advice to the governing boards prior to each board's adoption of its formal budget requests.[176]

Commenting on this timetable problem in 1964, Arthur Coons, chairman of the council's Committee on Finance, complained that his committee had been "confronted with decisions already made."[177]

Finally, the council's advisory role was further undercut by the fact that the individual segments maintained legislative relations offices in Sacramento and, bypassing the council, exerted

[174] Coons, *op. cit.* (n. 68, above), p. 110.
[175] Director's Report, "Agenda for the Coordinating Council for Higher Education," October 7–8, 1968.
[176] Coordinating Council for Higher Education, *The Budget Review Role of the Coordinating Council for Higher Education, op. cit.* (n. 167, above), p. 33.
[177] Coordinating Council for Higher Education, *Minutes*, November 24, 1964, p. 25.

political pressure on the various government agencies and committees responsible for budget preparation.[178] After reviewing these resistances to its budgetary-review role in 1967, the Coordinating Council concluded sadly that "[by] and large, the council's role in the formal budget review processes has failed to contribute significantly to the quality of decision making in public higher education finance."[179]

Thus the effort to decentralize coordination on the all important issue of institutional budgets for the system of higher education as a whole was a failure from the beginning. The council was mouse-trapped because of the reluctance of the legislative and executive branches to relinquish their budgetary roles and by the reluctance of the individual segments to relinquish their independent efforts to influence these branches of government. Coordination was still done through the politics of state government.

In 1967–1968, when the question of the budget for higher education became a political issue of critical proportions, the decision-making process became further centralized, and the Coordinating Council was rendered more impotent. By 1966 higher education had become an extremely hot political issue — largely because of the campus turmoil at the university — and Ronald Reagan built much of his gubernatorial campaign on that issue. Immediately after his inauguration, moreover, the Department of Finance proposed to cut 10 percent from the budget requests of the university and state colleges, and to set tuition charges for both segments. In the early months of 1967, the press was filled with the political debate over these proposed budget cuts and tuition charges, and the university and state college segments began to mobilize whatever political support they could to resist these proposals. The new governor, consulted directly with the regents and the trustees and for several weeks bypassed the Coordinating Council entirely in questions of budgetary policy.[180] Ultimately the Coordinating Council commented negatively on various provisions of the governor's budget, but these comments had little effect on the governor's ultimate decisions to cut requests and

[178] Paltridge, *op. cit.* (n. 111, above), p. 68.

[179] Coordinating Council for Higher Education, *The Budget Review Role of the Coordinating Council for Higher Education, op. cit.* (n. 167, above), p. 17.

[180] Coons, *Crises in California Higher Education, op. cit.* (n. 68, above), pp. 95–98.

to reduce the salary increases already enacted by the legislature.[181] In addition, although the council was asked to advise on tuition and related matters, the new governor announced his own tuition and student-loan and grant program before he received the council's report.[182] The issue of tuition became a political issue of major proportions, ultimately involving a division between Reagan supporters and those of his opponent-to-be in the 1970 election, Assembly Speaker Jesse Unruh.[183]

During the council's brief history, a number of efforts were made to bring it more under the influence of the state's political agencies and less under the influence of the individual segments. Most flagrantly, in 1970 the Ways and Means Committee of the assembly deleted the funds for the Coordinating Council for the forthcoming year. The money was later partially restored, but the deletion revealed how dissatisfied many legislators were with the coordinating apparatus of the state's higher education system. Finally, early in 1971, the board's composition was again changed, giving the public members a majority on the council for the first time.

The effort to decentralize the coordinating function of California's growing system of higher education, then, appeared to have failed as of 1970. The system's internal struggles, caused by its peculiar pattern of growth, clearly exceeded the capacities of the coordinating machinery created in 1970. The failure was due mainly to three sets of circumstances: (1) the tendency for the individual segments — especially the university and the state colleges — to bypass the council and take their competitive demands directly to the legislative and executive branches; (2) the reluctance of the political agencies traditionally responsible for many problems of coordination to relinquish their control over the budgetary process; and (3) the state of chronic political crisis that afflicted higher education in California during the latter half of the 1960s and has forced so many issues of higher education into the arena of partisan political conflict. In those years California reverted to an almost completely recentralized mode of allocating resources and adjudicating conflicts among the segments of higher education.

[181] *Ibid.*, pp. 117–126.
[182] *Ibid.*, p. 100.
[183] See the position taken against tuition by the Joint Committee on Higher Education (chaired by Unruh), *The Academic State, op. cit.* (n. 21, above).

The challenge of the 1970s appears to be whether the state can invent an effective decentralized apparatus for governance and coordination[184] or will continue to rely on the familiar mechanisms of partisan conflict and compromise in state politics.

Authority and Conflict in the University of California

To conclude this essay, I turn back to the university segment and discuss institutional patterns of authority and solidarity in the university. Then I analyze some of the pressures that growth and structural change typically exert on these patterns — pressures that tend to reorganize the system of authority and undermine the system of solidarity. Finally, I outline a typical pattern of conflict that emerges, illustrating it with several events in the university's recent history.

Types of authority and solidarity in a university. Like all formal organizations, a modern university has complex patterns of authority relations. Yet by virtue of the university's particular functions, its patterns of authority differ from those of other organizations. One distinctive type of authority in a university is *academic* authority, which the faculty holds in relation to students. That authority is grounded in the presumed academic experience and expertise of the faculty member. In exercising this authority he can demand specific kinds of academic performance from students (completing assignments, term papers, dissertations, and the like); he imposes the sanctions of intellectual evaluation on this performance, especially through grades. Normally, the student is expected to accept this kind of assessment, whether it is positive or negative. Administrators have other sanctions — they can dismiss the student or place him on probation for poor academic performance. In the early years of college the student is evaluated more frequently and in more detail than when he is in graduate training.

A second type of authority is *executive* authority, which is vested in the officials of the university as employers of faculty and nonacademic staff. In this respect a university is no different from any other formal organization that employs personnel; the available sanctions are orders, demands for performance of contractual

[184] For a discussion of a number of suggested alternatives to the Coordinating Council, see Coordinating Council for Higher Education, *Governance of Public Higher Education in California* (Sacramento: 1968).

duties, threats of discharge, and so on. Executive authority in a university, however, is structured in different ways for the different estates. The authority of administrative officers over tenured faculty members is general — because of the rights and privileges of tenure, and because the activities of a faculty member are not specifically defined. Furthermore, in the tradition of academic freedom, the faculty member is normally shielded from executive interference with his work.

The authority of university officials over nonacademic staff is much more direct and specific than over faculty, and thus resembles the line authority of industrial organizations. Also, ancillary staff positions are structured to facilitate the faculty's performance of academic duties and to free them from the housekeeping side of research and teaching. Consider, for example, the enormous aid of a highly organized library staff for research, and of administrative assistants, clerical workers, and so on.

The administrative officials of the university do not have executive authority over students, because students are not employees. Officials can, however, demand that students meet financial and other contractual obligations in their capacity as students, and the officials have sanctions if students fail to meet their obligations.

A third type is *moral* authority. This deals with the general conduct of different members of the organization — conduct not directly related to the performance of their academic activities. The principles regarding the general conduct of faculty members are seldom evoked, but moral authority over students is often extensive. The principle of *in loco parentis*, of course, is ample evidence of this broad control over the students' general moral conduct. But even where this tradition is weak, the university reserves the authority to deal with specific types of behavior — criminal, commercial, political, and immoral.

Formally, all these types of authority are held by the governing body of the institution, and ultimately — in the public university — by the state that has chartered it. In practice, the university functions in a complicated network of different kinds of authority. The functioning of the university relies, moreover, on more than superordinates applying sanctions to subordinates. In particular, it depends on a number of informal systems of solidarity, which sometimes facilitate and sometimes constrain the working of the authority system. I have in mind the following kinds of solidarity:

(1) The "old blue" link, involving some administrators, some (usually senior) faculty members, and some alumni. This kind of friendship and fellowship creates an intense loyalty to the institution and its traditions, and frequently a sentimental concern with athletics, the legendary figures of faculty and administration, and the university's traditions.

(2) The solidarity of colleagues, mainly in faculty relations with other faculty, but also among administration and faculty. The principle of colleagues assents to the myth that the faculty is a company of equals, that colleagues deserve respect, that they should be consulted on matters of university or departmental business, and that they should be permitted to influence — mainly through persuasion — matters that affect them. The principle is especially important in relations between the central administration and the faculty. The administration actually exercises very little formal authority over faculty members. The complicated system of advise-and-consent between administration and faculty is a functional substitute for authority based on the right to issue and enforce orders.

(3) Solidarity between faculty member and student. Although the relationship between a faculty member and student may in some respects be regarded as one of opposed interests — with the student wanting to be certified and the faculty member insisting on standards — it also has aspects of solidarity. It is assumed that teacher and student are engaged in the cooperative enterprise of learning and intellectual inquiry and that the faculty member has a simultaneously facilitative and evaluative role. It is assumed that the teacher will be objective but not arbitrary or vindictive.

(4) Solidarity between student and student. In this extremely important form of solidarity, students share a common experience during an important, formative phase in their life. Most generally it takes the form of being in "the class of '65," and this membership is periodically reaffirmed by newsletters, reunions, and so on. More intimately, however, solidarity among students is manifested by strong peer cultures which develop, in part, as systems of defense against the authority of faculty and administrators, but which independently evolve complex codes of conducts regulating study habits, classroom behavior, and styles of dress and leisure.

(5) Solidarity between administrator and student. This type of solidarity may seem specious, because relations between administrators and students have been so inimical in recent times. Nevertheless, relations between students and their deans and counselors have traditionally been important forms of solidarity, and they offer the student protection against the automatic exercise of authority. The quiet handling of criminal offenses (such as thefts from book stores), the widespread use of probationary penalties, the practice of talking to a student rather than immediately punishing him — all these point to assumptions of solidarity that are institutionalized in authority relations involving punishment and conflict.

Any given university, then, at any given point in time, is characterized by a network of several types of authority and several types of solidary ties. Their interrelations are very complex. One of the most important relations is that *an appeal to solidary ties is a way of avoiding the use of formal authority as a sanction.* If an administrator enjoys the support of his faculty colleagues, he can influence them to support a policy; the formal enactment of that policy, although an act of authority, is something of an afterthought. If a faculty member can talk to a student working on a term paper and offer criticisms and suggestions in a cooperative spirit, this process of persuasion reduces the necessity of grading the paper "cold" in its final form. If a dean can persuade students to desist from rule-violating behavior, this often removes the need to rely on formal disciplinary action. If student peers have evolved informal systems of regulating plagiarism or cheating, this reduces the need to for formal control over such behavior by faculty members and administrators. In other words, if solidary ties cannot be appealed to as a basis for coordinating activity, those in authority may have to rely more exclusively on the sanctions associated with the exercise of formal authority.

An appeal to solidary ties is often *a means of avoiding or reducing conflicts over the exercise of authority.* If an administrator is able to persuade faculty members, as colleagues, that a given policy is consistent with their common dedication to the pursuit of knowledge, then the likelihood of conflict over that policy is reduced because it has been legitimized by reference to the values of common membership and common symbols.

Growth and Its Impact on Authority and Solidarity Systems.

Earlier I examined the implications of the growth and structural change in the University of California for the development of conflict-prone estates.[185] In the remainder of this section I examine the implications of this growth and structural change for the systems of authority and solidarity in the university. I do not, however, attempt to discern the exact state of the authority and solidarity systems at any given point in history; rather, I establish the general trends associated with the university's growth. In particular, I discuss the pressure to decentralize authority that accompanied growth, and the institutional vulnerabilities that were exposed in connection with that process. I also discuss the ways that growth undermined existing patterns of solidarity and thus rendered the system less capable of resolving conflicts by appeal to common memberships and symbols. I posit a typical genesis and development of conflict, illustrating it with reference to such conflicts as the oath controversy and the Free Speech Movement.

Decentralization of authority. In a 1966 report on university organization, Clark Kerr reviewed the history of the University of California as a long process of increasing decentralization:

> The first decentralization within the university came reluctantly in 1891 when the regents gave the president authority "to employ, dismiss, and regulate the duties of janitors . . . [provided he] promptly reported his action to the board." In 1958, the university was administered essentially as a monolithic institution; it is now a pluralistic system with several major centers of authority related to each other.[186]

In the same report, Kerr cited a vast number of moves made between 1958 and 1961 to decentralize the authority of the statewide administration in budgeting, fund raising, personnel and admissions, and other activities.[187] The largest single series of decentralizing moves occurred in the summer and fall of 1965, when the Board of Regents delegated much authority for regular faculty appointments, approval for research grants and contracts, and budget transfers, as well as such activities as business services, student housing, and summer sessions.[188] Often the tendencies

---

[185] Above, pp. 78–111.

[186] Office of the President, *Development and Decentralization: The Administration of the University of California, 1958–1966* (1966), p. 6.

[187] *Ibid.*, pp. 1–2.

[188] *Ibid.*, p. 4. For an account of the events surrounding the move to decentralize in 1965–65, cf. Coons, *op. cit.* (n. 68, above), pp. 72–73.

toward decentralization have been less formal and have evolved as a matter of custom. To give only one illustration, faculty members, although formally responsible for designing courses of instruction, grading, and submitting grades to the registrar, have in fact turned over to teaching assistants the responsibility for evaluating undergraduates.

As a system grows and becomes more complex, it becomes progressively unmanageable if day-by-day authority continues to rest with the central agency; although ultimate authority may still continue to reside in that agency, it becomes imperative to delegate operative authority to lower levels. Often, however, the decentralization lags behind the realities of growth. In at least two dramatic instances, an extensive program of decentralization was enacted in the wake of a rapid period of growth and a crisis which shook the university's authority system. In 1949, the university had been strained by the flood of thousands of veterans in the immediate postwar period. Yet the university — which had long been under the effective leadership of Robert Gordon Sproul — had failed significantly to decentralize its authority. A provost for the Los Angeles campus had been appointed in 1945, but when Monroe E. Deutsch, provost of the Berkeley campus and vice-president of the university, resigned in 1947, he was not replaced. The administrative situation in the president's office was extremely cumbersome;

> Thirty line officers, exclusive of staff, had reported to the president even during Deutsch's tenure. To this number were added twenty-two deans, directors, and other administrative officers when Deutsch's retirement left vacant the provost's position in Berkeley. The organization and staffing of the president's office had not kept pace with the complexities facing it.[189]

In the period from 1949 to 1952 during the loyalty oath crisis — mainly a dispute between faculty and the Board of Regents — the inadequacies of this authority structure became evident. The Restudy Team of 1955 issued a plethora of recommendations calling for the removal of many detailed items from the regents' docket and the greater delegation of authority from the statewide ad-

---

[189] David P. Gardner, *The California Oath Controversy* (Berkeley and Los Angeles: University of California Press, 1967), pp. 5–6. For a general account of Sproul's reluctance to decentralize authority and the criticisms of him that developed in 1947, see Stadtman, *op. cit.* (10, above), pp. 271–279.

ministration to the individual campuses.[190] A decade later, when the Free Speech Movement revealed the ambiguities of the administrative relationship between the president's office and the Berkeley campus especially, the Byrne committee — commissioned to investigate the campus disturbances — came forth with sweeping recommendations for greater decentralization and campus autonomy. Although neither the president's office or the Board of Regents accepted these recommendations in full, the regents did accelerate the decentralization processes in a series of actions in 1965.

Erosion of the bases of solidarity. A university may be regarded as a network of different kinds of solidary ties which lubricate the decision-making apparatus, heads off potential conflict, and mediates actual conflict. But when the university experiences a period of rapid growth, structural change, and realignment of estates, new personnel is not automatically incorporated into this network. This is clearly illustrated by the state of the colleague relations among faculty and the advise-and-consent relations between faculty and administration during the later years of Sproul's presidency. Both the northern and southern divisions of the Academic Senate had faculty advisory committees to the president, but they met infrequently, were not kept informed, and did not have ready access to faculty opinion. In addition:

> The senate was . . . in the process of transferring power from the old guard to the younger men of promise. The senior men had for years worked closely with the president and knew many of the regents personally. On the other hand, they did not know well the newer men on the faculty, many of whom had been appointed since the close of World War II. At the same time, the younger men were less well known to many of their colleagues, were not experienced in working with the president, and were not widely acquainted with the regents.[191]

This lag in the development of the informal machinery of consensus and consultation was exposed during the loyalty oath controversy when, "in negotiations with the president and with the regents, those serving the senate were placed time and again in the position of representing opinion later found to be unrepresentative of the faculty majority."[192]

[190] Holy, *Restudy, op. cit.* (n. 28, above), pp. 222–258.
[191] Gardner, *op. cit.*, p. 6.
[192] *Ibid.*, pp. 6–7.

The university's enormous growth in size, internal complexity, and academic specialization in the years after World War II eroded the sense of community and fostered a "bureaucratic federation of departments, colleges, schools, business offices, and student personnel establishments."[193] And the increasing ties between individual scholars and extramural research agencies decreased the commitment of faculty members to — and their dependence on — the home university. The fragility of faculty solidarity, at least on the Berkeley campus, was particularly evident during the periods of crisis. In 1964–1969, during intense conflict, the faculty was forced to invent new modes of achieving consensus, such as hastily formed caucuses, an Emergency Executive Committee of the Academic Senate, and a changed role for the Senate Policy Committee, which formulated consensus positions after extensive consultation and bargaining with faculty groups, and attempted to secure their ratification in mass meetings of the faculty.

Earlier, I analyzed the effect on students of a number of trends associated with the growth of the university. Among these were the increasing size of campuses and classes, the decreased contact between faculty and undergraduate students and the correspondingly increased contact between teaching assistant and student, and the high rate of student turnover.[194] All these trends worked in one direction: to weaken the ties of solidarity between faculty and student and between student and student.[195] The same might be said of the relations between administration and student. In the face of increasing numbers and increasing bureaucracy, students were forced to rely more on standardized procedures than on individualized advice and counseling. The traditional disciplinary apparatus, which often involved a more personalized relationship between disciplinary authority and student, was also undermined, if for no other reason than that a dean and his staff simply could not cultivate that kind of relationship with masses of students.[196] On all

[193] Burton R. Clark, "The Role of Faculty Authority" (Paper presented at the President's Institute, Harvard Business School, June 20, 1963), *Papers, 1956–1964 of the Center for the Study of Higher Education, University of California, Berkeley*, vol. I.

[194] Above, pp. 79–101.

[195] In some respects the political mobilization of students in the crisis years 1964–1969 provided new bases for student–student solidarity.

[196] Michael Otten traces the long-term drift from paternalistic to bureaucratic authority in his *University Authority and The Student* (Berkeley and Los Angeles: University of California Press, 1970).

fronts, then, the distinctive pattern of growth and structural change in the university was exacting a cost in solidarity — and a corresponding cost in problem-solving and conflict-mediating machinery — and was surrendering the coordination of the university more and more to formal administrative mechanisms.

Authority, solidarity, and some dynamics of conflict in the university. In the broad historical development of the university, operative authority was increasingly decentralized, while ultimate formal authority remained completely centralized in the Board of Regents. In some respects this process created a very delicate structure, with both the central agency and the agency to which authority was delegated experiencing some sense of insecurity and impotence. On the one hand, delegation from the top gave the governing body less operative control over the affairs of the institution; on the other, although such control did devolve to lower levels of authority, the threat of intervention or revocation from above was always present. And with the simultaneous erosion of solidary ties, mechanisms of mutual trust and informal communication — important counterbalances to the instabilities inherent in a semidecentralized structure — were also losing force.

This uneasy balance between centralization and decentralization was the context for most of the major conflicts that shook the university between 1950 and 1970. In fact, *most of the conflicts erupted when a centralized authority (campus administration, Board of Regents, and so on) attempted to exert authority in an area that had not previously been subject to regulation, or in an area that had been formally or informally delegated to a subordinate level.* Consider the following examples: (1) In 1949 the Board of Regents "clarified" University Regulation #17, which dealt with the use of campus facilities for extracurricular activities. The clarification restricted the passing of handbills during political meetings on campus. A storm of protest immediately arose, and it was rumored that the real motive behind the revision was to deprive students of the right to circulate petitions. This particular conflict was short-lived, since President Sproul announced that the only restrictions on passing petitions were those required to prevent interference with instructional activities.[197] (2) The loyalty-oath controversy beginning in 1949 was initiated by the regents'

[197] Pettitt, *op. cit.* (n. 163, above), pp. 125–216.

effort to impose a requirement for additional affirmation in the oath of allegiance required of the university faculty. (3) The Free Speech Movement in 1964 was initiated by the Berkeley campus administration's prohibition of political activity on a specific part of the campus — activity that had been informally permitted for a number of years. (4) The conflict over the famous course, Social Analysis 139X — a course authorized by the Board of Educational Development on the Berkeley campus in 1968 and featuring Eldrige Cleaver as a lecturer — developed when the Board of Regents voted to withhold credit for the course, thus exercising authority traditionally granted to the faculty.

The reasons for this kind of intervention were usually mixed, and were subject to dispute by the contending parties in the ensuing conflict. Sometimes external pressure played a role: the anti-Communist atmosphere of the late 1940s and early 1950s obviously influenced the loyalty oath; and in the 1960s authorities intervened to prevent radical political activities. Sometimes the intervention resulted from the conviction of the higher authority that those at lower levels have behaved irresponsibly, as in the case of Social Analysis 139X. Sometimes the intervention was "provoked" by dissidents who challenged the relevant authority to "crack down" on behavior that was potentially defensible. Whatever the reason (or mixture of reasons) in any given situation, the act of intervention raised questions about the entire authority system — whether the intervention was legitimate, whether it weakened the lower level of authority or the legitimacy of the intervening authority, who really was intervening, and whether the attempt to exert authority should be complied with or defied.

If the intervention was defied, the conflict rose to a new level of magnitude. The intervening authority was faced with the problem of enforcement, if necessary by some disciplinary measure. The actual new magnitude of the conflict depended on a number of factors, some of which I have noted in this essay: One factor was the number and types of estates disaffected with the university, and the degree to which the intervention was interpreted by the constituted authorities as an actual or potential assault on them.[198] These estates were the base of mobilization for conflict with the

[198] For a discussion of the development of disaffected estates in the university during its period of dramatic growth, see above, pp. 100–112.

authority. A second factor was the degree to which the mechanisms associated with the solidary groupings in the university were able to manage or contain the conflict. As we have seen, the pattern of growth that affected the university seriously undermined these mechanisms; and without them, the conflict was more likely to break out in the open. A third factor was the degree to which the authority behaved — or was successfully accused by its opposition of behaving — in an authoritarian or arbitrary way. When this occurred, the conflict was magnified by drawing in with the under-dog, many sympathizers who might not have had particularly strong feelings about the substantive issue.[199]

Once a large-scale conflict broke out, this signaled a failure of authority at that level. It further marked the occasion for a recentralization of authority. Some "outside" authority, such as the Board of Regents or the police intervened in a variety of ways. Sometimes an attempt was made to "reestablish order," by direct management of the crisis. Sometimes the relevant authority — for example, a chancellor — was discharged for what was judged incompetent administration. As often as not, this intervention, although perhaps necessary and justified by the logic of maintaining order, fanned the flames of crisis and intensified the divisions in the university. For example, when police or soldiers were summoned — during the strike of November 1966, or the Third World Liberation Front strike in the early months of 1969, or the People's Park crisis in May 1969 (all of which took place in Berkeley) — this immediately heated up those situations and precipitated new mobilization and new actions by different campus groups. Also, when the regents' threatened to intervene in the obscenity crisis of 1965, that precipitated the statements by Kerr and Meyerson that they intended to resign and produced an enormous faculty mobilization in their support.

The recapturing of authority in the heat of crisis produced another important, and perhaps more constructive effect. It occasioned an investigation into the authority structure itself, into the archaic features that might have led to its breakdown, and into any possible restructuring that might prevent future occurrence of the

---

[199] Max Heirich describes a number of crises on the Berkeley campus in 1964–65 when administrative officers at different levels tried to enforce their authority by taking disciplinary measures. *Op. cit.* (n. 8, above).

same kind of crisis. An example of this is the increased decentralization of the authority of the statewide university administration and of the regents after the crises of 1964–1965. Often, however, the solution arrived at by the central authority created a situation of uneasiness that contributed to future conflict. I have in mind, for example, the simple reaffirmation of disciplinary regulations designed to prevent specific actions that occurred during the crisis; such actions tended to cast the authority in a menacing posture. A similar effect was created by simply taking back previously delegated authority, as the Board of Regents did in 1969 over the issue of Herbert Marcuse's reappointment on the San Diego campus. This action intensified the suspicions — and the readiness to enter the conflict — of many faculty members concerned with academic freedom.

One final point requires mention — the effect of crisis on the authority and solidary systems of the university. Most university crises in the past two decades have concluded peacefully, and authority has been formally reestablished. But this is never the end of the matter. The very occurrence of a crisis of authority creates new issues and aggravates the bases of conflict. New groups form during the crisis, groups prepared to raise heretofore neglected questions about the legitimizing values and goals of the institution as a whole, to rewrite history from their own perspective, to generate new definitions of the campus situation, and to square off against other groups who do not share their views. Moreover, when authority is openly challenged, old groups that until then were not visibly dissatisfied may generate new expectations about their place in the institution and their share in its authority system.

One issue — the viability of the campus administration's authority — seemed to dominate the Berkeley campus in the period immediately following December 1964. Under stable conditions, the main question about authority is *how* it is exercised — effectively, benevolently, repressively, or how. Once the legitimacy of authority has been successfully challenged, however, the issue turns into *whether* authority has been successfully challenged, *whether* authority can be exercised at all. Under these circumstances the authority struggles to rebuild and maintain the support of the constituencies who can bolster his claims to authority; and those who have successfully challenged that authority continue to deny it, partly by attacking the values that legitimate it and partly by prodding it and testing its viability. For almost a year after December 1964, the main issue on the Berkeley campus was whether authority could be exercised. Both Martin Meyerson in his brief eight-month administration and Roger Heyns in the early months of his administration fought to retain this ability. It was of great symbolic importance that Meyerson was able to discipline those involved in the obscenity crisis without stirring up a mass campus reaction.[200] It was also significant that this discipline was exercised shortly after an enormous show of support by the faculty. It was of great symbolic importance that Heyns was able to prevent the unauthorized placing of political signs in the fall of 1965 without triggering a serious challenge to his authority. In this year after FSM, many of the issues seemed petty. How many minutes after 1 P.M. could speakers go on using the microphone in Sproul Plaza? How large could political posters be? In reality they were very large issues, because they tested the legitimacy of the administration's authority.

Another phenomenon accompanying a major crisis is that various campus constituencies (students, faculty, teaching assistants, and the like) take sides and declare their loyalties. The fact of their doing so creates a new realignment of loyalties and antagonisms, layers of scar tissue that can be torn off in any new crisis. But because many of the constituencies are either heterogeneous or marginal or both — and therefore ambivalent in their loyalties — polarized political conflicts tend to split each constituency. Thus a university campus in crisis experiences a "multiplier effect," whereby any serious conflict *between* constituencies (for example, between students and administration) leads to the intensification of conflict *within* the various constituencies (for example, faculty members favoring the administration versus those favoring the students). And the effects on such conflicts on solidary ties are adverse. Crisis, especially prolonged crisis, having developed in part because of the inability of a deteriorated system of solidarity to prevent or contain the conflict, further erodes that system. This is an example of the capacity of conflict to aggravate the very conditions that gave rise to it.

[200] In fact, this crisis almost became the occasion for another major intervention, as certain regents attempted to persuade the Board to discipline the students directly, bypassing the chancellor's authority.

Summary

Most explanations of conflict-proneness and conflict itself on university campuses in the 1960s appeal to immediate determinants of either an *ideological* or a *psychological* variety.

The *ideologies* of protesters and counterprotesters — as well as explanations of conflict that incorporate bits of those ideologies — frequently try to explain why they are in conflict with their opponents. Spokesmen for student dissenters, for example, often accuse their opponents (campus administrations, political administrations, police) of belonging to a political establishment which, by virtue of its corrupt policies and repressive strategies, deserves to be destroyed. Counterprotesters frequently characterize student dissenters as Communist-inspired, or as revolutionary — qualities which, being evil, deserve to be destroyed. And although the ideologies accompanying conflicts among different kinds of educational institutions are not often highly developed, such ideological labels as "elitist," "populist," and "powergrabbing" are frequently used to explain the behavior of the parties in conflict.

Many other accounts of student protest in the 1960s make primary reference to the *psychological* characteristics of the parties in conflict. Richard Flacks and his associates, for example, stress the liberal, humanitarian attitudes of both protesters and their parents and argue that such attitudes make protesters more sensitive than nonprotesters to situations of injustice and authoritarian policies.[201] Lewis Feuer, although strongly critical of such an explanation, nevertheless also develops a psychological explanation, stressing that the students' destructive attitudes toward authority are inherited from the Oedipal situation.[202] And Kenneth Keniston — although acknowledging a diversity of causes of protest, including the characteristics of the besieged institutions — pays particular attention to the "protest-prone personality."[203]

Such accounts do much to explain why individuals and groups enter into conflict. Certainly individuals are prompted to act according to their own definition of a situation, and if they have

[201] Richard E. Flacks, "The Liberated Generation: An Exploration of the Roots of Student Protest," *Journal of Social Issues* 23 (1967) 3.

[202] Lewis Feuer, *The Conflict of Generations* (New York: Basic Books, 1970).

[203] Kenneth Keniston, "The Sources of Student Dissent," *Journal of Social Issues* 23 (1967) 3:108–137.

adopted an ideology that identifies some individual, group, or institution as inimical, they will be prompted to adopt a posture of conflict. And psychological differences are essential in accounting both for the differential participation of people in conflict situations and for the style in which conflict is carried out. Yet these immediate explanations also reach their limits and must be supplemented by other factors, such as the general political and cultural climate, social-structural situation, and so on.[204]

I have prepared this essay in the spirit of supplementing the more immediate accounts of the development of conflict proneness. More specifically, I have turned to the *social structure* to seek determinants of the particularly striking level of conflict proneness in California's system of higher education between 1950 and 1970. Even more specifically, I have attempted to trace the implications — for conflict proneness — of the pattern of growth and structural change that also characterized that system in those decades. In addition, I have attempted to supplement the more immediate accounts of conflict proneness by considering conflict in general, rather than limiting my scrutiny to vivid and dramatic episodes of student protest.

I have structured my argument in the following way: The main dependent variable throughout the essay has been conflict proneness. I began my analysis, however, with a set of determinants very remote from that variable — determinants that influenced the pattern of growth in California's system of higher education; then, in several steps, I attempted to trace the diverse implications of that particular pattern of growth, moving gradually toward the more proximate determinants of conflict proneness. In summary, I will now recapitulate the principal steps in my argument.

With respect to factors influencing the system's pattern of growth, I identified a particular confluence of pressures and opportunities for growth. The twin values of competitive excellence and egalitarianism, deeply embedded as legitimizing principles in California, predisposed the system to respond expansively to changes in its social environment. Those values — when combined with an extraordinary demand for education and training from

---

[204] Keniston considers other factors besides psychological protest-proneness. *Ibid.*

increasing numbers of young persons seeking education and from those who would subsequently employ their skills, and when combined with a great input of state and federal financial support — sent the system of higher education into a dramatic spiral of growth during the quarter-century following World War II.

This growth, however, occurred within an existing structure. The distinctive feature of that structure was a three-segment system — the university, the state colleges, and the junior colleges. Those segments overlapped in some functions (undergraduate education) but were rigidly differentiated in other functions (such as research and training for advanced degrees). In addition, the system of higher education in California was, in general, lacking in internal mechanisms that might regulate its growth, and was ultimately forced to rely on the central political apparatus of the state — the legislative and executive branches — as the arena in which critical decisions were made about the resources necessary for growth.

Thus programmed within an existing structure, the system, when pressed to grow, had to rely on a limited number of the possible structural responses that usually accompany growth. It could readily increase the size of its campuses, or their number; it could shift the functional emphases of its various campuses and add new structures (research units, graduate training programs). But it could not, within the legal strictures of the Master Plan (and the policies preceding it) develop qualitatively new types of institutions.

In short, the pattern of growth that was encouraged increased the number of campuses and the number of students at each campus within each segment. Because these types of growth took place within the functionally differentiated segments, the typical pattern of growth was the addition of like-function campuses for each segment. With respect to the functional shifts, junior colleges took over an increasing proportion of lower-division education; the university retained exclusive control of the doctorate, but the state colleges surpassed the university in numbers of master's degrees granted; and the remarkable growth in research activities took place almost exclusively within the university segment.

Having identified these distinctive patterns of growth and structural change, I then traced their impact on several academic estates within the system and their implications for group conflict. My first line of argument had to do with the consequences of growth within a system that is simultaneously stratified on the basis of values of competitive excellence and legitimized on the basis of values of equal opportunity. Under such circumstances, those lower in the stratified system have a defensible claim on the resources available for growth, because they can argue, with justice, that they should have the opportunity to become as excellent as those above them; those higher up, however, can defensibly resist these claims and venture their own, because they can argue that they must maintain their excellence. Conflict, in short, is endemic, because both sets of values cannot be simultaneously realized in such a stratified system. Within this line of argument, I traced the continuous struggle between the university and the state-college segments — a struggle over students, resources, programs, and, above all, those functions reserved for the university and prohibited to the state colleges. I also identified a parallel pattern of conflict over resources and programs among the university campuses.

Turning next to the university segment alone, I traced the implications of the irregular pattern of its growth for its several academic estates. Each campus of the university began to experience an increase in the proportion of graduate students and a decrease in the proportion of lower-division students, although the larger, older campuses began this process earlier and carried it further. Faculty became increasingly involved in research activities; and undergraduate teaching, particularly by senior faculty, was deemphasized. This went furthest at Berkeley and UCLA, with the other campuses following more slowly. In line with these changes, two sets of ancillary personnel began to increase sharply — teaching assistants whose major service was to fill the teaching gap at the division level, and nonfaculty research personnel, who contributed to the burgeoning research enterprise. Relying on the insights of Tocqueville, I argued that the changing fortunes of students, faculty, teaching assistants, and research personnel generated increased experiences of relative deprivation in all these groups, although it took a different form for each group. These feelings of deprivation, moreover, predisposed these groups — again, in different ways — to enter into conflict with the university and with one another.

Finally, to shed further light on conflict proneness, I investigated the ability of the educational system to absorb competition and conflict, and I examined how this ability was affected during periods of rapid growth and structural change. At the level of the system as a whole, I traced several historical episodes in which the pressures to grow — and the competition that accompanied them — bypassed the ineffective and outmoded efforts to coordinate the system's growth. The last and most vivid of these was the establishment of the Coordinating Council on Higher Education under the Master Plan and its subsequent decline in effectiveness, particularly in its function of budgetary review. Then, at the level of the university, I explored briefly how the processes of growth and structural change had rendered some authority structures obsolete and eroded some solidary relations, thus making the university more vulnerable to the conflicts that beset it in this memorably turbulent quarter-century of its history.

Financing California's System of Postsecondary Education*

by F. E. BALDERSTON

Who is the piper? What is the tune that he who pays the piper wants to call? Adapting the old adage, I wish to consider the questions of money for California higher education, but this must be done with appropriate attention to the predictable influence that money brings with it, and to the consequences, broadly considered, of the alternatives available for financing California's higher education system.

Just about the only fiscal proposition on which all opinions are united is that higher education is too important to forget about and too costly to leave to the natural devices of the marketplace. All else is controversy. The basic fiscal alternatives are:

(1) to make private the offering of educational services and the decisions to buy them, leaving entirely to students and their parents the financing of both educational services via tuition and the cash outlays and implicit costs of investing in an education;

(2) to make the offering of educational services a nongovernmental function organized and offered entirely by nonprofit (and possibly profit-making) corporations, with whatever legislated conditions for the offering of educational services and regulation of educational operations may be needed for broad public-policy reasons, and with the institutions financed by fees received from students and the students individually receiving financial aid from tax sources;

(3) to provide tax support for institutional operations and

*Ford Foundation Program for Research in University Administration, Office of the Vice President — Planning, University of California, Berkeley, *Paper P-15*, (January 1970).

whatever degree of subsidy to the other costs of attendance may be felt necessary on public-policy grounds.

Each of these basic alternatives, pursued to its logical conclusion, would have implications for those students from each segment of society who would obtain education beyond high school, for the mode of operation of educational institutions, for the extent of public-policy control and responsiveness to perceived public-policy needs, and for the incidence of cost. In short, the fiscal pattern that should be chosen depends on one's view of what individuals and society seek to accomplish via higher education. It also depends on one's view of the effectiveness with which the goals sought can be served and of the risks of something going wrong.

In the United States, and in California, we actually have a mixture of all three financing patterns and of several modes of organization of educational institutions: private for profit; private nonprofit; and governmentally organized and operated. In fact, it all looks like a fiscal and organizational crazy quilt, and it is tempting to believe that it should all be reorganized and straightened out, both fiscally and organizationally.

· Most of the students in California go to educational institutions organized and paid for by the government, although there is a vital private nonprofit sector (some of whose operations are financed by federal funds and many of whose students receive help via federal and state aid programs), and, in some vocational areas of postsecondary education, a considerable amount of proprietary activity for profit. The old tradition in the public sector was to charge the student nothing for the educational services received, but to expect him to pay the other costs of attendance.

Nobody is actively attacking the private nonprofit sector. Nor is much attention being paid to the proprietary sector right now. But the status quo of the public sector is being criticized, right, left, and center.

The radical critique is exemplified by Ivan Illich in *Deschooling Society*. He would dismantle the institutional operation of education (*all* education) and ban the use of all educational certification for jobs or anything else. Why? Because he believes that the very act of institutionalizing the educational process strips it of the student's necessary self-chosen initiative for learning and opens the way to control of society's and the individual's values by

wrong forces. His proposed answer is to deschool, to make education private, voluntary, and nonformal, for the seeker of learning
and for its provider. He does not want education to serve government, which he mistrusts, or business, the labor market, or technology, which he finds evil.

The conservative critique has surprising parallels to Illich.
Milton Friedman would also dismantle governmental operation of
higher education, although he would be willing to have private
organizational initiatives and markets for educational services. In
principle he also approves of decertificating society (leaving it to
the marketplace to determine whether a doctor is a genius or a
fraud, and whether each individual is fit to do a job for a market-
determined wage). And on the whole he wants to leave it entirely
to the individual whether he decides to obtain an education or not.
Ideally, the individual would pay for a choice of education (whether
for cultural or professional reasons) out of personal assets and (to
whatever extent he chooses) loans from perfectly operating capital
markets. But there *is* inequality of income and assets, and there is
no perfect capital market; therefore Friedman concedes, grudgingly, that governmental assistance may be needed for the capital
investment, ideally as a loan.

Illich denies that broader social purposes are served by the
institutional establishment of education, because he believes that
society is corrupt and in need of radical Christian reform and that
the educational establishment helped make society corrupt and
helps keep it so. Friedman simply denies that education produces
benefits beyond those received by the individual and capitalized by
the individual in the form of greater current and lifetime satisfaction, either as cultural consumption or as an income-producing
increase of his own productivity.

And then there is the center-liberal critique, which at times
echoes some themes common to conservatives and radicals, but for
very different reasons. The liberal critique tends to concentrate on
the following issues:

(1) Hansen and Weisbrod claim that public education is paid
for by the poor and that its benefits are obtained by the rich. Thus,
far from serving to redress the evil of inequality, governmentally
supported education adds to it. Joseph Pechman, using Hansen
and Weisbrod's data for California (1964–1965), demolished this

argument. He showed that the dollars' worth of higher education received by those of lower incomes considerably exceeds the tax dollars they contribute to higher education. And he did so before the California income tax was made much more steeply progressive in the Reagan tax program of 1967, which bore down heavily on the middle- and upper-income groups.

(2) Hansen and Weisbrod join Friedman in soft-pedaling if not quite denying the possibility that social benefits exist over and beyond the individual benefits received by students who attend institutions of higher education. They try to put the burden of proof on those who argue for the existence of these externalities — to show what they are and how big and valuable they are — before admitting that public subsidy should be used to buy them.

(3) Other center-liberal thinkers take a very different tack, arguing that the fiscal and organizational status quo fails on the grounds of both efficiency and opportunity, and that fiscal reforms would enable it to be reorganized and realigned. Here, two schools of thought go in contradictory directions. The one would like the whole system put under more direct obligations of streamlined systemic control, to eliminate duplications and inefficiencies and produce a better response to public (governmentally defined) requirements. The other prefers sharper decentralization and the release of new organizational incentives; this approach often takes the form of proposals for voucher financing, with the parent or student selecting the educational mode, on the presumption that educators would at least be forced to deliver what the customers would want.

SPECIFIC OBJECTIVES AND THEIR FINANCIAL IMPLICATIONS

It is all too easy to get bogged down in abstract philosophizing about education, although such philosophizing fails to come to grips with tangible issues. In his testimony to the Select Committee on the Master Plan, on December 21, 1971, President Charles Hitch defined four specific objectives. Each of these influences the scale and total cost of the system, the financing available to the student, and the organizational modes of our colleges and universities. These four objectives are:

(1) *Universality of opportunity for higher education.* This

implies that the total capacity of educational services should be large enough to meet the needs of all who are qualified, including both the conventional college-age group (roughly 18 to 24) and older people in search of further education. It also implies that financial assistance will be provided for those who need it.

(2) *Greatest possible diversity.* This means that there is no one best or most efficient pattern for all students and all programs, but rather that there should be a large variety of campuses and programs, of differing sizes, shapes, and styles. This objective is in part met by preserving and enhancing the private institutions of many types, and assuring financially that there is wide access to them. A spectrum of publicly supported institutions, not a single dominant model, is also important.

With California's emphasis on large scale public higher education, for reasons of economy, a fully adequate diversity has been neglected. It is difficult to find a university campus or state college or community college where truly small-scale educational experience is available.

If campuses are large, they can contribute to the objective of diversity by encouraging and sustaining internal diversity through experimental colleges and the like. Some types of budget formula or budgetary control tend to inhibit diversity, particularly where they inhibit different methods of organizing the educational process.

(3) *Maximum freedom of student choice.* There are now four kinds of constraint on student choice. A student may not have adequate information about goals and valid alternatives. Or he may lack the financial means to do what he decides is in his best interest. Or the admission standards may keep the student with a poor high school record from going immediately to a state college or the university. Finally, there may be more eligible applicants than places in a particular program or campus. In this event, the student is given the opportunity to apply to another program or campus.

Whether it would be wise to lower the present minimum admission standards for state college and university is a matter for reexamination. In numerous postbaccalaureate program areas, students are now constrained by two additional factors: limited capacity and higher-than-undergraduate admission requirements.

In his testimony to the Select Committee, President Hitch said:

> I would recommend that the committee take the position that higher educational institutions should counsel students about apparent manpower needs and job markets but should otherwise seek to meet informed student demand for curricula except for certain costly and highly specialized professional programs where enrollment limitations may have to be imposed.

We are, however, aware that emerging long-term manpower needs, although difficult to estimate, are a real factor both in what the student needs to know when he embarks on a long period of study and in the plans that the state colleges and the university may devise for program expansion in some fields.

(4) *Optimum flexibility to meet change.* As President Hitch remarked, this objective is "imperative today because of the period of innovations in higher education we find ourselves entering." Tight and highly detailed budgetary standards, together with the resistance of vested interests, inhibit experiments and innovations.

Historically, two broad principles have guided the financing of public higher education in California: the state (sharing, in the case of community colleges, with local districts) would pay for the institutional costs of education; and the student would meet the direct and implicit costs of attendance. In recent years, the former principle has been modified at the University of California through the adoption of an education fee, but this is only a very small fraction of the average costs per student year. The second principle has also been modified as we sought to enlarge access to higher education on the part of the poor. Therefore, we stepped up financial aid in the university. From all sources of funding (federal and university), the total awards were $48 million in 1970–1971. The allocations from regents' funds rose from $2.4 million in 1967–1968 to $10.6 million in 1971–1972; in the latter year, $4.7 million of registration fees were also used for financial aid. The University of California has nearly reached the limit of its ability to increase these financial-aid allocations from regents' overhead and endowment funds, and from now on the money for improving access must come from the state and federal governments.

Beginning with the 1969–1970 academic year, students have had to pay approximately $300 per year for tuition. As matters now stand, neither community nor state colleges charge California residents for tuition, though nonresidents pay a stiff $1,500 at the university and $1,100 at the state colleges, apart from other fees.

A SUGGESTED PRINCIPLE: NO TUITION FEES

There is still controversy among the university's Board of Regents about tuition fees. In the above-mentioned testimony, President Hitch said:

> I strongly opposed the sharp increase in educational fees — in effect, the institution of tuition — at the University of California, and when I finally agreed to accept the new fee schedule, it was only because the present fiscal pressures left no alternatives except the even more serious consequences of grave and far-reaching impairment of university quality or denial of university instruction to substantial numbers of students.

What broad principles should control California higher education for the next decade or two? I personally believe that the state should meet, to the extent the federal government does not, the costs of public higher education, which should be tuition-free in all types of publicly supported institutions, for all degree levels and all student ages. Such present financial resources as local property-tax support of community-college budgets and the university's educational fee should be replaced with state funding, for the following reasons:

(1) Tuition-free offer of education is an excellent basis for a policy of universal educational opportunity, although it does not in itself *assure* access.

(2) A recently enacted California law makes eighteen the legal age of majority, including various rights of contract and the right to vote. Eighteen is also the age at which most people enter college. This implies that young people will make mature decisions at eighteen and that the income and assets of parents should not, in principle, be considered relevant to college attendance. At this young age, most people still lack the employment skills necessary in a postindustrial society, and if they are in college they cannot do more than part-time work. Their own incomes and assets are, for the overwhelming majority of students, severely limited.

(3) Those who left school to work, and women who have been at home rearing children, have another kind of educational need at

a later time: to redirect career energies, to rebuild educationally based skills, or to prepare to reenter the working force. The state must recognize these needs as an explicit responsibility, and encourage, not discourage, further education for men and women of mature years.

At present the state does not recognize this obligation. Even very highly trained scientists and engineers have suffered from rapid changes in federal research and development budgeting in recent years, and special federally supported programs have been organized to aid in the retraining and redirection of this group. The same dislocating forces affect many other workers and technicians, and for many people in contemporary society the need for renewal appears after an extended interval away from formal education.

(4) The *Seranno vs. Priest* decision points to another aspect of the same problem. Because elementary and secondary education is financed from property taxes, the quality of such education varies according to the wealth of the locality. While the state of California is grasping the holly bush of school finance, it might as well grasp the nettle of community-college finance, if the state is indeed committed to the principle of universal opportunity for postsecondary education. With this basic principle in mind, I do not think it wise to have tuition based on costs of instruction, or differential tuition based on differential costs.

There are good old reasons and some good new ones for affirming this principle. I believe that the individual student or his parent should not be expected to pay the institutional costs of public higher education. The state should be prepared to pay them, assisted by whatever federal programs are available. Localities, following the *Serrano* decision, should not have to pay the institutional costs of community-college operations. The state, with whatever help can be derived from federal programs, should accept responsibility for financial aid to students attending public postsecondary institutions wherever such aid necessary to permit attendance.

What is the state's obligation to students attending private institutions and to the private institutions? First, I must again stress the crucial importance of preserving private educational alternatives. There is now ample evidence of the cost-income squeeze on higher education generally throughout the United

States. The situation is especially difficult for private institutions, which face a large differential between what they must charge in tuition and what is available, both in cost and quality of education, from nearby public institutions. The squeeze is even greater for those institutions interested in students from low-income and minority families.

Private institutions in California add a great deal to the diversity of the state's higher education; they also ease the educational burden on the state budget. But if they received direct institutional support from the state on a formula or other basis, the danger of increased governmental influence could diminish the distinctive contribution they make. I would instead favor a substantial expansion of the California State Scholarship and Loan Commission's program to help students who elect to go to private institutions.

AID TO STUDENTS AT PRIVATE INSTITUTIONS

The aid program should be expanded to cover more than the present 3 percent of high-school graduates, and to permit more complete funding of tuition-aid grants. Because the tuition fees charged in many private institutions do not cover the full cost of instruction and must be supplemented with increasingly limited institutional resources from endowments and current gifts, the state should also consider providing a cost-of-education supplement to the institution accepting a student supported with a tuition-aid grant. This approach is one of several being considered to improve federal aid to higher education.

ANALYSIS OF STUDENT LOAN PROGRAMS

Loan programs to students and their families make much more effective use of taxes to cover the costs of education than other aid programs. Numerous proposals have been made along these lines: the Educational Opportunity Bank (the so-called Zaccharias Plan), which on a limited scale is being tried out by Yale University with the assistance of the Ford Foundation; the proposal by a governor's commission in Wisconsin for full-cost tuition in all public institutions, offset by loans repayable over the earning lifetime of the student; and, in California, various forms of "learn, earn, and reimburse" — proposed by Assemblyman L. E. Collier and others — which have been considered in recent sessions of the legislature.

The traditional approach to administration of undergraduate financial aid has long included some use of loans as part of the package. The institution in which the student expects to enroll first estimates the cost of attendance. This includes tuition and fees, living costs, books, transportation, and incidentals. The figure varies with the student's individual circumstances. If the student is an applicant for financial aid and is dependent on his parents, the parents are asked to provide detailed information about their income and assets, and the amount they can reasonably contribute to the cost of education is then determined. The student's projected summer earnings (net of summer living costs) are also estimated. The remainder is the student's need — to be met by a combination of fee deferments (if the institution's policy permits this) — work/study arrangements during the academic year, loans, and grants-in-aid or (if the student qualifies) scholarships. The loan component of these financial-aid packages has usually been held to a modest total amount (per year from all loan sources) of $200 to $1,000 per student.

Even as it is, if two young people marry just as they finish college and each of them has a debt averaging $1,000/year for each of five college years, they will have a total debt of $10,000. At a greatly subsidized interest rate of 3 percent, a ten-year $10,000 loan would have a monthly payment of $96.56. If the interest rate they pay is 6 percent — double the subsidized rate and much closer to the market rate — the monthly payment is $111.02, or just one sixth more. One proposed approach to higher-education finance is to set a full-cost tuition; the student is expected to borrow money to cover the tuition (and, if necessary, his other costs), and to repay these loans over a reasonable amortization period.

I have discussed this problem in a report entitled "The Repayment Period of Loan-Financed College Education," which shows that the high school graduate who goes to college will later earn a cumulative income that requires some years to catch up with the cumulative income he would have earned had he gone straight to work from high school. Especially if his education is to be loan-financed, he should apply a discount rate to the future stream of income in order to determine whether he will gain or lose financially by investing in a college education. The larger the debt, the higher the borrowing rate, and so *loan financing cannot fail to have a deterrent effect on college attendance.* Furthermore, if the student faces a short repayment period, he will repay his debt mainly during the early years of his working life, the years prior to the break-even point of cumulative income. These are also the years of establishing a family and going into debt for housing and consumer durables. Most families do their net savings when the head of household is between ages forty-five and sixty-four — preceded by the years of heavy household responsibility and fol-lowed by the years of retirement. Thus, a program based mainly or entirely on loan financing of college attendance would need to be based on a very long amortization period in order to avoid serious deterrent effects on attending college.

Students from families with low incomes and little education are characteristically fearful of debt. They also are likely to feel uncertain about job and income prospects, and they may in fact have to forecast a lower income if they are Black, Chicano, or American Indian, because job discrimination has not been elimi-nated from American society. Special programs of grants-in-aid, as well as counseling and tutoring, have been found necessary throughout the nation to broaden the actual access of low-income and minority students to higher education. If loan financing be-comes the sole or dominant means of providing college education, it would inevitably mean a reduction in the rate of college attend-ance by low-income and minority students.

Similarly, loan financing would probably reduce the rate of college attendance by women. First, women are paid less for equal work. Second, many women expect to be raising children during a good many theoretically income-earning years, between the ages of twenty-five to forty or forty-five. Recognizing this, Assemblyman L. E. Collier and other California proponents of loan financing have amended earlier proposals so that the debt liability of women would be deferred or forgiven if home and child-rearing respon-sibilities take them out of the labor market.

For all students, males and females of every income and edu-cational background, the choice of a career is accompanied by un-certainties about future income from each career alternative. An early objection to the Collier Plan was that it would increase the financial penalty of choosing a socially worthwhile but economically modest career. On the other hand there are the scientists and engineer who *were* aiming at high-income occupations but found that recent federal and corporate research and development cut-backs had dried up many job opportunities.

To relieve this hazard, some proponents of loan-financed college education have suggested that each former student pay back some given percentage of this later income — large if that income is high, and small if not — so that the student's risk will be averaged over low as well as high incomes. In California, where about 80 percent of high-school graduates go on to at least some post-secondary education, the overwhelming majority are in publicly supported institutions. Nearly all of them stay in California after completing their education. Thus, we already have an approximation of this sort of risk-averaging: the state income tax. California will lose the future state taxes of students whose education it finances if they leave California on completing their education. For many years, of course, California has imported large numbers of people whose higher education was obtained elsewhere, often at public expense, and California legislators do not complain about this.

California now receives the greatest amount of federal assistance in higher education financing for two purposes: the broadening of access through work/study programs, loans, and grants; and, at the other end of the spectrum, university research and graduate education, without which the University of California and Stanford could not function as they do in doctoral and graduate professional education. The latest federal move provides substantial cost-of-education grants to medical schools on a per student basis. When and as this new federal approach becomes fully funded, it will be of great help to California in financing the operating costs of expanded education in the health professions.

Yet as a general principle it would not be to California's fiscal advantage to shift the burdens of higher education finance to the federal level, because California is a high-income state and will bear more than a proportionate share of expanded federal programs. Also, the California tax structure is partly subsidized at the federal level, and California taxpayers have a lower federal tax liability.

VOUCHER PLANS

A voucher system for higher education permits the individual student to choose which institution to attend and which program to choose within that institution (subject to its rules of eligibility); the institution and the student will be reimbursed by the voucher-providing agency for all or part of their costs.

The G. I. Bill, after World War II, was a classic voucher system and had an enormous social impact on a whole generation of American society. In the administration of the G. I. Bill, the federal government had to set statutory standards: Once the student was in a program, the administrators had to determine how long the rights to claim payment would last, for both the institution and the student; and there were questions of the amount of G. I. Bill eligibility the individual had.

How does California's present higher education system relate to a voucher system? Much of what I have already discussed is pertinent. First, as to the question of adequate access to post-secondary education, the California student's financial burden is in effect eliminated if he attends a community college or a campus of the California state university and colleges. If the educational fee of the university is a financial barrier, fee deferral can be arranged. And aid should be provided to students attending private colleges or universities in California. Thus, with our present system and my recommended improvements, the burden of institutional costs on the student would be no greater than in a voucher system.

Second is the question of differing eligibility and enrollment-taking capacity standards in publicly supported systems and individual campuses. The enrollment-taking capacity of a campus or program depends on the availability of staff and facilities. Eligibility standards for undergraduate admission are a matter of public policy and acutely affect a high school graduate's chance of attending a state college or university campus if he does not at present qualify. The university has experimented successfully with exception admissions for students under the "2 percent plus 2 percent" plan approved several years ago by the Coordinating Council for Higher Education. The chief effect of a voucher system at the undergraduate level, along with the admission of students who do not meet specific eligibility standards of the state colleges and the university, would be to increase the numbers of academically less qualified students choosing these two segments at the lower-division level. How many of these there would be I do not know, but the amount and quality of counseling would have to be considerably increased in order to keep students out of courses they would find too difficult.

For graduate professional and academic education, California's state colleges and university campuses have long had far fewer places than applicants. The expected standards of academic performance in the graduate professions and in doctoral programs are quite high. If students could use vouchers, without reference to eligibility standards and capacity limitations, to decide whether to go on to graduate study, some graduate areas would need to be substantially expanded and the rates of attrition in graduate study would be considerably higher than they are now.

Advocates of voucher systems often claim two special merits for this approach: increased student influence (1) on program expansion and (2) on content of academic programs when students affect the size of programs and institutions through their choices. But in fact public institutions have already done much to increase student participation in decision making, and this has been done quite independent of the mode of financing.

Its proponents also claim that the voucher system leads to an efficient market for educational services, putting more pressure on each institution to attract students and do well by them, and creating an opportunity for new educational institutions to be organized along new lines. In the past decade, three new campuses of the University of California — at San Diego, Irvine, and Santa Cruz — have developed very differently from one another and from the previously well-established campuses of the university. As we know, an infant campus costs much more per student than a mature one. It took these campuses far less time to reach viable (although not mature) size than is usually true for new private institutions. Student enrollment demand and academic standards and accreditation have been high. I doubt that a voucher scheme could have improved on this record.

Great organizing effort and skill — and a large, risky, start-up investment — are required to get a new institution started. A voucher system, unless accompanied by commitments for this initial investment, would fail to stimulate new institutions. A voucher-approving agency would have to decide whether and how to approve and finance such investments in new institutions if they were to be encouraged: in short, it would have to engage in chartering and capital funding. Also, the voucher agency would have to decide whether to approve students' use of vouchers for the educational programs offered by new institutions. It would either have to rely on the present accreditation machinery or set up its own.

To set in motion a new design for education also requires a good new idea, one which effectively anticipates what will be worthwhile to students and to society on a long-term basis. The most striking kind of innovation is the occasional formation of a whole new institution or campus according to a new concept of education. In either new or existing institutions, there can also be new or revised curricula, and a most important incremental form of innovation goes on all the time by means of updating of courses, addition of new courses, and experiments with teaching approaches. These flourish if the faculty and administration are imaginative and if energy and resources are available for changes and improvements. If a voucher system is to be truly receptive to change, it must be generous enough to provide this resource margin.

There is also another issue: what kinds of innovation would student choices *via* vouchers stimulate? Students are now often involved in highly constructive ways of modifying curricula and courses. But most often major new fields and topics of study emerge from scholarly research and new perceptions of how to organize professional training, not from shifts in student taste.

For existing public institutions in California, a voucher system might have one great advantage. If the legislature provided full financing of the cost of educating each student, it would increase the independence of institutions and of their administrations and faculties, and would decrease the hazards of political intervention and bureaucratic management of academic budgets.

A FORMULA BUDGET FOR HIGHER EDUCATION

How desirable is formula budgeting? At present, many other state programs *are* formula-based, but the state colleges and the university are not, to their disadvantage. This means that the higher education part of the general fund budget is a major focus of state fiscal pressure.

We know that costs per student year of the various types of postsecondary programs vary tremendously. Laboratory science, engineering, and many technical-vocational programs have high equipment, support, and space costs per student compared with humanities and social science programs. Advanced programs, and those with small enrollments, tend to have high costs. To achieve the important goal of simplicity in fiscal relations, a single formula might be devised for the enrollment-related costs of all public higher education.

As an illustration, a simple formula budget for operation (not for capital) might allocate to each segment $1,000 to $1,200 for each lower division full-time-equivalent (FTE) student, $1,800 to $2,200 for each upper division and master's degree student, and $2,800 to $3,200 for each graduate student in the graduate professions and advanced doctoral programs. The actual amounts would depend on detailed cost studies. (The especially expensive programs in the health professions would of course require much more.) A formula of this kind would simplify fiscal relations between the public academic institutions and the state and would give the institutions greater choice of programs to push or cut back.

A more dramatic change would occur if a new budgetary approach were to emphasize the quality and quantity of educational results, rather than enrollment. The enrollment-based approach reflects the amount of educational exposure available, but it ignores questions of quality, of educational "value-added" (for example, helping a student who had been poorly qualified to do well in his education), and of program completion and attrition. Access — the opportunity to try — is one essential public goal. Our present educational budgeting does not stimulate the amount and the quality of educational results, which are worth serious effort. When a student successfully completes a program, he has accomplished something qualitatively different from simply serving time in an educational institution. He thinks so, and the world of work thinks so, and they are both right.

Some external validation of the quality of the program and the student's work — for example, standardized achievement tests at each level of degree or certificate — would be necessary with this approach. Otherwise, there might be temptations to let achievement standards slip in order to get more students through. But as a general principle, I believe that an orientation of educational budgeting to educational results would bring new and refreshing attention to the reform of indefensible program requirements; it would focus attention on improved teaching and potential drop-outs.

HOW MUCH FOR HIGHER EDUCATION?

Two questions remain: What amount of the state's resources should be allocated to public higher education? How should this be apportioned to each segment in the present structure? The first question is deeply political. In my view, society generally and California in particular benefit enormously, and not only in economic ways, from the educational stimulus that our people of all ages can receive. I would therefore favor a considerable expansion of state support to postsecondary educational functions that the state does not now underwrite. I also believe that a greater state role in the financing of the community colleges and of access to private colleges and universities in California would be desirable. But these additional financing burdens would require additional state revenue of several hundred million dollars per year.

When Masters Plan

by O. MEREDITH WILSON

Of the several themes that are woven into Neil Smelser's analysis, the one that interests and concerns me most is master planning. Such planning is endemic to the United States.[1] The impulse to plan, and after planning to coordinate, is alleged to arise in one or more of several power centers. The motivation is usually efficiency, which, strictly interpreted, is money-saving. And, of course, there need be no close coupling between efficiency determined by a measure of dollars spent and efficiency measured by educational imagination or even by conventional goals magnificently achieved.

First, as to the centers of power or interest that may have generated the move to plan: it is commonly believed that the political agencies have wanted structural reform to relieve them of the lobbying pressures from disparate educational units. But as Smelser suggests, in California, at least, the political agencies that had traditionally handled many of the problems of allocation or withholding of resources — namely, the state Department of Finance and the Office of the Legislative Analyst — were reluctant to give up their controls even after the new structural machinery had been created and was in place. Perhaps individual legislators wanted the protection afforded by a coordinating council, but existing bureaucracies felt threatened. And even individual politicians were ambivalent.

A fact-gathering agency that a legislator could depend on to provide accurate data and disinterested recommendations about

[1] Lyman Glenny, *Autonomy of Public Colleges; The Challenge of Coordination,* New York, McGraw-Hill, 1959), *The Carnegie Series in American Education;* M. M. Chambers, *Voluntary Statewide Coordination in Public Higher Education* (Ann Arbor, Michigan: University of Michigan, 1971).

education has been every politician's dream. The fad or the mode
of the sixties was to resort to coordinating councils within or without master plans. Not infrequently the politician began with the
idea that the coordinating council should be given decisive authority which could relieve the legislature of the awkward necessity for
making discriminating and politically unpopular decisions. However, it took only a little experience with such delegated legislative
authority to persuade the more powerful legislative leaders of the
wisdom of Teddy Roosevelt's dictum: "You can't tie a man's hands
for evil and leave them free for good." If a coordinating council
protected the legislature from having to make unpopular decisions,
it also foreclosed the possibility of courting constituents when
favorable judgments could be made. After several years of interested observation, I have concluded that good public servants,
whether in the governor's chair or in legislative committees, want
and need easier access to information. They are less certain that
they also want automated decisions that deny them the limelight
when dramatic educational decisions are to be made.

My own experience with the Minnesota legislature and its
state agencies is consistent with Smelser's findings in California.
Although one should not overgeneralize from personal experience,
what has been personally experienced should not be ignored. The
political powers that could affect higher education in Minnesota
were the governor and the legislature. Each was friendly to the
university; each occasionally criticized particular programs; each
grumbled at costs; each believed itself too little informed about
higher education. At one time or another a house committee, a
senate committee, or the governor would urge or demand a buffer
organization between the educational institutions and the political
process — a buffer that could guarantee unbiased, completely re-
searched recommendations, so that legislative decisions could be
lifted out of the climate of self-serving, logrolling, politically oppor-
tunistic relations into a dependable world of facts. New institutions, they thought, should be established only where unbiased
research showed them to be needed; new programs allotted only
on the basis of firm data about individual wants and society's manpower needs. After one dramatic instance in which the authority to
locate a new college was delegated by the legislature to an ad hoc
committee of educators who were intimately acquainted with a

coordinating council's demographic data and its findings on the geographic distribution of educational opportunities, I doubt that such a delegation would ever take place again. Statistical decisions are too antiseptic. Political goodwill does not grow in such sterile soil.

A second power center within which the drive for coordination has arisen is the educational community within the elite institutions. My observations suggest that the drive has most frequently been motivated not from a hope of attaining the best of all possible worlds, but rather by the fear that the only alternative to coordination may be a deteriorating one. Most American educational institutions exhibit the "university syndrome." The syndrome is, for the academies, a faith in the infinite perfectibility of man and the unquenchable urge for upward mobility which Tocqueville observed as characterizing the typical American, and which led him to say:

> . . . of all armies, those most ardently desirous of war are democratic armies, and of all nations, those most fond of peace are democratic nations; and what makes these facts still more extraordinary is that these contrary effects are produced at the same time by the principle of equality. . . . In either case, the restlessness of the heart is the same . . . the ambition of success as great; the means of gratifying it alone are different.[2]

What makes privates aspire to become generals makes junior colleges aspire to become full-service universities. And the fear that there would soon be no room at the top, or that new young institutions would compete for the scarce educational dollar and when successful reduce the allocation to the elite universities, often turned educational administrations in the direction of coordination. At the same time the heads of the new state colleges joined in a cry for coordination. The two sets of educators sought quite different benefits from the proposed new bureaucracy. The elite sought an ordered hierarchy of institutions, and the intent of their proposals was usually to protect the doctoral programs of the university; the effect was to perpetuate the status quo. They spoke of coordination as the means, but they had no expectation that the system would make *coordinates* of the educational units. Webster defines "coordinate" as "(adj.) equal in rank, quality, or

[2] Alexis Toqueville, *Democracy in America* (New York: Knopf, 1945), vol. II, pp 32–34, 266–267.

significance; similar in order or nature; not subordinate; (n.) one who is of equal rank, authority, or importance with another."

The intent of the master planner has usually been expressed as an organic theory of education. Some institutions should serve as the head, some the hand, some the leg, and so on. And please will each of you find honor and dignity in your own role and not all crowd into the head? (Translated, this means let us get on with graduate education while you content yourself with lesser roles.) The *underdeveloped* segments perceived the new council as a possible lever they could use to break into the select university circle. They aspired to be coordinates and most of them eagerly wait to be coordinated. In the California context, Smelser refers to new campuses within the university system as *under*developed, requesting standardized policies that would afford equal treatment on all campuses: "Let us strive for excellence too!" "Don't put artificial limits on our aspirations in order to leave only Berkeley and UCLA free." Meanwhile the state colleges asked, "Why are we prohibited from striving to be as excellent as the university?" The university response — "to avoid wasteful duplication and decline in quality" — is reasonable enough, unless the constraints on style or program at San Francisco State, as an example, prevent San Francisco State from full use of the skills and talents of its faculty out of respect for the new master plan — that is, unless the bureaucratic smothering of aspirations leads San Francisco State to produce less than it could.

Initiative arises from a third center of interest: men who have become students of higher education because it presents an interesting administrative problem. Some of these students have had experience with the political forces that enliven public higher education. Some, out of the largeness of their hearts, and without the chastening influence of experience, offer advice. One such, the most vigorous and most respected, is Dr. Conant. He hailed coordinating councils with great hope and the California Master Plan as a rational approach to educational policy-making beyond the high school, and he concluded that if we could join the New York Board of Regents and the New York Commission of Education with the California Master Plan, we would have "American public education at its best."[3] Having thus been caught up in the enthusiasm for

[3] J. B. Conant, *Shaping Educational Policy* (New York: McGraw-Hill, 1964), pp. 81–82.

coordination, his ultimate contribution to the field was his recommendation of an Educational Commission of the States in the creation of which he takes much pride and satisfaction.[4] Among my own colleagues in the Big Ten and the AAU, the proposal was considered a disaster of proportions directly related to the prestige enjoyed by Dr. Conant. With no experience in the delicate relations between university and state officials, he devised a plan that at best would add to the unproductive meetings we would be required to attend; at worst, the new agency could force an entirely new relationship between academies and politicians under circumstances which were certain, if not calculated, to increase the political element in the business of educational planning. Part of his motivation for a national commission seems to have arisen from his drawing the wrong lesson from a social observation. On page 114 of *Shaping Educational Policy* he says, "Therefore one might say that it is a happy accident that in all states, at present, there are free public schools and at least one state university and several state colleges. It is further a happy accident that in all but a few states children must attend school (public or private) from approximately six years of age until at least sixteen. . . ." The implication is that social behavior not mandated by law is accidental. In fact the real roots of social behavior and social creativity lie deep in the culture, and the law is only a pruning instrument used to shape the edges, to snip off stray or aberrant growth, or a prop to brace a weakening limb. The first laws enjoining the New England township to provide education were written because socially expected patterns of family and apprentice instruction had broken down. It is the function of the law to step in to repair failure, or to enjoin desirable but nonexistent social behavior, not to endorse what already exists; and social behavior enjoined by law is generally considered less secure than behavior arising naturally from the customs and the experience of the society.

It may well be true that some coordination is desirable, but the tide in its favor now runs so strong that a cautious view of the matter will not check it. We should think more realistically about the virtue of controls of and for educators that arise from coordinating councils. To that end I should like to include two paragraphs of dissent which I wrote when I served on an advisory committee on the Study of Statewide Systems of Education:

[4] J. B. Conant, *My Several Lives* (New York: Harper, 1970), p. 649.

1) At a recent conference that included primarily university presidents, I heard reluctant acquiescense in the proposition that since [the] move toward coordination was general, it was inevitable and perhaps good. However, those who spoke most positively went on to say that what is required and required desperately is that the coordinating agencies get better staff. Universally it seems assumed that the cause of the shortcoming of the coordinating agency is the poor quality of staff. Perhaps one should ask whether it is not the position and the general conception of a coordinating agency which is the cause of the poor staff. The coordinators are expected to think about important educational problems that seem to have eluded the wisdom of university officers who are generally conceded to have good staffs. Yet almost anyone in the United States who looks at higher education candidly will say that in a competition for a particular potential university officer, a university can readily win over any coordinating council, with the consequence [that] the university will continue to draw the best staff. Under your accepted and apparently urged solution, we are condemned to try to solve our most rugged educational problems with our least satisfactory educational minds.

2) The premise on which you begin is that while education is good and the people who serve it do have a status which needs to be protected against the rest of society, nevertheless perhaps the chief value which we should seek now is greater systemization and therefore greater economy in operation. Economies can be directed toward a variety of goods. In my judgment, even in this tight economy, good minds are in shorter supply than dollars and good ideas about education are in shorter supply than dollars. A system of educational organization that excludes or discourages many minds or invites (only) a few minds to think on the problem is less efficient than one which leaves the field for thinking and creativity open, if the objective is more bright ideas instead of the spending of fewer dollars. You acknowledge that at one time the free market was the best environment in which to develop education but announce that the frontier has passed and now order is required. I suspect that the problems that we have to resolve now are the more difficult than they were then and that the kinds of bright creative ideas that are required now will be no more congenial to bureaucratic or conservative government agencies or governors than they were then. The cleaner and tidier the blanket of coordination you throw around my shoulders the more oppressed I feel.[5]

Apart from the issue of efficiency, but related thereto, there lies behind the movement toward coordination only a modestly

[5] Appended in Robert O. Berdahl, *Statewide Coordination of Higher Education*, (Washington, D.C.: 1971), American Council on Education, pp. 273–74.

disguised indictment of the integrity of university leaders. They are portrayed as too self-centered, too involved in empire building to be trusted to serve the public weal. But the fact is, they are quite capable of educational statesmanship and are more likely to perform that role if they are not hedged with the constraints that project doubt and suspicion. The following statement by M. M. Chambers seems a good summary of the circumstances:

> The spirit which underlay the institutional rivalries of the early part of this century was far from being wholly bad. Today college and university presidents are not all rampant "empire builders" bent upon the aggrandizement of their own institutions and heedless of the statewide system. To be sure, they have a primary interest in seeing their institutions grow in service with the times — if they had not, they would not be worth their salt. But the notion that by and large they are incapable of grasping statewide problems, that they invariably allow local self-interest to override the general public interest, that they are a feral species which somehow must be netted and caged and held within the restraints of a rigid bureaucracy, is not only erroneous to begin with, but also, if effected, destructive of the essential spirit without which colleges and universities do not thrive. . . .
>
> We live in a day when vigorous and prompt expansion of the service of a higher education is paramount. Shall we hastily fashion additional stumbling blocks to be placed in the way of the men who see the need and have the energy and courage to act promptly? How can we lightly accuse them of improper motives, when, in the large, the urgency of what they are doing is so great?[6]

Once established, a university, more than any other corporation with which I have acquaintance, has a life of its own. Its curricular characteristics and its style are its spiritual force and personality, and unless these authentically reflect the nature of the faculty and administration, the university will be in trouble — perhaps schizophrenic. If there is a distortion of this reflection as the result of constraints occasioned by a master plan or a coordinating committee, we should be very sure that the constraints are necessary and that the blessings they bring adequately compensate for the sense of frustration and the death of aspiration they visit on the institution thus constrained.

As with people and their governments, so with universities

[6] M. M. Chambers, *Voluntary Statewide Coordination in Public Higher Education* (Ann Arbor, Mich.: University of Michigan, 1971), p. viii.

and coordination. Edmund Burke provides cause for reflection and, I think, counsel as wise for us as it was to Parliament:

> The extreme of liberty obtains nowhere, nor ought to obtain anywhere, because extremes . . . are destructive to both virtue and enjoyment. Liberty too must be limited in order to be possessed. The degree of restraint it is impossible in any case to settle precisely. But it ought to be the constant aim of every wise public council to find out, by cautious experiment and rational, cool endeavor, with how little — not how much — of this restraint the community can subsist. For liberty is a good to be improved and not an evil to be lessened. It is not only a private blessing of the first order, but a vital spring and energy of the state itself which has just so much life and vigor as there is liberty in it.

Flexibility, Quality, and Authority in Coordinated Systems of Higher Education

by T. R. McCONNELL

Eric Ashby, analyzing American higher education generally, and Neil Smelser, looking at California particularly, ascribe the evolution of post secondary education to the tension between two values — competitive excellence and egalitarianism. Sir Eric, unabashedly emphasizing the necessity of elitism, wrote:

> All civilized countries . . . depend upon a thin clear stream of excellence to provide new ideas, new techniques, and the statesmanlike treatment of complex social and political problems. Without the renewal of this excellence, a nation can drop to mediocrity in a generation. The renewal of excellence is expensive: the highly gifted student needs formal instruction, intimate contact with other first-class minds, opportunities to learn the discipline of dissent from men who have themselves changed patterns of thought; in a word (it is one which has become a five-letter word of reproach) this sort of student needs to be treated as elite.

To bolster their thesis, both Sir Eric and Smelser cite Tocqueville, who, said Ashby, "long ago predicted that elite treatment would be anathema in an egalitarian society." And he continues:

> It is commonly assumed that America has to choose between one or other of two patterns of higher education: mass or elite. I would deny this assumption. It is America's prime educational challenge to devise a coexistence of both patterns. There is already sufficient evidence to demonstrate that this could be done without dissolving and redesigning the whole system.[1]

[1] Eric Ashby, *Any Person, Any Study: An Essay on Higher Education in the United States* (New York: McGraw-Hill, 1971), pp. 101–102.

CALIFORNIA'S RIGID SYSTEM

California's method of resolving the antipodal values of competitive excellence and egalitarianism, as Smelser recounts, was a
three-tiered system in which the junior colleges, the state colleges,
and the University of California were assigned differential, and to
some extent overlapping, functions. These functions were set forth
in the Master Plan of 1960. During the negotiations leading to the
formulation of the plan, the University of California, in an effort to
contain the efforts of some of the state colleges to achieve university status, proposed that the differential functions of the three tiers
of institutions should be incorporated in the state constitution.
Fortunately, in my view, the university could not mobilize support
for this method of perpetuating the functions and statuses of the
three sectors. However, the leading proponents of the Master Plan
succeeded in persuading the legislature to give statutory sanction
to the functions designated for the three groups of institutions.
Smelser calls attention to a highly significant point in the legislation
which established the boundaries for the three segments of the
system: the pattern of functional differentiation not only specified
what functions a given sector could perform, but also specified
what functions it *could not* perform.[2] Thus, the statute fastened a
high degree of rigidity on the system.

The report of the Joint Committee on Higher Education in
1969 did not exaggerate the system's inflexibility when it declared
that there is presumably no way of altering an institution's course
of development, no matter what new social and economic needs
emerge, because this course is determined by the overriding functions and sanctions of the sector to which the system belongs.[3] It is
not an overstatement to say that the California Master Plan and the
statute which incorporates it have, in effect, engraved the functions
and statuses of the sectors and their constituent institutions on
tablets of stone. It is particularly significant that the law prevents
an institution from moving from one sector to another. The statute
thus brings even orderly and planned evolution to an arbitrary halt.
But the Master Plan did not stop the determination of some of the

[2]N. J. Smelser, "Growth, Structural Change, and Conflict in California
Public Higher Education, 1950–1970," p. 32. Paper prepared for a meeting of the
Western Secretariat of the American Academy of Arts and Sciences held at
Stanford, Calif., Feb. 17–18, 1972. (See p. 30, above.)
    [3]*Ibid.*, pp. 31–32 above.

state colleges to join the university club. Stung by what they considered to be the second-class status to which the Master Plan relegated them, the colleges continued to strive to redress their deprivation by pressing for equivalent salary schedules, time and support for research, lower teaching loads, and designation as universities. The colleges were able to circumvent some of the constraints placed upon them. (During the restudy in 1954, I found that the new science building at San Diego State College provided laboratories for faculty research.) The colleges devised ingenious ways of reducing teaching loads. Some faculty members secured research grants from outside sources. Finally, in 1971, the colleges succeeded in persuading the legislature to authorize the California Coordinating Council and the state College Board of Trustees in unison to designate particular colleges as state universities; in signing the bill the governor said he hoped that the council and the board would move quickly to change the names of all nineteen institutions. The governor, the legislature, and the chancellor of the state college system all declared that in changing the names of the colleges, there was no intention of changing the functions assigned to them in the Master Plan legislation. One may assume, however, that whatever the formal professions of adherence to stated differentials, the institutions will redouble their efforts to attain university status in organization and function as well as in name.

I think it is unfortunate that the law makes it impossible for an institution to move from one sector to another if the state's comprehensive plan for the development of higher education should make such transfer appropriate. In Illinois, such change in role is possible if it is approved by the Board of Higher Education, the state's coordinating agency. Illinois's Master Plan for Higher Education states that "the system of systems concept is not intended to type institutions indelibly or to predetermine their ultimate destiny."[4] This policy does not condone unrestrained institutional entrepreneurship. The fact that the Board of Higher Education has power to approve all new academic programs effectively restrains an institution, even if it is dubbed a university, from diverting large portions of its financial resources to the creation or expansion of doctoral programs and expensive professional schools.

[4]*A Master Plan for Higher Education in Illinois, Phase II* (Board of Higher Education, Springfield, Ill., 1966) p. 57.

Although planned movement from sector to sector may be desirable in a limited number of instances, new roles and functions should be designated by a planning and coordinating agency which is powerful enough to approve change of sector for a selected few institutions and to disapprove it for the many others. The California Coordinating Council has neither the power nor the influence to control selective reassignment. I shall return to this point later.

THE BRITISH ANALOGY

Although Smelser confined his study to the development of higher education in California, he suggests that some of the processes he identified — such as the relationship between the rapid growth of the system and its inability to invent new integrative machinery — might also exist elsewhere. Many of the factors at work in California are playing an increasingly significant role in the development of British higher education. Although the current controversy over the binary (as contrasted with a unitary) system of higher education exploded with the creation of the polytechnic sector in 1966, Britain in fact has long had a dual pattern. The universities have comprised the elite degree granting sector, and an extensive network of area and regional technical colleges have offered a wide range of advanced courses for students over eighteen. Some of these led to Higher and Ordinary National Certificates for technicians, and others led to examinations for the London external degree. In 1956, a white paper of the Department of Education and Science announced that ten of the regional colleges of technology would be designated as colleges of advanced technology and would then offer work exclusively at an advanced level, including postgraduate and research courses. These were to be university-level institutions, although they were not empowered to grant degrees, over which the universities had the monopoly. However, students could qualify for the Diploma in Technology, a national award of honors degree standard granted by the specially chartered National Council for Technological Awards.

The colleges of advanced technology rapidly embraced the university tradition and began turning their backs on their technical college heritage. In the end, according to Burgess and Pratt, "only in their adherence to sandwich courses, in the continued intimacy of their links with industry and perhaps in their continuing acceptance of ONC [Ordinary National Certificate] entrants, did the CATs retain a recognizably technical college outlook and a link with social or industrial need." In 1963, eight of the CATs were transformed into technological universities, and the other two were incorporated in existing universities. This implied that status was to be attained only as universities, that joining the university club meant abandoning technical college attitudes and traditions, and that part-time and working-class students should be diverted to a second-rate group of institutions.[5] Burgess and Pratt concluded that the creation of the colleges of advanced technology failed to produce university-level institutions effectively related to commerce, industry, and public administration. Thus, institutions that conceivably could have developed in the spirit of the American land grant colleges and universities opted to embrace the traditions of the existing university system.

Frustrated in its attempt to produce more technologists and applied scientists through the CATs, the Department of Education and Science inserted a new sector between the elite university sector and the further education system. In 1965, in a famous — many would say infamous — speech at the Woolwich Polytechnic, Anthony Crosland, secretary of state for education and science, declared:

> There is an ever increasing need and demand for vocational, professional and industrially based courses in higher education — at full-time degree level, at full-time just below degree level, at part-time advanced level, and so on. This demand cannot be fully met by the universities . . . It therefore requires a separate sector, with a separate tradition and outlook within the higher education system.

He declared, too, that if every institution which attains high academic standards moves automatically into the university sector, "the residual public sector becomes a permanent poor relation perpetually deprived of its brightest ornaments, and with a permanently and openly inferior status." Therefore, he asserted, a substantial part of the system of higher education should be under public control, directly responsive to social needs, and should lead to appropriate diplomas and degrees. "Let us now move away," Crosland orated somewhat pretentiously, "from our snobbish

[5] Tyrrell Burgess, and John Pratt, *Policy and Practice: The Colleges of Advanced Technology* (London: Penguin, 1970), pp. 172–173.

caste-ridden hierarchical obsession with university status." He
then promulgated the binary doctrine: "The university sector will
continue to make its own unique and marvelous contribution. We
want the public sector to make its own equally distinguished but
separate contribution."[6]

Following the Woolwich speech, the Department of Education and Science announced that it would designate thirty technical
colleges as polytechnics — university-level but presumably not
university-type institutions. The one white paper issued by the
Department of Education and Science declares that they are to be
primarily teaching institutions; that they will serve both full-time
and part-time students; and that they will maintain direct links
with industry, business, and the professions. In the eyes of the
universities and the schools, and in the public mind, the polytechnics were immediately considered to be second-class institutions,
and the proponents of the public sector became concerned with
how it might attain that British preoccupation, "parity of esteem."
In announcing the creation of the polytechnics, Crosland slammed
the door shut for a decade at both ends of the sector; he foreclosed
the possibility of movement at the top into the university system,
and he dashed at the bottom any hope that other technical colleges
might have of becoming polytechnics. However, slamming the
door did not extinguish what Crosland had called the rat race for
status. Straws in the wind foretell that, just as the colleges of
advanced technology turned their backs on the technical college
tradition, the polytechnics will do the same. Although officials of
the ministry have invariably declared that the polytechnics are to
be teaching institutions primarily, they have also emphasized that
the polytechnics are to engage in applied research. With the university model in view, polytechnic faculties are pressing ever more
strongly for time, equipment, and funding for research.

As part-time students were the casualties of the transition of
the colleges of advanced technology to university status, so they
may become the forgotten students in the polytechnics. Early in
the history of these institutions, it was apparent that — as full-time
enrollment and full-time courses expanded — the number of part-

[6] For a more complete discussion of the controversial binary cleavage, see
Martin Trow, "Binary Dilemmas — An American View," *Higher Education
Review*, 1 (Summer 1969): 27–43.

time students and courses declined. In one of the best of the polytechnics, part-time enrollment had declined from three thousand to one thousand by 1970. In 1970–1971, only 4 percent of the students in first-degree courses approved by the Council for National Academic Awards were part-time.

One of the most cherished British traditions is the equivalence of university degrees. This is a myth, although obviously degrees from the forty-four British universities are much more nearly equivalent than those from American colleges and universities. Although he emphasizes the equivalence of degrees, Eric Ashby admits that not all entrants to British universities are comparable in academic ability. He explained the situation as follows:

> Thus, on the five-grade scale (A-E) at A-level, an applicant to Cambridge would need to have one or two As; an applicant to Birmingham would get a place in some departments on B grades or less; an applicant to Essex might get in on D and E grades alone. But — and this is the significant difference between the American and British systems of admission and degree levels — all these British students will, three years later, be sitting examinations of similar difficulty in which the grading will have similar merit.[7]

British universities must be far more effective educationally than American ones if entering students at the low end of the A-level grade distribution can equal those of the opposite extreme at graduation.

The Council for National Academic Awards strives to make polytechnic degrees equivalent in level of accomplishment to those in the universities. Likewise, the council requires entrants to degree courses to have at least the minimum level of capacity required for university admission, even if their particular abilities differ in kind (a difference not yet documented).[8] In fact, the capacity of polytechnic students is increasing rapidly. One informant estimated that the percentage of entrants to the polytechnics with two or more A-level passes or equivalent has increased over the last five years from about 40 percent to 65 percent and is still rising.

In the meantime, many of the polytechnics covet the right to award their own degrees. Although the University Grants Committee would probably be receptive, the Department of Education

[7] Eric Ashby, *op. cit.*, pp. 53–54.
[8] *London Times Educational Supplement*, July 23, 1971.

and Science is unlikely to favor such a transfer. It would prefer to establish a polytechnic grants committee, and maintain the binary system. Belatedly, the department is at work on more explicit guidelines for polytechnic development in an effort to maintain a sector of higher education with at least some distinctive characteristics. But perhaps it is already too late. A university vice chancellor has declared that, with the exception that polytechnics offer courses at varying levels for students with different types of ability, all the reasons given for differences between the polytechnics and the universities seem to be bogus.[9]

Eric Ashby found a streak of frustrated aspiration running through the whole system of American higher education. Turning back to the British scene, he saw evidence of the same kind of relative deprivation and the same struggle for status. "Our system of higher education," he wrote, "is very different from the American, but we have embarked on a course which leads to similar dilemmas."[10] The current debate in Britain over the future of the colleges of education — whether they should be incorporated in the universities or the polytechnics or both, or established as a third sector of higher education — has complicated the controversy over functions and statuses. And so one finds in Britain's transition from elite to mass higher education the same underlying mechanisms which Smelser has detected in California's evolution toward universal higher education: feelings of relative deprivation, generalized dissatisfaction, and diminished loyalty. So far, there has been little overt conflict between the university and the polytechnic sectors. The universities, once fearful of competition for students, have relaxed; they may get more students than they really desire. But if the polytechnics and possibly the colleges of education evolve into a system of mass higher education, competition for limited resources may be expected to engender heightened competition and ultimately conflict between the universities and the other sectors of higher education. Smelser is correct in assuming that some of the processes he has delineated would also characterize other educational systems.

[9] C. F. Carter, "Towards Comprehensive Higher Education," pp. 87–93 in *New Horizons for Education*, ed. Brian MacArthur (London: Council for Educational Advance, 1970).

[10] Eric Ashby, "Meeting the Cost of Universal Graduation Without Knowing Why," *London Times*, April 5, 1971.

STUDENT SELECTION AND TRANSFER IN THE SYSTEM

Smelser points out that to implement the value of competitive excellence would entail highly selective admission policies. California attempted to solve the problem of selectivity by establishing graded standards of admission among the three tiers of institutions: the junior colleges are open to all, the state colleges admit students from in the upper third rank of high school graduates, and the university limits its entrants to those in the highest eighth. However, the students are not irretrievably distributed in this fashion. Those who, at the time of high school graduation, are not eligible for admission to a state college or to a University of California campus may become eligible for one or the other, or both, by appropriate selection of courses and level of academic performance in a junior college.

To some degree, retrieval of opportunity for higher education is possible in the British system. For example, students who leave school without completing the sixth form may take A-level courses in technical colleges. Furthermore, there are other avenues of entrance, to at least some of the technological universities and to the polytechnics, than the usual A-level courses; students who have earned the Ordinary National Certificate or the Higher National Certificate at a technical college may be admitted. However, it has been almost impossible for British students to transfer from one institution or one sector to another. There are some changes in the offing which should enable a student to move about more freely. For example, the Council for National Academic Awards has proposed that polytechnic courses be organized on a so-called modular plan, which would enable a student to apply work done in one institution to the completion of a program in another. A more sweeping proposal for restructuring British higher education — one less likely to be adopted in the foreseeable future — is for establishment of a network of tertiary colleges throughout the country. These colleges might be terminal for many students, and for other students they would be preparatory to courses in the universities, the polytechnics, or other institutions of higher education.[11]

[11] Alex Ross, "Restructuring Higher Education," May 1970 (mimeographed).

Transferring from one institution or sector to another is much easier for the American student than for his British counterpart. A study of the flow of students in California higher education has revealed an enormous amount of movement among the segments of the tripartite system.[12] Among California state college graduates, only about one student in four was graduated from the institution he entered as a freshman. Thirty-eight percent of the graduates had transferred once, 22 percent twice, and 13 percent three times or more.[13]

This flow of students in and out of institutions and sectors shows that in this regard, at least, the complicated California system possesses considerable flexibility. It also indicates that in a highly diversified system a student may have difficulty finding a place appropriate to his interests, abilities, and expectations.

OPEN ADMISSION TO THE SYSTEM

American higher education has responded in a variety of ways to egalitarian pressure for admission of students. The ordinary response of public four-year institutions which, by legal necessity or by choice, practice open admission is to eliminate a large proportion of entrants during the first two years. A few institutions have made significant internal adaptations to diverse student bodies. For example, the University of Minnesota established within its structure a two-year General College open to all Minnesota high school graduates who had taken a specified pattern of secondary school courses. After the General College was established, the College of Science, Literature, and the Arts and the Institute of Technology raised their standards for admission. A study made some years ago indicated that the College of Science, Literature, and the Arts had become as selective as the University of California at Berkeley. As one would expect, the General College, in spite of the fact that it devised innovative and imaginative courses for general education, was relegated to second- or third-class status in the

[12] California Coordinating Council for Higher Education, *The Flow of Students in California Higher Education*. (Sacramento: Coordinating Council for Higher Education, 1968).

[13] Division of Institutional Research, California State Colleges, *Those Who Made It: Selected Characteristics of the June 1967 California State College Baccalaureate Graduates* (Los Angeles: Office of the Chancellor of the California State Colleges, January 1969).

university. Its faculty and students suffered intense feelings of relative deprivation and inferiority which persist to the present day. Thus, whether adaptation to a highly diverse student population takes the form of internal differentiation or of a pattern of institutions performing different roles and functions, a hierarchy of statuses, reputations, and services seems to be inevitable. One would like to erase invidious distinctions among institutions and students in a diversified educational system. That we shall probably be unable to do so does not mean, in my judgment, that we should forego all efforts to sort students among institutions and programs. I am quite ready to support open access to a diversified *system*, but I find no compelling reason to repudiate the statement I made a decade ago, that "a democratic system of higher education need not accord all students the privilege of attending the same kinds of institutions, any more than it need permit all to pursue the same curricula."[14] That proposition, it seems to me, is not incompatible with the conviction that America's problem is to adapt its institutions to the full range of backgrounds, abilities, and interests of students, with standards appropriate to each kind and level of higher education, and to assure every person, whatever his social background and economic resources, the opportunity to reach the highest educational level for which he is fitted. If this is to be accomplished, no ultimate educational or professional opportunity should be closed to a student at early points in his schooling. What I said earlier about individual accomplishment seems relevant today:

> Within the present limits of our knowledge about the "fit" between students and institutions, it would be indefensible, even in a coordinated and differentiated system, to assign a student once and for all to a particular institution or a specific curriculum. The system must be flexible enough to enable each student to reach the highest level for which his aptitude and performance qualify him.[15]

FITTING STUDENTS TO THE SYSTEM

When one reads that the top third of high school graduates are eligible for admission to the state colleges and the top eighth for admission to the University of California, one may thoughtlessly

[14]T. R. McConnell, *A General Pattern for American Public Higher Education* (New York: McGraw-Hill, 1962), p. 83.
[15]*Ibid.*, p. 190.

assume that the state colleges accept students up to the university threshold and that all of the top cream may be found on the nine university campuses. Such, of course, is not true. Students in the highest eighth may be found in all three segments of higher educa- tion. How much overlapping there is between the state colleges and the university in the highest band of student ability I do not know, but I would guess that a considerable number of California's ablest students choose to attend the state colleges. A study made several years ago showed that these colleges were attracting more members of junior college scholastic honor societies than the uni- versity. Thus, the system makes it possible for the sectors to com- pete for talent. It would be wholly undesirable, in my judgment, to exclude exceptional students from the state colleges. Because they can attract such students, the colleges could attain high academic distinction if they chose to capitalize on their teaching mission. In fact, the colleges have developed pockets of distinguished perform- ance. For example, before Clark Kerr — as chancellor and presi- dent of the University of California — strengthened Berkeley's work in music, art, and theater, San Francisco State College greatly overshadowed Berkeley in the performing arts. Individual excellence is not defined and measured solely by grades in so- called academic fields, or by scores on a general scholastic aptitude test. Furthermore, although over the whole range of intelligence and creativity there is a positive relationship between these two variables, the relationship may essentially disappear for selected groups of people. For example, researchers at the Institute of Per- sonality Assessment and Research at Berkeley found that there was a slight, but probably negligible, correlation between intelligence and creativity.[16] Thus, a state college might find within its third of high school graduates some students of high creative potential or creative performance.

The fact that there are significant personal attributes other than those ordinarily — and imperfectly — measured by grades or scholastic aptitude test scores leads one to ask whether the Univer- sity of California succeeds in attracting students who possess the characteristics that fit them to meet the intellectual demands of an

[16] D. W. MacKinnon, "Selecting Students with Creative Potential," in *The Creative College Student: An Unmet Challenge* ed. Paul Heist (San Francisco: Jossey-Bass, 1968), pp. 101–116.

institution heavily oriented toward graduate education and research. Two specific questions are pertinent: 1) Is the University of California student body actually as homogeneous in academic ability as its band of selection suggests? 2) Are there other attributes than those revealed by grades that are particularly relevant to intellectual excellence?

The answer to the first question is "No," at least for the Berkeley campus. A recent report on the characteristics of Berkeley undergraduates through the 1960s pointed out that these students were in fact much more heterogeneous than would be suggested by the grade level required for admission. The report characterized the situation as follows:

> Both high school grades and total scores on aptitude tests are multidimensional measures, and the mere fact that they provide the assessor with a single number tends to obscure the fact that the number represents, quite imperfectly, a huge range of diverse abilities and modes of academic behavior. Thus merely by limiting registration to those students who command a B average in any of a rather impressive variety of high schools leaves still a very broad range of incoming talent, as much as four times the range of "tested ability" which enters an institution like Cal Tech or Swarthmore.[17]

Turning to the second question, the Berkeley report summarized data on an index of intellectual disposition derived from several scales of the Omnibus Personality Inventory.[18] The index focuses not on verbal skills and problem-solving ability, but on characteristics which combine to produce a disposition toward high intellectuality — "an intrinsic and broad interest in intellectual subjects and the world of ideas, a willingness to deal with complexity, and enough freedom from traditional patterns of thought to enable imaginative and creative responses to occur in a variety of situations." Students' scores on the index were distributed among eight categories; at one extreme were students with broad intellectual and aesthetic interests, openness to new ideas, and intellectual independence; those at the opposite extreme had little interest in ideas as such, were more concerned with the

[17] K. L. Jako, *Dimensions of the Berkeley Undergraduate Through the Sixties* (Berkeley: University of California, Project for Research on Undergraduate Education, 1971), pp. 29–30.

[18] P. Heist, G. Yonge, T. R. McConnell, and H. Webster, *Omnibus Personality Inventory.* (New York: Psychological Corporation, 1968).

concrete and practical than the general and abstract, and were relatively more conventional and less flexible in their thinking. What strikes one is the relatively small percentages of Berkeley students who exhibited an interest in abstract ideas, who were theoretically rather than pragmatically oriented, who were critically disposed and open to new ideas. The authors of the Berkeley report observed that "brilliance and intense intellectuality . . . are *included* in this student population, but are by no means typical or highly characteristic."[19] In 1959, almost as large a proportion of men at San Francisco State were in the highest three categories as at Berkeley — 10 percent and 14 percent. In the same year, 21 percent of the men at Cal Tech and 35 percent of those at Reed, Swarthmore, and Antioch combined were in the highest three categories of intellectual orientation. In both 1959 and 1966, incoming Berkeley freshmen were asked to check in a list the most important reason for choosing UCB rather than another college or university campus. In 1959 more than three-fifths, and in 1966 more than four-fifths, indicated that the most important consideration was the academic standing or reputation of the institution. If this is the Berkeley image, should it not attract a much larger proportion of students who possess the intellectual attributes that fit the perceived character of the institution? Is it unreasonable to expect that at least as large a proportion of Berkeley students as those at Cal Tech and the three selective liberal arts colleges should be in the upper reaches of intellectual orientation?

Eric Ashby has defined the "inner logic" of the university as critical rationality: "The only authority recognized in the world of scholarship," he wrote, "is the convincing statement, supported by evidence and attested by logical argument. . . . It is an attitude which accepts the supremacy of reason and disciplined imagination as the technique for solving intellectual problems; which resolves differences by persuasion and willingly tolerates dissent from those who are not persuaded. . . ."[20] If this is the ethos of the university and the spirit of the Berkeley campus, and if the University of California is to live up to its high calling in the tripartite system, surely it should attract and nurture students who possess the intellectual and moral qualities which will enable them to participate in the inner life of the institution.

[19] K. L. Jako, *op. cit.*, p. 36.
[20] Ashby, *op. cit.* (n. 1, above), pp. 96–97.

AN INTELLECTUAL COMMUNITY

However, simply attracting more students who are intellectually and creatively disposed will not be sufficient to enable the university to translate its public, its professed values, and its intellectual resources into living reality. It is not enough for young scholars to come to the campus. They need to find one another, to stimulate and support one another intellectually, to engage in vigorous intellectual and moral dialogue, to question, to dissent, to strike out in new directions, and to generate new ideas. Important as this student culture itself can be, it needs to be enlivened, enriched, and stimulated by association with faculty members. A campus which concentrates on scholarship and investigation need not ignore its responsibility for good teaching. One can envision groups of students with common interests taught by like-minded faculty in small seminars throughout their university careers. To teach these students would not be a burden but an opportunity. One can at least imagine the day when such outstanding students as many of those who were caught up in the Free Speech Movement of 1964 would commend the university as a scholarly community instead of denouncing it as cold and impersonal.

Although the number of intellectually and creatively oriented students should be large enough to put its stamp on the university's educational environment, not all students need to profess the same interests and dispositions. I suspect that, within reasonable limits, variety rather than homogeneity may be productive of both intellectual attainments and humane sentiments. Ideas, attitudes, and values take shape from challenge as well as support, from invalidation as well as confirmation. The clash of diverse subcultures is preferable to the concordance of ideas and attitudes. In spite of all of its disadvantages, a multiversity may be more fundamentallly educative than an intense place like Reed.

QUALITY AND DIFFERENTIATION

In soliciting support from the legislature and the people of the state, the University of California has emphasized the importance of maintaining the institution's academic quality. It has defined quality not only in terms of the ability of its students, but also in terms of its assigned functions. Thus, Smelser writes, "The university has taken the stance of a conservative elite, attempting to safeguard its custody over those functions — research, the doc-

torate, and training in the liberal professions — that guarantee it a
lead in realizing the values of competitive excellence."[21] In order
to carry on research of high quality, the university found it necessary to recruit a highly talented staff. "In general," as Smelser
points out, "the national competition for the most distinguished
talent was a competition for distinguished *research* talent. . . ."[22]
Thus, by and large, the university has equated quality with its
research function and with a staff distinguished primarily for research and only incidentally for teaching. In 1971, Vice President
Frank Kidner of the University of California adduced the principle
of competitive excellence as an argument for prohibiting the state
"colleges" from becoming "universities". He said:

> I would hope that the staff [of the Coordinating Council for
> Higher Education] would pay particular attention to the question of
> quality so that the council can be assured that whatever action is
> taken the level of quality can be maintained in every segment of
> California higher education.[23]

On first reading, this statement seems to imply that *equivalent
levels* of quality should be maintained throughout the California
system. On second reading, however, it seems that what Kidner
called for was the maintenance of *different levels* of quality between the state colleges and the University of California. At any
rate, the latter interpretation is consistent with the university's
practice of equating high quality with the distinctive functions assigned to it in the Master Plan. The university's habit of ascribing
high quality to its functions and lesser quality to those of the state
colleges has been unfortunate; one consequence has been to make
the colleges more determined to ape the university instead of performing their assigned missions with distinction.

In urging the change in name, the chancellor of the state
college system declared that calling the colleges universities would
aid in recruiting faculty and in securing federal and foundation
funds for research but would not alter their basic role. But now that
the change has been authorized, we may expect to see the faculties
redouble their efforts to reduce teaching loads, to secure research
support, and to offer doctoral degrees. Yet the financial austerity

[21] Smelser, p. 74, above.
[22] *Ibid.*, p. 86, above.
[23] *Minutes*, Coordinating Council for Higher Education, May 6, 1969.

now afflicting California higher education — an austerity that is likely to be only partially alleviated even if the state elects a governor more generously disposed toward public higher education — has made it painfully apparent that California cannot support a large number of institutions heavily engaged in research, graduate work, and advanced professional education. Shortage of funds has led the university to review its policy of turning all nine campuses into general institutions offering a full range of professional schools and graduate programs. The university is revising its plans for the development of several campuses by reducing estimates of future enrollment, lowering the proportions of graduate students, and limiting the number of fields in which the doctorate will be offered. The apparent current and anticipated overproduction of doctorates will postpone for some time to come the realization of the state colleges' doctoral ambitions. Any other course will condemn both the university and the state colleges to serious dilution of quality.

Across the Atlantic, Britain is about to face the same choice between uniformity and mediocrity, on the one hand, and differentiation and distinction on the other. As noted above, the Council for National Academic Awards has approved courses for the doctorate in several polytechnics, in effect turning these places into research institutions. This is happening at a time when it is becoming increasingly clear — although it is seldom acknowledged — that not all the forty-four universities financed under the University Grants Committee can become distinguished centers of research and postgraduate education. It has been suggested that the UGC might select a limited number of universities for such eminence, but this proposal evokes widespread opposition.[24]

It is difficult to suggest ways in which institutions whose primary mission is teaching can aspire to high normative standards consistent with that role. As Smelser points out, our present normative standards of excellence, not only in California but across the country and abroad, are tied to research and graduate instruction. On many occasions I have asked sociologists to suggest what support might be given for difference rather than conformity, but I have received few ideas. Perhaps the minimum reward might be to

---

[24] T. R. McConnell and R. O. Berdahl, "Planning Mechanisms for British Transition to Mass Higher Education," to be published in *Higher Education Review*, Autumn 1971.

equate the salary schedules in research institutions with those devoted primarily to teaching. Whether this would establish new and
different norms of academic excellence is uncertain. I think it is fair
to say that the vast majority of college teachers do not really want to
engage in research. Again and again, students have shown that
relatively few persons do research after attaining the doctorate.
Therefore, we might begin to establish new norms by destroying
the myth that nearly everybody is straining to do research. Next,
we might try to demolish another myth perpetuated by researchers; namely, that research is essential to good teaching, or even
that research assures good teaching. I have seen no evidence for
either assumption, and I seriously doubt that any such evidence
could be adduced.

A NEW COORDINATING BOARD ESSENTIAL

The need for new normative standards speaks to the functions
and the effectiveness of the California Coordinating Council for
Higher Education. There is a widespread belief that the council
has been ineffective in planning the development of higher education and in mobilizing legislative and public support. The reasons
for the council's ineffectiveness are many; what follows are comments on a few of the most important ones.

The major inadequacy is in planning. A recent study of the
coordination of higher education in four states, including California, concluded that planning had been mainly quantitative, with
little attention to issues of substance and quality, rather than qualitative, with more attention to issues ultimately related to students,
teaching, and learning. Looking more particularly at California, the
report declared: "Much of the Coordinating Council's work has
gone into management-oriented studies, such as those on faculty
salaries, space utilization standards, budgeting procedures, need
for new campuses, flow of students among the segments, and similar topics."[25]

Another serious deficiency is that the Coordinating Council is
purely advisory rather than regulatory. The present director of the
council is reported to have said recently: "There is no effective
statewide planning and coordination in this state. There's a vacuum

[25] E. G. Palola, T. Lehmann, and W. R. Blischke, *Higher Education by
Design: The Sociology of Planning.* (Berkeley: Center for Research and Development in Higher Education, University of California, 1970), pp. 538 and 575.

at the top. We can't fill the vacuum with our weak little agency, so the politicians [of both parties] move in."[26] It is now generally accepted among students of coordination that a statewide coordinating board should have the power to approve or disapprove any proposed new unit of instruction, research, or public service; to review the educational and economic justification of all existing programs; to approve new institutions or additional campuses of existing institutions; to set minimum admission standards for the several sectors; to make detailed analyses of the budgets proposed by institutions or sectors; and to submit to the executive and legislative departments of government recommendations concerning appropriations for current operation and capital outlay.[27] These are very considerable powers, and they should be exercised only after consultation with advisory committees and task forces composed of university presidents and faculty members, representatives of many organizations, and citizens at large. It has become increasingly obvious that California's system of higher education cannot be planned, monitored, and coordinated successfully unless the Coordinating Council is given the powers enumerated above. Berdahl's recent study of statewide coordination has shown clearly that the trend in most states has been to give coordinating boards regulatory rather than purely advisory responsibilities. The choice, wrote Berdahl, is "between having a stronger coordinating agency or being ingested into the executive branch of state government."[28]

Looking to the British scene again, one finds that although the functions of the University Grants Committee are formally stated less in terms of authority than of guidance, the committee nevertheless has steadily become more directive and regulatory. By convention rather than explicit delegation, the UGC actually exercises more authority than nearly all of the coordinating boards in the United States. For example, only the Oklahoma coordinating board and the Georgia statewide governing board receive

[26] William Trombley, "Master Plan," *The California Professor* 6 (November 1971): 3.
[27] See, for example, L. A. Glenny et. al., *Coordinating Higher Education for the Seventies* (Berkeley: University of California, Center for Research and Development in Higher Education, 1971).
[28] R. O. Berdahl, *Statewide Coordination of Higher Education* (Washington, D.C.: American Council on Education, 1971), p. 146.

lump-sum legislative appropriations which they then distribute among the institutions; the UGC exercises this de facto power by virtue of its "advice" to the government on the distribution of funds among the universities. The UGC has allocated high-cost fields of specialization among the universities instead of permitting wasteful duplication. It has established uniform faculty salary scales and has imposed an upper limit of 35 percent on senior faculty ranks. It has attempted to regularize costs by moving high-cost and low-cost departments toward the average of all the universities. In effect, it has eroded the system of making block grants by indicating to each university the factors it considered in arriving at its grant. There are signs that the UGC expects the universities to follow these indications faithfully. For example, the committee recently wrote what was described as a rather curt letter to the vice chancellor of one university, calling attention to the fact that it had admitted more postgraduates than the committee had specified in its letter of intent. Without question, the British universities are experiencing, in Eric Ashby's words, "an increase of influence from the center and a decrease of autarchy at the periphery."[29] The same trend will occur in the United States. Central influence should be exerted to the greatest possible extent by an intermediary body standing between the institutions, on the one hand, and the executive and legislative branches of government, on the other.

The third major deficiency in the California Coordinating Council is its lack of effective leadership. As I wrote on March 5, 1965, in a memorandum to President Clark Kerr of the University of California:

> . . . any reading of the responsibilities and opportunities of the Coordinating Council would indicate that a great deal of initiative and leadership on the part of the director is essential to the success of the council and to the development of higher education in the state. . . . The voice of the director, and perhaps of the chairman of the council, should be heard where the cause of higher education needs clarification and emphasis. . . . The future of higher education in California — certainly the future of coordination — depends on having as director of the council a man of the highest academic and administrative qualifications. . . . He should possess the background of scholarship, experience, and administrative talent possessed by the president of a major university or university system. . . . A

[29] Eric Ashby, *Hands Off the Universities* (London: Birkbeck College, 1968), p. 14.

short-range view might suggest that the university would more nearly have its way if the director were relatively weak, or at any rate, were a person who did not attempt to exercise leadership or take much initiative. . . . In the long run this would be greatly to the disadvantage of the university and to higher education in the state.

Most students of educational planning believe that periodically a blue rubbon commission should make a full-scale study of a state's needs for higher education, review the governance patterns of institutions and systems, and update the mechanism for continuing planning and coordination. Such commissions, as Clark Kerr recently suggested, should be composed of persons who are familiar with higher education and are deeply and impartially devoted to it.[30] Although the majority of the members of such a commission should be drawn from higher education, persons selected to represent the public interest should be included. It is only realistic to recognize that neither the governor, the state finance department, nor the legislature, in California or any other state, is alone competent to rearrange the pattern of higher education. Certainly, the state should make final decisions on broad questions of educational policy, but it should make these decisions only after considering carefully the recommendations prepared by what Berdahl calls a "suitably sensitive mechanism."[31] This mechanism would make a determined effort to reconcile the public interest with the aspirations of the institutions or sectors that form the state's system of higher education. One intermediary agency is the so-called blue ribbon commission. The body which should be charged with continuing mediation between the interests of both parties is the coordinating board. Glenny has characterized the process as follows:

> The coordinating process is a political one involving powerful social agencies, such as colleges and universities, with their historic intellectual independence and autonomy on the one side, and the central public policy-formulating authorities of the governor and legislature on the other. The coordinating agency, situated between these two powerful political forces, seeks to identify with both in order to achieve satisfactory solutions.

In Glenny's view, the coordinating board does not perform its essential function merely by serving as an arbitrator among

[30] Clark Kerr, in an interview in *College and University Business*, 51 (November 1971) 5:5–57.
[31] R. O. Berdahl, *op. cit.*, p. 15.

conflicting forces; it plays its fundamental political role by providing leadership in planning the development of higher education, and in devising a pattern of institutions and programs that will economically and effectively serve the needs of the state and the lifelong educational aspirations of its people.[32]

Because the California Coordinating Council is unable to accomplish this task, we need the leadership of a new coordinating board during the next decade.

[32] L. A. Glenny, "Politics and Current Patterns in Coordinating Higher Education," in *Campus and Capitol*, ed. W. J. Minter (Boulder, Colo.: Western Interstate Commission for Higher Education, 1966), pp. 27–46.

Law and Higher Education in California

by ROBERT M. O'NEIL

Late in the spring of 1965, after calm had returned to Sproul Plaza and Mario Savio had retired from campus politics, the University of California received claims for special police costs from the cities of Berkeley and Oakland and the county of Alameda. The amounts were substantial, reflecting many hours of arduous duty clearing Sproul Hall during the December sit-in. For several reasons, the legal posture of these claims was quite uncertain. An obscure provision of the California Government Code obligated the mayor or police chief to "direct a sufficient number of policemen to attend and keep order at any public meeting at which, in his opinion, a breach of the peace may occur" — a prescription which arguably covered the finale of the Free Speech Movement. Yet the university, unlike many institutions of higher learning that rely on the local police, had its own security force. Some fifty uniformed officers were assigned to the Berkeley campus alone, and they were on duty during the sit-in. Thus the university's liability for supplemental police services was problematical.

Scarcely had the claims been presented, however, than the Vice president and general counsel advised the regents that they need pay only the city of Oakland; Berkeley and Alameda County, he argued, were legally required to police the campus and thus could claim no extra compensation for the unusual services rendered at Sproul Hall.

Several important lessons emerge from this episode. First, it suggests that more vital decisions concerning the legal status of the university are probably rendered by the judge in University Hall than by the judge in city hall. Like many university and college attorneys, the regents' general counsel has the power and authority to determine when the university's decisions and policies will be tested in court, and under what circumstances. On countless occasions, in negotiations, in the writing of briefs, and during argument in court, he and his associates must represent the legal views of the regents on questions about which there has been little or no time for actual consultation.

Second, this process of lawmaking and adjudication occurs almost exclusively in University Hall. Although many, perhaps most, large state systems of higher education have decentralized legal services along with other aspects of administration, the University of California (and the state colleges) have kept a very tight central rein. Moreover, the tendency has been to impose on the other eight campuses a set of legal principles responsive to the special problems of Berkeley, because the flagship campus generates the bulk of the difficult legal controversies. There is neither mechanism nor occasion to determine fully the appropriateness of such principles for the vastly different needs of Riverside, Santa Cruz, or Santa Barbara. Once the law has been made for Berkeley, it applies, however imperfectly, to the rest of the system.

Third, and perhaps most important, the general counsel's advice in 1965 reveals much about the University of California's legal status. The much vaunted autonomy of the university has in fact been invoked when convenient or necessary, but is often disregarded when unnecessary or inconvenient. If the issue in 1965 had been the right of city or county police officers to enter a campus building without invitation, the official response would likely have been quite different. But for the question of which governmental agency should bear the cost of several thousand hours of overtime police pay, the protective aspect of the constitutional autonomy was conveniently overlooked.

These observations suggest several pertinent themes in the relationship between law and higher education. At the heart of the matter is the concept of autonomy, to which I devote most of my attention here. Autonomy exists or occurs in California at two distinct levels. The role of autonomy within the public sector — deriving from the special constitutional status of the regents — tends to be considerably exaggerated. Yet another form of autonomy — that which differentiates the private institutions of higher learning from their tax-supported counterparts — is largely neglected in studies of California higher education. We shall consider both the intrasystem and the intersystem aspects of this elusive concept.

AUTONOMY: THE UNIMPORTANCE OF BEING CON-STITUTIONAL

It is widely believed, at least among educators, that the University of California derives some mystical independence from Article IX, Section 9 of the state constitution. In recent testimony before the Constitutional Revision Commission, President Hitch argued that this provision has given the university "a necessary measure of autonomy for one hundred years" and that "constitutional protection [is] vital to the University. . . ." This view is widely shared throughout the state, among faculty and students as well as citizens, parents, and taxpayers. Were the constitutional status of the university seriously jeopardized, a cry of opposition would doubtless arise. The vital question for consideration here is what justifies the faith in constitutional autonomy.

Whose autonomy? First, it must be understood that whatever autonomy the constitution does confer extends directly to the regents rather than to the university — much less to the individual campuses. In an ideal world, of course, the interests of university and governing board would be virtually identical, so that a guarantee enjoyed by one would be fully shared by the other. However, few persons would be naive enough to claim that such a harmonious relationship exists in California.

A few recent examples will suggest how grave is the threat to campus autonomy from the governing board. Having delegated to the chancellors all responsibility for reviewing and approving nontenure academic appointments, the regents nonetheless withdrew that authority in the summer of 1970 just long enough to terminate the employment of Angela Davis — well before any charges arose from the Marin Courthouse shoot-out. About the same time, the regents withdrew curricular responsibility delegated to the faculty. Some years ago the board had invested the Committee on Courses of the Berkeley Division of the Academic Senate with broad authority to review and approve new courses for academic credit. As against the campus chancellor, this power substantially limited administrative initiative in curricular innovation. Yet when the regents learned that Eldridge Cleaver was scheduled to give several lectures in Social Analysis 139x during the fall of 1969, they withdrew that authority from the Committee on Courses and denied credit — not only for the originally scheduled course, but also for a hastily devised independent study option offered by a regular department. This action soon became the subject of a lawsuit, brought by a group of aggrieved students and faculty members.

Such incidents suggest that there may in fact be an inverse correlation between the governing board's legal independence and the effective autonomy of the university. Two explanations are plausible. The regents may feel that because of the constitution they are less likely to be held accountable by judges or legislators for violations of campus or individual freedom. Alternatively, the board may fear that a failure to keep their own house in order — even to the extent of anticipating the demands of hostile constituencies — would ultimately jeopardize their constitutional stature. Ironically, the regents' autonomy may have been diluted and cheapened by the very process of trying to preserve it. Whatever the explanation, the evidence does suggest that the University of California campuses may be less autonomous than their counterparts in other states precisely because the body that governs them enjoys a special constitutional status.

Autonomy *within* the systems — both California systems — is diminished in another important way. Unlike most large and complex state university networks, the vital function of legal counseling and representation remains wholly centralized. No provision is made for quick rendering of legal advice by a local attorney, or for the handling in local courts of small matters that may involve a campus several hundred miles from Berkeley or Los Angeles. The fact is that campus autonomy is only as substantial as the chief administrative officer's capacity to make his own decisions and defend his actions when challenged. Even if all other administrative functions were to be decentralized in both systems, the continued reliance upon a single legal office would measurably circumscribe campus autonomy.

Ultimately, whatever autonomy the regents or the university may enjoy is *gubernatorial*, because the governor retains the sole authority to appoint all but the ex officio members of the board. When the Michigan constitutional model was borrowed and adapted, the provision for popular election of regents was omitted. Subsequent attempts to require senate approval as a check have been resisted, although the state college trustees must now be confirmed and the proposed new California constitution would add this step to the selection process. The vesting of exclusive appointment power in the state's chief executive is a mixed blessing, to be sure. Popular election of regents works quite well in Michigan, giving the university a striking degree of real autonomy. Yet in Colorado, a popular election several years ago subjected the university to the ultraconservative hegemony of a Denver brewer and precipitated a crisis in academic freedom. Moreover, one need hardly point out that the sixth of the California board that *is* popularly elected — four of the ex officio Regents — has caused a disproportionate share of the university's problems in the last decade.

Senate confirmation or legislative assent is not a complete guarantor of integrity. The University of Minnesota discovered this several years ago, when the state senate declined to confirm several nominees for reappointment because of apparent pique with the board's tolerance for student and faculty activism. Had the governor had exclusive authority, these renominations would have gone through unchallenged.

Clearly the result in each state depends very much on the vagaries of partisan politics and other rapidly changing realities. But a special risk inheres in the California system. A governor can, in four years, effectively impose his political and educational philosophy on the university to a degree that other constituencies may not undo for eight to ten years. (In fact it may not even take that long. Governor Reagan had working control of the regents — sufficient at least to obtain the discharge of President Kerr — within weeks of taking office.)

Recent events provide dramatic confirmation of the extent of gubernatorial control over the university. Few issues have been more troublesome of late than the level of faculty salaries. First the legislature refused to act, although University of California compensation was falling behind that of competitive institutions in other states. Then, after the 1970 election, a new liberal majority twice passed salary increase appropriations, only to have them vetoed by the governor. This experience suggests how far the fox has been entrusted with custody of the chickens; what the governor cannot accomplish in his role as president of the Board of Regents, he may nonetheless be able to achieve as chief executive of the state.

Autonomy and the courts. Any review of court cases would suggest that the University of California has fared quite well before the bar of justice. Seldom has a lawsuit against the regents gone much beyond the threshold. Countless claims have been dismissed on demurrer or by summary judgment after review of relevant policies and documents. From the successful suit by Berkeley students challenging compulsory ROTC in the 1930s to the unsuccessful suit by former ASUC President Dan Siegel to regain the campus office from which disciplinary action had removed him in 1970, the pattern of litigation has been quite uniform. Thus the general counsel argues with some force that the judicial deference of the thirties survives into the seventies, even if the university is not absolutely immune from suit for its acts and omissions.

The real explanation for the university's relative invulnerability to suit lies somewhat deeper. A vital difference between California and other states may lie in the relative accessibility of legal remedies. In New York, by contrast, institutions of higher learning — both public and private — are often brought to bar. Courts have required that degrees be granted, that courses be rescheduled, that students be reinstated, and even (although ultimately reversed) that tuition be repaid for classes missed during the Kent-Cambodia aftermath. But there is a special explanation for the New York pattern: Article 78 of the Code of Civil Procedure makes the acts of a wide range of public agents, corporate officials, and others readily reviewable in the state's trial courts. Institutional accountability is thus built into the procedural laws of the state, although the draftsmen of the code had no thought of universities when they framed Article 78.

There is a rather substantial deterrent to lawsuits against the University of California. A new section added to the Education Code in 1967 provides that the regents, when sued, may demand that a plaintiff post security to cover the probable costs of the litigation. The amount of the security is to be set at $100 for each plaintiff, or more if the court deems appropriate. If judgment is rendered in favor of the regents, "allowable costs incurred by the regents in the action shall be awarded against the plaintiffs." Thus one now sues the university at his peril.

It is difficult to measure the impact of such differences in state procedural laws, for the *volume* of potential litigation varies widely among states according to the number of litigable issues arising on campuses, the availability of legal services, the applicable substantive law, and other factors. At least it can be said that getting into court is somewhat more difficult and probably costlier for the aggrieved faculty member or student in California than in many other states, and that once in court the scope of review is likely to be narrower.

There is a second factor that tells more about the *integrity* of California institutions of higher learning than about their *autonomy*. Throughout the 1960s, California deans (both student and academic) were generally ahead of the courts with regard to procedures employed for student discipline and faculty termination cases. Thus the warrant for judicial intervention was lessened by the impression of fairness and tidiness within the academy.

When Arthur Goldberg and three other students brought suit challenging their suspension for leading the Filthy Speech Movement in the spring of 1965, the courts may have had some doubts about the looseness of the substantive regulations, but they were so favorably impressed with the thoroughness and impartiality of the Committee on Student Conduct that the suit was dismissed. A year or two later, when a former teacher at San Jose State College (by then a state assemblyman) sued to regain his position, the courts abstained for similar reasons after reviewing the exhaustive procedures followed on campus prior to the termination. A student at the College of San Mateo brought suit in the federal district court after he had been suspended on an interim basis pending a disciplinary hearing; again probable fairness of the procedure awaiting him led the court to dismiss without critical analysis of the substantive issues. Examples of such judicial deference are legion, and suggest that abstention reflects a basic confidence in the fairness of California public colleges and universities far more than it reflects the phrasing of the constitution. Were that confidence to be shaken by summary or arbitrary dismissals — a most unlikely prospect in California higher education — the judicial response would doubtless change to accommodate different conditions.

One very recent case will suggest the limits of constitutional autonomy in the courts. A third-year medical student at the San Francisco campus brought suit claiming he had been denied entry to the fourth year on arbitrary and improper grounds. The general counsel for the regents simply filed a demurrer — a legal claim that even if all the facts alleged in the complaint could be proved, no cause of action would be made out entitling the plaintiff to relief. The matter was obviously a sensitive one, because the suit asked in effect for a judicial inquiry into the fairness of an academic judgment about a student. Nonetheless, the Court of Appeal reversed the summary dismissal of the complaint. For the first time, a court held that even the *academic* judgments of the University of California are potentially subject to judicial scrutiny upon a showing of arbitrary, capricious, or malicious criteria. However unlikely it may be that the plaintiff could ever bring his claim within these criteria, the precedent is nonetheless important.

Autonomy and the legislature. Whatever the constitution may say, the university's actual autonomy extends only as far as the legislature is willing to respect it or the courts are willing to protect it when it is threatened. The practical differences between the university and the state colleges in this regard tend to be exaggerated. (The comparison may be imperfect. The university has been a more frequent target of criticism in recent years and thus perhaps more vulnerable to external threats because of its greater visibility. But recent events have begun to shift the focus from one system to another.)

There are essentially two ways of measuring the independence of the university from the legislature. The first and most obvious is to examine the legislation, to appraise the areas in which the lawmakers have deferred and those in which they have regulated. The pattern is quite mixed. One example of apparent deference concerns academic tenure and faculty promotions. In 1970, the legislature apparently felt the university was too lax about hiring senior faculty from outside the system without a probationary period. Rather than abolish initial tenured appointments, however, the lawmakers passed a joint resolution "call[ing] upon the University of California to alter its academic tenure policy" in the suggested manner. Apparently the regents duly received this advice, considered it, but took no steps to act on it.

Perhaps the strongest manifestation of legislative respect was the failure of the threatened investigation of the Berkeley campus to materialize after the Free Speech Movement. Yet the explanation for inaction at that time appears to lie much more in political realities than in constitutional autonomy. As speaker of the assembly, Jesse Unruh was an ex officio regent, and was thus called upon to authorize an investigation of events and actions he had partially condoned. Moreover, the regents had taken the initiative in launching a major investigation of their own, headed by a Los Angeles attorney seemingly satisfactory to both conservatives and liberals. Third, and perhaps most important, Unruh had developed early rapport with and strong confidence in the acting chancellor of the Berkeley campus. To have sanctioned the investigation while a new administration was trying to restore calm and order might have seriously undermined that relationship. Thus the investigation never did in fact materialize — and to this extent an important aspect of the university's integrity was apparently preserved.

It is also true that the University of California has been somewhat freer from legislative intrusion than large public systems in other states. There have not been the kinds of full-scale investigations launched in 1970 by the legislatures of Ohio, Indiana, Illinois, and Virginia, among others. The University of California faculties have been spared the work load conditions and restrictions imposed in Michigan, Florida, New York, and Washington — although the reprieve may be only temporary. The California legislature has never imposed on student financial aids the sort of attaint imposed by Pennsylvania's lawmakers in 1969. Nor have the officers of the relevant California legislative committees ever given gratuitous "advice" to the campus presidents and chancellors, as was done in Minnesota after the close of the 1971 regular session. In these respects, a measure of autonomy seems to have accompanied the special constitutional status of the regents.

However, the impression is partly deceptive. A substantial, and apparently increasing, number of potentially intrusive California laws apply indiscriminately to all three public systems. The definition of resident student status is supplied by the legislature for all systems. The Coordinating Council has the power to "require" all public higher institutions to "submit data on costs, selection and retention of students, enrollments, plan capacities, and other matters pertinent to effective planning and coordination," and this applies equally to regents and trustees. All governing boards are required by recent legislation to keep records of rejected applicants, to develop and utilize "an information system" to

reflect redirection patterns, and the like. All systems are to report
regularly to the legislature "on the progress made on the implementation of the enrollment plans and admissions priorities system." In these and other respects, the university receives no special immunity from state legislation that reaches into internal affairs
and system management.

There is a risk in looking too closely at the trees, however, and
forgetting the forest — some might say jungle — that is the Master
Plan itself. By the very process of insulating the university from the
other two systems, the legislature has restricted flexibility and
closed options. If the Master Plan tells the university what it may
do (and what others may not do), it also tells Berkeley and UCLA
what they may not do. Moreover, as Smelser has shown so forcefully in his paper, "in the last analysis the authorization for growth
must come in large part from the state legislature." Without the
assent and support of the lawmakers, there is very little the regents
can do on their own to shape or change the character of the system.

To look simply at statutes, as we have done up to this point, is
to neglect a major artery of legislative intrusion, the budget and
appropriation process. Soon after the Kent-Cambodia crisis and the
"reconstitution" of classes, key committees of both houses in Sacramento took clearly punitive measures against the university.
First, the Finance Committee of the state senate struck from the
budget a proposed 5 percent cost of living increase in University
of California faculty salaries. A few days later the Ways and Means
Committee of the assembly deleted an item earmarked for the
support of the Academic Senate. This latter action, explained the
committee chairman, was designed "to shake them up." "What
does the Academic Senate do," he queried, "but make themselves
obnoxious? Why don't they fund themselves out of their own
dues?" With a stroke of the legislative pen, the mightiest organ of
faculty self-government in the United States was badly crippled; a
body that could terrify chancellors and worry regents was no match
for the state legislature. (Some of the cuts were later restored, and
the senate limped through the year on a meager austerity budget.)

What may be the sharpest blow of all has been reserved until
last, because it is a glancing blow — the legislation to invest the
state colleges with the nomenclature of universities. Superficially,
this has no bearing on the university's status. Yet the relationship is

too clear to require elaborate demonstration. Despite the insistence of supporters that the name change portends no abandonment of the Master Plan's structural distinction between systems, the prospects are ominous. Chancellor Bowker properly fears that a "state university" may soon be authorized to develop new doctoral programs, when "even within the University of California, Berkeley faces strong competition for scarce funds from new and growing campuses with their own plans for doctoral programs." Yet the governor, on signing the name change bill, claimed to be mystified by the university's anxiety, adding — as though to assuage the fears — "I love the university; I show no favorites."

The lesson is fairly simple: The autonomy of one entity can be impaired as much by strengthening a competitor as by weakening the original beneficiary. Whether or not the state college trustees ever attain constitutional status (as proposed by the constitutional revision), the major battle may already have been won simply by altering a single word in the title. The actual decision as to which campuses may become universities has been left to the trustees and the Coordinating Council — the very Coordinating Council that recently suggested dismantling the smaller foreign language programs at Berkeley, UCLA, and Davis.

How has the university's autonomy fared in the courts? Although this is not the place to examine the cases at length, a brief summary of the law may be useful. A group of early cases have been cited as establishing nearly absolute university autonomy in the face of conflicting or threatening legislation. But careful review suggests that the early decisions were rather narrow in sustaining the university's claims and that their holdings have been inflated by several later cases, and especially by a series of attorney general's opinions in the 1940s and 1950s. In 1913, for example, the California Supreme Court recognized that the regents possessed "a larger degree of independence and discretion with respect to [matters covered by general state law] than is usually held to exist in such inferior boards and commissions as are solely the subjects of legislative creation and control."

When the critical showdown came, forty years later, the limits of the regents' autonomy were clearly marked. The conflict was between the loyalty oath required of all state employees and the special supplemental oath the regents had imposed on the univer-

sity faculty. The California Supreme Court held that a supervening
statewide concern (loyalty of all public employees) gave the general
law primacy over supplemental regents' orders. (It is possible, of
course, that the court was simply making bad law in a good cause,
lacking the votes to declare the oath unconstitutional, as the state's
high court did fifteen years later. Bad law or not, the decision in
the oath case is nonetheless important law on the issue of autonomy.)

The two issues that will really test the extent of university
autonomy have yet to reach the courts. One of these is the validity
of the Master Plan itself, which may someday be challenged because of the distinctions it draws between institutions and systems.
Precisely such a challenge has already been mounted in the federal
courts of New York against the CUNY-SUNY stratification. In a
brief opinion several months ago, a district judge sustained the
corresponding New York legislation. The judgment is rather
superficial, however, and the last word remains to be spoken on
this issue.

The other issue lurking around the corner is the applicability
to the university of general public employee collective bargaining
legislation which is almost certain to be enacted within the next
five years. Perhaps for the first time in the autonomy struggle,
challenges to such a law would pit the regents against the legislature, with the university faculties sharply divided. The dilemma for
the professors would be acute: Those who most clearly favored
collective bargaining would probably also be most reluctant to see
the university's autonomy waived for other purposes, and those
who opposed collective bargaining might be more willing to forfeit
autonomy on other issues. Yet ultimately sides would have to be
chosen, depending essentially on the relative importance of the
immediate conflict versus the future value of the university's special status.

Autonomy and the Regents. I began this section by suggesting
that whatever autonomy does exist is more the regents' than the
university's. If the original autonomy has been squandered, therefore, the governing board is primarily accountable, at least in its
lack of vigilance.

There is, first, the matter of the charges for supplemental
police services. Seemingly to avoid payment of a rather substantial
bill, the general counsel declared that Berkeley and Alameda

police were supposed to be on the campus anyway and could not claim overtime. Later, when an Oakland housewife demanded to see the confidential lists of officers and bylaws of student political organizations on the Berkeley campus, the files were opened on orders from University Hall — apparently in the belief that these were "public documents" made accessible to any applicant by a general state law. (Later, when a Berkeley law student brought suit to enjoin the university from disclosing such information, the university formally — and successfully — defended its open-file policy, thus in a sense making a virtue of its waiver of autonomy.) Then, on two occasions, demands for information from the Internal Security Committee of the United States House of Representatives and its predecessor have gone unchallenged by the university; in fairness it should be noted that very few institutions of higher learning have responded to these requests with much vigor or protection.

Finally, the regents have not consistently protested even serious incursions by the legislature, the governor, the Division of Finance, the Coordinating Council and other external bodies. The experience of Michigan stands in stark contrast. This comparison is appropriate, not only because the California constitutional provisions were patterned largely after those of Michigan, but also because the universities of California and Michigan are generally regarded as the two great constitutional state universities. From time to time, the University of Michigan has been beset by an angry or a parsimonious legislature. Most recently, the 1970 higher education appropriations bill contained a variety of intrusive and restrictive conditions, on such matters as faculty work load, class size, level of student tuition and fees, accounting and reporting requirements, student conduct and discipline, and related matters. The regents of the university, joined by the governing boards of Wayne State and Michigan State, immediately filed a lawsuit in the state court challenging these conditions as invasions of the universities' constitutional autonomy. The governing boards won at least the first round of their current suit. Early in December 1971, the circuit court held the conditions imposed in the 1970 budget to lie beyond the constitutional powers of the legislature because they invaded the constitutional province of the respective governing boards.

The analogy between California and Michigan is not quite

perfect. It is true that the California legislature has not used budget conditions of the Michigan type to control the conduct of the university and its disbursement of funds. Yet the selective budget cuts that have become increasingly fashionable of late serve essentially the same purpose, and just as effectively remove discretion and flexibility from the governing board. If the legislature can take away teaching assistants one year, the Academic Senate another, and faculty salary increases a third year, the result is the same.

The differences between the statuses of these two constitutional governing boards reflects a fundamental contrast in philosophy and outlook. The Michigan regents apparently regard themselves as a fourth branch of government and behave accordingly, while the California regents do not. Although a university governing board lacks the checks and balances of the other branches — the veto, the power of the purse, the injunction — Michigan's regents have protected and bolstered their autonomy by seeking the aid of one agency against another. The California Board of Regents has simply not acted as a fourth branch of government, even though it may believe it enjoys that status under the constitution. The power that has not been exercised may some day be found to have atrophied.

COORDINATION: THE IMPORTANCE OF BEING PRIVATE

It is impossible to talk of higher learning in California without taking note of the private colleges and universities. The state's system of postsecondary education includes two nationally eminent private universities, one of the most comprehensive private consortia, a number of smaller universities, and a large group of private two- and four-year colleges. Although the vast majority of California college students attend publicly supported campuses, the role of the private sector far exceeds its numerical proportion. Thus it is pertinent to consider ways in which the law affects relations between the two sectors.

Less coordination or control exists between the two sectors in California than in many, perhaps most, other states. Clearly the private colleges and universities are freer than in New York, where the regents possess the constitutional power to charter and accredit every private institution, to approve every new degree program, to make visitations and require written reports as often as they wish, to set specific standards for the qualification and compensation of faculty members, and to grant or withhold permission for a private institution to close its doors. The independent higher institutions of California are also freer of state control than their counterparts in Massachusetts, where not only general health and safety requirements but even a loyalty oath (recently invalidated) have been imposed on employees of private colleges and universities. Nor do public officials hold ex officio seats on the governing boards of private universities, as in Connecticut, Louisiana, and Pennsylvania.

Where many other states have undertaken extensive studies of the private sector and the relations between tax-supported campuses and those that are not tax-supported, California has been relatively unconcerned. Late in the 1971 session, the legislature enacted a bill to create a Council on Private Postsecondary Educational Institutions, which would have made a modest start toward evaluation and coordination. But the governor vetoed the bill on two grounds: first, that the state already had enough commissions and agencies; and second, that the proposal "creates another board without changing the substance of the laws to be administered." Thus even this first and rather tentative step will not be taken, at least for a while.

The difference between California and other states might appear to be essentially a fiscal one. It is true that the state constitution precludes direct support of private colleges and universities — a ban which the proposed new constitution would dissolve. Yet this explanation is inadequate for two reasons. On the one hand, the *indirect* support of the private sector is quite substantial. Roughly half the state scholarships, accounting for an estimated 85 to 90 percent of the funds, go to students attending private institutions which enroll only 10 to 12 percent of the total California student body. Moreover, the governor recently signed into law a bill to create a medical contract program for the support of students in the private medical schools. This arrangement comes about as close to direct subvention of the private sector as would be possible under the present constitutional constraint. One additional factor is potentially relevant: The California constitution raises an unusually high wall between church and state, thus effectively precluding any direct support of church-affiliated colleges and universities. The California courts would not, for example, tolerate anything like New York's system of per capita payments to institutions of higher learning — a system initially extended to some Catholic colleges and denied to others but recently held available to most.

The relatively primitive relationship between public and private sectors in California must find an indigenous explanation. Surely the framers of the California constitution were not oblivious to the private institutions; the section immediately following the provision creating the University of California regents deals extensively with the Leland Stanford Junior University, conferring special status and tax exemptions on the property of the trustees. Doubtless the clear constitutional constraint against direct support of the private sector partially explains the current separation. Perhaps, too, the relative financial health of the private institutions and the steadily rising demand for higher education in California have deferred the issues of coordination and support. Moreover, the political strength of the two great private universities would probably have averted legislative conditions and exactions to which private universities in other states have been more vulnerable.

It seems unlikely that the present state of affairs can continue indefinitely. The situation may not yet have reached the critical pass of New York, Pennsylvania, and Ohio, but the private sector is clearly in trouble everywhere. Thus, the final comments of the Constitutional Revision Commission on a proposal permitting direct public support of private colleges and universities clearly point up the changing realities of the times:

> The proposal reflects the view that these existing prohibitions are unduly rigid and may actually increase the cost of higher education to the public. In the decades ahead, the financial needs of private institutions are likely to exceed existing or forseeable resources. If private institutions begin to close, or become unable to expand, the number of students that must be absorbed by the public institutions will increase. In these circumstances it may prove less costly for the state to assist existing private institutions than to build new state facilities at public expense.

The end of an era is in sight. Some form of assistance to the private sector will almost certainly be sanctioned. Once that is done, the political pressures to appropriate the funds will be intense and cannot long be resisted. With this new infusion of state aid to the private colleges and universities, a measure of coordination and perhaps greater control seems inevitable. Thus, within a matter of years the one real form of autonomy that now exists, and which sharply differentiates the two sectors, may well come to an end. For a university, being private may someday be as relatively unimportant as being constitutional.

The Humanities in The Multiversity*

by HENRY NASH SMITH

Adopting the role of devil's advocate, I wish to argue that the position of the humanities in the multiversity is necessarily uneasy. The reasons for this state of affairs are complex, but the principal difficulty can be stated rather simply: The multiversity is an institution designed to meet the needs of American society, and this society is basically indifferent to humanistic studies or, so far as it notices and understands them, hostile. The multiversity is more directly responsible than are the major private universities to the business community and to a majority of the electorate. It is therefore peculiarly subject to pressures from popular culture that have been conspicuous at least since the time of Andrew Jackson: on the one hand an admirable egalitarian idealism, but on the other a virulent strain of anti-intellectualism (which of course does not mean a hostility to reason in the service of practical goals, but a suspicion of pure theory and complex forms of art).

Both the idealism and the anti-intellectualism were evident in the campaign to secure the first federal subsidies for higher education that resulted in the passage of the Morrill Act of 1862. This legislation, enacted in the exalted mood generated by the victory of the Republican party in the election of 1860 and the outbreak of a

---

*The term *humanities* is open to objections that I shall mention, but it is widely used (as for example in the program drawn up for this conference) and one can hardly discuss the topics proposed without it. *Multiversity* is a word introduced into the language, so far as I know, by Clark Kerr in his Godkin lectures of 1963. He used it to refer to a type of institution of which the University of California is the most fully developed example. I shall use it in the same way, but I should note here that the University of California has given relatively greater support to the humanities than have other state-controlled institutions at which I have taught. Because I rely rather heavily on the term *popular culture*, let me say that I mean by it the values and attitudes most widely shared in a society at any given time.

war regarded as a democratic crusade, was a landmark in the rise of the common man. Senator Justin B. Morrill and the other men who fought for the act had a strongly anti-aristocratic ideology. They assumed that American society was made up of two numerically unequal parts: "the industrial classes" constituting the great bulk of the population, and a small minority that they called "the professional classes."[1] This elite was thought of as consisting mostly of clergymen and lawyers and wealthy merchants who had typically been educated in long-established private colleges by being subjected to a traditional liberal curriculum emphasizing the history and literature of Greece and Rome, together with moral philosophy. Because such a curriculum trained men to manipulate symbols rather than material objects, the professional classes could be described as "sedentary," in contrast to the people who worked with their hands.[2] The classical curriculum of the private colleges was derived ultimately from the Renaissance ideal of the courtier, or gentlemen, who was educated to be a ruler by having all his capacities developed harmoniously, and who was exempted as a matter of course from manual labor. In the United States the ideal of the gentleman had been modified by the Puritan conception of a theocracy, in which members of the learned professions constituted a caste of lawgivers and rulers of the state, whether in the pulpit or out of it.

Senator Morrill and his colleagues proposed to establish a new, radically different kind of college, intended for the common people rather than the elite. In the language of the Morrill Act, its "leading object" would be to teach "such branches of learning as are related to agriculture and the mechanic arts. . . ."[3] This implies that the industrial classes consisted mainly of farmers and artisans or handicraftsmen (in the mid-nineteenth century usually called mechanics). Each of these occupational groups was represented by a familiar image in American popular culture. The farmer was the protagonist of a powerful agrarian myth which the Republican party had exploited through its promise to exclude slavery from the territories beyond the Mississippi in order to

[1] Edward D. Eddy, Jr., *Colleges for Our Land and Time: The Land-Grant Idea in American Civilization* (New York: 1957), pp. 27–28.

[2] *Ibid.*, pp. 3–5, 28.

[3] *Ibid.*, p. xiii.

preserve these lands for settlement by midwestern farmers. George W. Julian, a Republican leader who was instrumental in the passage of the Homestead Law in the same year the Morrill Act was passed, declared:

> The life of a farmer is peculiarly favorable to virtue; and both individuals and communities are generally happy in proportion as they are virtuous. His manners are simple, and his nature unsophisticated. . . . His life does not impose excessive toil, and yet it discourages idleness. The farmer lives in rustic plenty, remote from the contagion of popular vices, and enjoys, in their greatest fruition, the blessings of health and contentment.[4]

These were the images evoked by the proposal to provide an advanced practical education for cultivators of the soil.

In laying hold of the agrarian myth, the farmers of the land grant program could draw on the emotional charge of attitudes dating from a remote past. In providing for the education of artisans and mechanics, they recognized the forces of economic change.[5] It is true that in the mid-nineteenth century the modern myth of the machine was only beginning to take shape. But the New England Yankee who had a gift for whittling and tinkering with machines had been celebrated in folklore since before the Revolution. This jack-of-all-trades was related to the mythical Uncle Jonathan, imaginary ancestor of Uncle Sam; and he also had some kinship with Benjamin Franklin's thrifty artisan, Poor Richard.[6] The image of the mechanic was destined to grow in vividness and importance as that of the yeoman farmer slowly faded with the declining role of agriculture in the nation's economy. It is not without significance that the term *industrial*, which in the 1850s referred to manual labor, had come by the end of the century to refer primarily to the use of power-driven machines in transportation and manufacturing.

The subjects we now call the humanities are related to the traditional education of the professional classes rather than to the new education designed for farmers and mechanics. The archety-

[4] Henry N. Smith, *Virgin Land: The American West as Symbol and Myth* (Cambridge, Mass.: 1960), p. 171.

[5] Frederick Rudolph, *The American College and University: A History* (New York: 1962), pp. 264–265.

[6] Walter Blair, *Native American Humor (1800–1900)* (New York: 1937), pp. 17–18, 45–46.

pal yeoman, nourished by daily contact with unpolluted nature, had nothing to do with the philosophy of the schools or with history, for his strength lay precisely in the fact that he was a new man, free of the burden of tyranny and corruption his forefathers had left behind in Europe. From this perspective, the fine arts of belles lettres, music, sculpture, and painting were associated with the decadent Old World aristocracy. The mythical counterpart of the yeoman, the hero-type of the mechanic, had similar attitudes. Mark Twain's Connecticut Yankee, the most fully developed portrayal of the type, declares: "I am a Yankee of the Yankees — and practical; yes, and nearly barren of sentiment, I suppose — or poetry, in other words."[7] His highest reach of appreciation in the graphic arts is a machine-produced chromolithograph, which he pointedly prefers to the tapestries on the walls of King Arthur's palace in Camelot. In his program for industrializing medieval Britain, he places great reliance on the education of former peasants in what he calls "man-factories" — technical institutes where he trains the engineers needed to maintain his industrial system. We may be sure these schools do not offer instruction in literature or the arts.

The creators of the land grant colleges, however, had in mind a less doctrinaire cultural revolution than Mark Twain's Yankee tried to bring about. They recognized that the common man who was the focus of nineteenth-century democratic ideology was determined to rise in the world, and this meant not only making more money but also improving his social status. Senator Morrill understood these matters thoroughly. He insisted that the new colleges should not be merely "agricultural schools." With a very American blend of idealism and pragmatism, he said that the program of instruction should be "broadly scientific" and at the same time proposed to offer higher education to all "those at the bottom of the ladder who want to climb up, or those who have some ambition to rise in the world." Indeed, Morrill even supported the notion that federal subsidies should be used to provide "an opportunity in every state for a liberal and larger education . . . to those destined to sedentary professions" as well as to "those much needing higher instruction for the world's business, for industrial

---

[7] Hamlin Hill, ed., *A Connecticut Yankee in King Arthur's Court (1889)* (San Francisco: 1963), p. 20.

pursuits . . . ."[8] The Morrill Act as finally passed provided that although the colleges formed under its terms should emphasize "agricultural and mechanic arts," "other scientific and classical studies" should not be excluded.[9]

Thus from the outset the new colleges exhibited a kind of eclecticism, not to say incoherence, in their goals. Their primary purpose was to serve the needs of a rapidly developing economy by instruction in scientific agriculture and in various types of engineering. It soon became apparent that the technical education, which had been advocated on behalf of the common man in opposition to a social and economic elite, was capable of creating a new ruling class; for the economic interests served by the land grant colleges (routinely developing into state universities) were the dominant forces in an industrialized society. At the same time, these institutions offered courses in the arts, especially in English and other modern literatures, which in the later nineteenth century gradually supplanted study of the classical languages and literatures. Such courses were elected mainly by women — coeducation being now taken for granted in accord with the pronounced midwestern trend.[10] Study of the humanities came to be thought of as a feminine pursuit, one of the ornamental accomplishments that Thorstein Veblen would describe in *The Theory of the Leisure Class* (1899) as forms of vicarious consumption and ostentatious waste.[11] The arrangement corresponded to the conventional contrast between use and beauty, the functional and the decorative.

In this fashion, liberal education (that is, the nonutilitarian, nontechnical parts of the university curriculum) became identified with a genteel tradition in American thought. Arnold's conception of a higher culture that fostered a free play of mind in social criticism tended to become the rationale for a narrowly complacent middle-class point of view, and the study of the humanities was made to perform a function exactly opposed to the one Arnold had assigned to it. Senator Morrill had favored offering higher educa-

[8] Eddy, *op. cit.*, pp. 28–29.

[9] *Ibid.*, p. xiii.

[10] *Ibid.*, p. 61.

[11] It is amusing that Veblen's hostile term *the leisure class* picks up the implications of the epithet *sedentary* applied to *the professional classes*. The rational, strictly functional engineers that he approved of were descendants of the artisans and mechanics honored in the ideology of the land-grant colleges.

tion to all "those at the bottom of the ladder who want to climb up."
The program of technical education for men and literary and artistic education for women corresponded to an ideal model of social
mobility in which the American husband works his way to wealth
while his wife and daughters exert themselves to acquire the social
graces appropriate to a higher station in life. For it was a notorious
American assumption that women were the custodians of the arts
as well as of morality. The pattern was a standard theme of fiction
from the time of Howells and Henry James onward.

But to explore this topic would take us too far afield. The point
I wish to make is that the lingering association of the humanities
with social mobility has operated over a long period to pull teaching in these areas off center. A particularly striking illustration is
the standard course in composition for freshmen. The fact that
speech is perhaps the most sensitive index to social status has
fostered an immense confusion on this subject. The cosmetic exercise of drilling students in correct usage is not distinguished from
the training in logic that is the functional basis for good expository
prose, and both Sisyphean tasks have been considered part of the
general refining process assigned to the humanities, usually the
department of English. Although unknown in Europe, this arrangement is so familiar in American universities that it seems
almost a part of the order of nature, even to many teachers of
English. But training students to write effective prose, although
essential to their education, has neither more nor less logical connection with the teaching of literature than with the teaching of
political science or paleontology; for scholarship in these fields
must also use the medium of language. It is significant that the
examination in composition taken by freshmen entering the University of California is carefully labeled "Subject A" in order to
indicate that it has no special relationship to the Department of
English. The question is of greater consequence than the casual
observer might imagine, because training in composition for every
student by means of special courses requires a large staff somewhere on the campus engaged in a menial task. This creates for-
midable problems of budget and morale. The California All-
University Conference in 1966 on "The Arts and Humanities in the
University" devoted a considerable part of its opening session to
debate about whether departments of the humanities should be

expected to bear responsibility for "elementary and service courses" in "freshman writing."[12]

Such controversies indicate that humanists themselves cannot concur on the proper goals of their scholarship and teaching. The first report brought up for consideration at the conference began by acknowledging that "The term *humanities* does not have an exact, generally accepted meaning, even among people concerned with curriculum planning," and went on to present, vaguely, the "general idea that humanistic studies are concerned with aesthetic and ethical values and with the concrete experience in which these values originate."[13] As chairman of the committee that prepared the report, I can certify that his phrasing was a deliberate effort to produce a formula ambiguous enough to accommodate views that were still irreconcilable after several hours of discussion. Even so, one distinguished member of the committee submitted a dissenting minority report objecting to the interpretation, in the document approved by the majority, of the term *humanistic*.

How can confusion on this scale exist? John Higham has dealt with the question from the historian's standpoint in an incisive article in the *American Historical Review*.[14] He shows that the term *humanities* can be understood only through careful attention to the development of American higher education. The word had relatively little currency before 1900, and when it was used it ordinarily referred simply to the study of the literature and culture of Greece and Rome. In the tradition of Arnold, however, it acquired a broader meaning, referring to the study of man as contrasted with nonhuman forces. Under the influence of the pronounced historical cast of much nineteenth- and early twentieth-century scholarship, the humanities were also understood to be (in the words of President William R. Harper of the University of Chicago) "those subjects which represent the culture of the past." This emphasis often suggested turning one's eyes away from the turbulent and chaotic present to serene vistas of bygone times.

The notion that the term *humanities* designates a broad but

[12]*The Arts and the Humanities in the University* (Proceedings of the University of California Twenty-First All-University Faculty Conference, University of California, Davis, April 3–6, 1966), p. 12.

[13]*Ibid.*, p. 6.

[14]Higham, "The Schism in American Scholarship," *American Historical Review*, 72 (October 1966) 1–21.

clearly defined area of scholarship and teaching gained currency only in the 1920s. The semantic change was occasioned by the rapid development of the fields of study now called the social sciences. When the American Council of Learned Societies was established in 1919 it included organizations of economists and sociologists as well as historians, philosophers, and literary scholars, but the momentum of the newer academic enterprises led to the establishment of the Social Science Research Council in 1923 as a body standing in an approximately symmetrical relation to the ACLS. This secession left behind an untidy residual category containing what remained of the vast area once called moral philosophy plus the traditional fields of belles-lettres. Schematic neatness has continued to foster the notion of a tripartite segmentation of the university curriculum (apart from professional training) into natural sciences, social sciences, and humanities. But this pattern corresponds neither to departmental organization (history for example, seems to be partly humanistic, partly a social science) nor to a common subject matter or methodology.

The confusion about boundaries and the lack of a clear sense of purpose within departments of humanities lend a special irony to the notion, now a commonplace outside the fields in question, that they have a unique responsibility for values in our society. Higham suggests that the currency of the idea may be related to the proclamations of social scientists that their inquiries are truly scientific and therefore value-free: the heritage of moral philosophy had to be given shelter somewhere in the curriculum. The influence of Arnold has also drawn literary studies in this direction. With only a moderate degree of distortion, he can be understood as maintaining that literary masterpieces of the past can be used instead of the Bible as a source of ethical guidance.

When the appropriation for the National Foundation on the Arts and Humanities was being debated by the House of Representatives in 1968, the foundation was defended by Representative Frank Thompson, Jr., of New Jersey on the ground that "someone must constantly remind us of the basic values of right and wrong."[15] Another supporter, Representative John Dellenback of Oregon, asserted that:

[15]*Congressional Record — House*, February 27, 1968, p. H 1405.

The humanities can make it possible for us to channel our enormous technical capacities in directions that free us to realize our ideals, rather than trap us in the complexity which technical skill creates. . . . The role of the humanities is crucial, because they enable us to make judgments of value, to weigh quality as well as quantity, to ask and answer what it means to live well and to live with purpose. . . . We derive our notions of freedom from the humanities, our notions of justice from the humanities, and our notions of compassion from the humanities. . . . We are dealing with the study of our reasons for being — the direction in which we are going and should be going.[16]

The vision that these well-meaning speakers call up — of the president or the Secretary of Defense consulting professors of literature about the morality of invading Cambodia or bombing North Vietnam — falls in the category of black humor. But the friendly congressmen were merely doing their best with the ammunition provided for them by academic spokesmen. They were essentially paraphrasing the report that had been submitted in 1964 by the Commission on the Humanities sponsored by the ACLS, the Council of Graduate Schools in the United States, and the United Chapters of Phi Beta Kappa.[17] And the Commission had labored under difficulties. It faced the same predicament that is faced by all spokesmen for the humanities who are obliged to give an account of themselves to the public at large or to agents of government. The commission was trying to explain, in the idiom of public relations and lobbying, two matters that the increasing dominance of technology has apparently made less and less comprehensible to Americans generally: the significance of history and the significance of the imagination. Both have a decisive bearing on the image of man that any given society uses as a guide in determining what quality of life it demands for its members and how it will allocate its resources to achieve that quality. The dimension of history, of collective memory, reveals what it means to be human by reminding us of what the race has shown itself capable of thinking and feeling and making and doing in the past. The dimension of the imagination expressed in art gives us direct access to infinitely

[16]*Ibid.*, February 27, 1968, p. H 1413.
[17]"Statement and Recommendations," *Report of the Commission on the Humanities* (New York: 1964), pp. 1–9.

various hypothetical possibilities of experience and action, not anchored in time.

The domains of history and art are not congenial ground for popular culture, which expresses a perennial yearning for the psychological security of fixed, familiar patterns and forthright, unambiguous categories such as right and wrong. In contrast, the historians, the artists, and the critics and interpreters of the arts are dedicated to exploring the inexhaustible complexities of experience. This is not to say, of course, that these men and women are not eager to find or invent forms that can contain the concrete materials with which they work; exactly the reverse is true. But the forms they create are not subject to measurement and thus cannot be quantified. Furthermore, because such craftsmen's ultimate allegiance is given to the irreducible concreteness of human experience, they are never ready to conclude, to balance the accounts and close their books. They are concerned at least as much with the residue of experience that spills over the edges of the form as they are with the part that can be contained and brought under control.

I realize that these rather pompous observations are far from being a satisfactory account of what historians, artists, and critics are up to, but they may help to explain why historical and literary studies are suffocated by the kind of moralism that knows only two categories, "the basic values of right and wrong." There are many nuances of rightness and wrongness, some of them far from obvious; and none of them retains its meaning when it is lifted out of context. Right and wrong are basic categories, but the data of experience never fit into them comfortably. Did the creation of the Union armies at the outbreak of the Civil War represent the glory of the coming of the Lord? Or another example: it is basically wrong for one man to kill another; Hamlet kills Polonius and Claudius; yet at the end he is "sweet prince" and we approve Horatio's demand for an escort of angels to speed him to his rest. Basic categories are too simple. The first effect of historical, literary, or ethical analysis is to disturb the strong, unqualified, emotional responses dictated by our unexamined beliefs and prejudices. This is irritating because at the outset it replaces a pleasurable experience with an unpleasant one and forces us to postpone consummation in order that in the end we may achieve a satisfaction more durable because it is based on a wider range of data.

Furthermore, the major historical crises and great works of art are so complex that different investigators come out with conflicting interpretations of them. These are some of the reasons why humanists resist the notion that they can supply values on demand.

By way of summary, let me quote a celebrated critic of American society, George Santayana, who declared in 1911:

> America . . . is a country with two mentalities, one a survival of the beliefs and standards of the fathers, the other an expression of the instincts, practice, and discoveries of the younger generations. In all the higher things of the mind — in religion, in literature, in the moral emotions — it is the hereditary spirit that still prevails, so much so that Mr. Bernard Shaw finds that America is a hundred years behind the times. The truth is that one-half of the American mind, that not occupied intensely in practical affairs, has remained, I will not say high-and-dry, but slightly becalmed; it has floated gently in the backwater, while, alongside, in invention and industry and social organization the other half of the mind was leaping down a sort of Niagara Rapids. This division may be found symbolized in American architecture: a neat reproduction of the colonial mansion — with some modern comforts introduced surreptitiously — stands beside the skyscraper. The American Will inhabits the skyscraper; the American Intellect inhabits the colonial mansion. The one is the sphere of the American man; the other, at least predominantly, of the American woman. The one is all aggressive enterprise; the other is all genteel tradition.[18]

The address from which I quote this famous passage was first delivered in the Greek Theater on the Berkeley campus, and I am tempted to suggest that Santayana was thinking about the University of California when he composed it. But the aptness of the setting was probably no more than an accident; the visiting philosopher doubtless had in mind New England and New York rather than California and San Francisco. It is true, however, that whereas in his day the older private universities of the east might still be thought of as representing a genteel tradition — a colonial mansion, in contrast with the skyscraper of economic and technological enterprise — the state universities were already so fully committed to meeting the technological requirements of American society that they incorporated within themselves both the sky-

[18]"The Genteel Tradition in American Philosophy," in *The Genteel Tradition: Nine Essays by George Santayana*, ed. Douglas L. Wilson (Cambridge, Mass.: 1967), pp. 39–40.

scraper and the colonial mansion in their contrasting programs of traditional humanities (representing the beliefs and standards of the fathers) and the practical, aggressive ethos of the Industrial Revolution.

The result has been a continuing sense of estrangement and isolation on the part of teachers of the humanities in the face of the phenomenal expansion of scientific and technical research and teaching. An even roughly adequate outline of the development of the state universities, leading toward the creation of the multiversity in the 1950s, is beyond the scope of this paper. Nor can I do more than gesture toward the historical forces that have brought about the political tensions of recent years within the multiversity. But it is evident that the insecurity of the position of the humanities has been accelerated by the staggering increase in federal subsidies for research since World War II. This trend has brought about a collaboration of the scientific and technical segments of the multiversity with outside enterprises that seems almost to amount to a merger. Who can say where industry and government end in the area of technological research, and where the multiversity begins?

The chronically bad morale in departments of the humanities generated by confusion about goals and functions has fostered various and often contradictory impulses of political protest among students and younger faculty. Because these impulses seem to be generated mainly by forces beyond the control of the universities themselves, I see no reason to believe they will lessen in the future. And it would not be surprising if the parts of the university that exist in a kind of symbiosis with industry, the Department of Defense, and the Atomic Energy Commission should feel a growing resentment toward departments that seem to develop and shelter troublemakers, fomenting discord within the institution and arousing hostility in the general public. Prediction is contrary to the mores of my professional community, but I shall end with the question whether, in the years ahead, the increasing conservatism of the country as a whole may not make the position of the humanities even more uncomfortable.

Humanistic Studies and the Large Public University

by ROY HARVEY PEARCE

The problem — I am tempted to say, the dilemma — of the humanities in the multiversity is precisely that of the humanities in American society at large. That problem derives essentially from the difficulty in defining, in conceiving of, the humanities as a profession or set of professions. For the substantive concern of the humanistic disciplines is life lived through day-to-day (and, increasingly, night-to-night). What results is more often questions than answers, discriminations rather than choices among alternatives. As often as not, the humanist must rest satisfied with knowing things as they were and are, not as they might, much less should, be. Humanists study the documents (and I mean that word in the largest possible sense) which record man's attempts to make sense of his life. Those documents may well be intensely and formally structured — works of art, of music, of literature, scientific experiments, political writings, sermons, and the like. And study of them may require an exacting and exquisite sense of their structure. But in the end, as at the beginning, the humanist wants to know and to expound them as they are, however intensely and formally — expressions of lived-through life, with all the ambiguities of that life. The humanistic studies, then, take so much of human experience into their purview that they run the risk of seeming to lack that disciplinary focus which has increasingly given the physical and biological sciences and the social and behavioral sciences their great strength and made for their great advances.

No matter that among my colleagues there is a historian whose "field" is nineteenth- and twentieth- century Spain, another whose "field" is satire, another whose "field" is modern and postmodernist painting, and that my "field" is American literature and intellectual history — no matter, because we all operate in a context and with a goal which in the end, if we are true to our vocation, militates against that extreme specialism which would enable us sharply to discriminate between our lived-through life and that expressed in the documents we study. That, I think, is precisely the source of the strength of our vocation. But it is a strength whose force and rationale it is often difficult to communicate to our colleagues in the multiversity — I mean those whose vocations are defined exactly so that they may be systematically abstracted from the concerns of lived-through life. And of course that difficulty becomes all the greater when one tries to construct an apologia for the humanities in the multiversity, and also in that great world which the multiversity serves.

Still, it is our task again and again to construct that apologia — if only in the hope that university planners might attend to it. Properly constructed, of course, that apologia might answer some questions which — for me, at least — are raised by Smelser's study. How does one differentiate what a humanist does in the university, in the state colleges (or whatever they are to be called), and in the community colleges? If the university's function is to lead in research and doctoral study, what specifically should characterize the humanist's share of that function? What is the difference, for a humanist, in teaching undergraduates in each of the three segments of higher education in the state? And how should the humanities be structured so that they do their proper job in each of the three segments?

There are answers to these questions, I think — and good ones. Here I shall not attempt them but, rather, give a basis for the answers. The questions derive, paradoxically enough, from the relative diffuseness (from the point of view of disciplinary concerns) of the humanities taken as a whole. Let me venture a definition: The humanities are together that complex of disciplines which are centered on the discovery and preservation, the understanding, and the interpretation of the record of human belief and commitment. Their substantive center, as I have said, is the documents which constitute that record — paintings, music, poems, political speeches, sermons, scientific experiments, and the like. Every humanist is in part a textual scholar — so far as he wants to discover and preserve the documents exactly as they were, or should have been. Every humanist is in part a critic–explicator — so far as he wants to understand those documents exactly as they say what they said. Every humanist is in part a historian — so far as he wants to comprehend those documents as being at once integral to their original sociocultural matrix and, because they still exist and have force, integral to his own. Every humanist is in part a philosopher — so far as, in the totality of his functions, he is necessarily concerned with the theory and method whereby he exercises his humanistic expertise. Whether the humanist professes literature or musicology or the history of science, he will still have in part to be textual scholar, critic–explicator, historian, and philosopher.

But the span of human life being what it is and the capacities of the human mind being what they are, most likely the humanist will specialize. He will not only profess literature, but his perspective will be primarily that of the textual scholar, or critic–explicator, or historian, or philosopher. Moreover, he may well be a "period" man. Thus he will make out his specialism. And as a researcher he will concentrate on that specialism. As a graduate teacher he will perhaps also try to concentrate on it; but, the humanities being what they are and the graduate students (particularly in this age) being what *they* are, he will find himself in significant part necessarily functioning according to his ideal vision of himself, as a "whole" humanist. And this latter situation will obtain all the more if he is an undergraduate teacher. Indeed, I think, it is the demands of undergraduate teaching in the humanities (and of undergraduates!) which constantly and forcefully remind the humanist of his commitment to wholeness.

This commitment of course carries great dangers and risks. The humanist can yield to the temptation to become one who knows a little bit about a great number of things, so that the learning he would put to the use of his students becomes nothing more than a homogenized mass. Moreover, he can image himself as a member of a modern clerisy, a man with more insight into values than his nonhumanist peers. It is true that the documents he deals with are nothing if not value-charged. But knowing those documents, sensing and expatiating upon their charge of values, the humanist does not necessarily thereby become a man himself more valuable than other men. Indeed, his vocation should entail his controlling his own private sense of values in the interest of getting objectively at those of the documents he studies and teaches. As Lionel Trilling has put it: He doesn't read the poems; the poems read him.

I am insisting, then, that the relationship in the humanistic studies, between having a specialism and being obliged to teach well beyond the limits of that specialism, ideally makes for disciplined self-control in the face of the documents studied and taught, from whatever perspective. There must always be in the humanistic studies what Coleridge called vis-à-vis literature a "willing suspension of disbelief." This can derive only from a sense of the humanities as rigorous disciplines, as the means whereby the scholar–teacher and his students can, through the knowledgeable interpretation of documents, submit themselves to whatever charge of values, whatever mode of life lived-through, those documents express. Only at that point can the scholar–teacher and his students justifiably judge the documents and the modes of life they express. The judgment must come, because the documents, as I have said, have force in the present lives of the scholar–teacher and students even as they had force in the past lives of those whose documents they originally were. To comprehend as authentically human, as altogether possible, beliefs, commitments, valuations, forces, expressive forms, ways of life — this is a prime goal of the humanities. And this can be achieved only when humanistic study is rigorously disciplined.

It is the role of the university to teach the modes of discipline required and to teach others to teach those modes. Further, and crucially, it is the role of the university to develop those modes. This is inseparable from its research function in the humanities. For it is a characteristic of the humanistic disciplines that they must change from generation to generation. The documents studied do not change; but those who study them — granting their commitment to the wholeness of experience — do change. Characteristically, the humanistic disciplines, as formal structures of knowledge, change accordingly. With modern textual study (itself a product of university-sponsored research), we now have a better text of *Moby-Dick* than Melville himself had. With modern exegetical and explicatory methods, we now know more about what *Moby-Dick* exactly said and says than did Melville's contem-

poraries, perhaps (because we have ways of getting at his precon-
scious intentions) than Melville did. But generation to generation,
we have changed. And, having established the text of *Moby-Dick*,
having more precisely understood it, we are free to ask of it any
questions we please. This is a matter of determining its relevance
to ourselves and our present condition. A disciplinary rule of interpretation obtains, however — a rule hopefully being inculcated
in graduate seminars in the university: that any answer we get to
our questioning of *Moby-Dick* must be consonant first with the text
as we have established it and second with what the text actually
says. One often concludes by saying: How am *I* relevant to *Moby-
Dick?*

My literary example is meant to indicate one way in which
one of the humanistic studies can be as exact and exacting as any of
the nonhumanistic disciplines. It has less to do with humanists as
being somehow particularly close to human values than it has to do
with defining as precisely as possible how the humanities function.
And this, I think, is a task much neglected by university planners
and by those charged with overseeing the Master Plan for Higher
Education. What I would hope is that a study like Smelser's would
lead to a study of the university and its purpose from the *inside* —
in terms of the structural–functional modes of the segments of
human knowledge it would promote. The humanities in the multiversity suffer not from a lack of sympathy but from a lack of
understanding.

Such understanding, I think, would lead to proper definition.
And such definition would spell out the relationship between
humanistic research and the upper levels of graduate training. One
element of that training is the development of appropriate skills in
textual study, criticism and explication, and interpretation; another
is the inculcation of the idea that it is necessary continually to
refine and redefine those skills. Such refinement and redefinition
are part and parcel of research in the humanities, so that such
research, whatever its substantive concern, is in truth at the heart
of graduate training. Further, such research would have grave implications for the organization of the humanities at all levels of
higher education. Present departmental structures, I am persuaded, would be found to be not at all in accord with the present
structural–functional nature of the humanities. We would need to

develop more flexible organizational structures, adaptable to the necessarily changing form of that structural–functional nature — itself a product of the abidingly central fact of the humanist's vocation: that the objects of his study do not change but that he, and those on whose behalf he does his work, do change, Such change would extend beyond graduate training to the various levels of undergraduate training.

I am unable to spell out the specific changes called for, although — as one involved in planning and developing one of the "underdeveloped" University of California campuses — I have some local ideas. But I do think it true that the changes, to be authentic, must derive ultimately from the nature of research in the humanities and must be in good part presided over by the graduate students who share in that research effort with us. Hence the role of the university as defined by the Master Plan remains central. But it is a role, as regards the humanities, which must be assumed on behalf of all higher education in California. In short, I hope for a Master Plan — and for a multiversity — which will pay due attention to the sociological and economic factors Smelser outlines only after it has paid prior attention to the structure and function of research and teaching.

The Social Role of the University and its Science Departments

by KENNETH V. THIMANN

The University of California, like all universities worthy of the name, is much more than a teaching institution. At the time of the great disturbances (1964–1969), it was common practice to upbraid the university for its devotion to research, as well as for its size and resulting impersonality. What follows is an attempt to evaluate some of the social and economic consequences of its size and its research, especially in the sciences, and to assess what role they may have played in the development and prosperity of California.

First, consider the matter of size. We must not overlook the importance of the university as one of the state's major employers. A university campus employs on the average, for secretarial and managerial assistance, including staff for structural supervision, planning and maintenance, one person for every ten students. Thus, the university campuses with 110,000 students employ around 10,000 nonacademic people on salary, with a total payroll around $100 million. If we add the workers at the university-wide offices and the additional nonacademic staff in university hospitals and the many research institutes, we approximately double these figures. Indeed, the University of California budget for 1971–1972 lists 17,000 permanent and 13,000 temporary employees with a payroll of $216 million. A payroll of over $200 million compares with those of Lockheed, Douglas, Twentieth Century Fox, and other major employers in California. (It is, of course, far less than that of such giants as General Motors, with almost 700,000 employees, or IBM, with 269,000.)

In addition, until the recent change in legislative sentiment about higher education, the university was building at an average expenditure (during the period 1957–1967) of over $60 million per year. Although the bulk of this expenditure actually went for the wages of construction workers resident in the state, it was by no means all derived from state sources. Indeed, up until 1960 more than half of all the university's land and buildings was paid for from nonstate funds,[1] and nonstate funds have continued to make major contributions ever since.

It follows that the current limitation of the university's budget must be contributing to unemployment among nonacademics. This is felt especially among clerical and constructional workers. Cuts in the university budget must, therefore, be compensated to some degree by increases in the welfare budget; in this way the cuts do not wholly accrue as net savings to the state or to the taxpayers. This may not always be understood by economy-minded legislators.

The second consideration is more important. The university's support of employment in the state extends far beyond its direct role as employer. Much of this influence is clearly traceable to its early development of strong departments in the sciences, and I shall limit myself to the science aspect. Daniel Coit Gilman's inaugural address in 1872 included the words: "Science is the mother of California. Give us more and not less science."[2] Accordingly, science faculty were appointed early and well supported. A powerful graduate school in chemistry developed early in this century, especially under G. N. Lewis, who came to the university in 1912 to be dean of the College of Chemistry. A group of world famous chemists, including Richard Tolman, Joel Hildebrand, W. F. Giauque, and Wendell Latimer, was added in the following years. Several of these men, as well as at least two of their graduate students (Harold Urey and Melvin Calvin), have won Nobel prizes. Berkeley shares with Illinois and Harvard the credit for producing the bulk of the nation's leading professors and practitioners of chemistry.

In physics the growth has been at least as spectacular and influential. The present Berkeley faculty in physics numbers 69,

[1] University of California Budget for Current Operations, Departmental Allocations, (1971–72).
[2] V. A. Stadtman, ed., *Centennial Record of the University of California* (1968).

that at UCLA 58, and those at the other campuses together about 140. Nobel prize winners include Owen Chamberlain, Ernest Lawrence, Emilio Segre, Edwin McMillan, Louis Alvarez, Edward Teller, and Glenn Seaborg (who was professor of chemistry but worked on radioisotopes and transuranic elements); the Berkeley campus alone has 11 of the 109 members of the physics section of the National Academy of Sciences.

These powerful science schools have had far-reaching importance for the state. The availability of federally financed graduate scholarships and fellowships has made it possible for students of high ability to go virtually wherever they please for graduate study, and many of them, from all over the country, have chosen the California campuses. Until the recent limitation, their support has been liberally supplemented by state-financed teaching assistantships. Because a number of teaching assistants participated in the Berkeley riots of 1964–1969, the funding of this general category was greatly reduced, although, typically the administrators overlooked the fact that very few of the rioters were teaching assistants in the natural sciences. Because many of the young men and women of scientific ability who are trained in California elect to stay here after graduation, there has been a steady "brain-drain" into California from many of the forty-nine continental states, especially those on the eastern seaboard.

The second consequence is that the output of young scientists has also made possible the initiation and development of a variety of science-based industries in California. These young scientists have not been limited to graduates of the University of California — Stanford and Cal Tech have also been notable contributors. Among industries based mainly on chemistry are the Cutter Laboratories (San Francisco), Syntex (Palo Alto), Calbiochem (Los Angeles), and Montrose Chemical (Los Angeles), which makes, *inter alia*, most of the nation's supply of DDT. Physics-based industries include Hewlett-Packard, which contributed David Packard to the Nixon administration; Beckman Instruments, founded by a former Cal Tech professor; and a number of smaller scientific-instrument companies. Engineering companies of importance include the worldwide Bechtel Corporation, directed by several members of the Bechtel family who were students at Berkeley, and the T. Y. Lin Associates, a large structural steel company founded by a Chinese immigrant who became a graduate student at Berkeley. The state's great airplane industry undoubtedly owes its inception to several factors, including the climate, but the availability of a supply of well-trained engineers from the Berkeley and Los Angeles engineering departments was undoubtedly important.

The university has also fostered scientific agriculture. Research and teaching in agriculture constituted an integral part of the university from its start and became prominent as early as 1874, when Eugene Hilgard began his extensive studies of California soils. The College of Agriculture narrowly survived a strong move to separate it from the university in 1876, and shortly thereafter initiated the first Agricultural Experiment Station in the United States. The University Farm at Davis, opened in 1907, added a variety of facilities and staff and was for many years the center for the more practical aspects of the work. Many of its students became county farm advisers and extension specialists. Together with the federal government, the university set up the Citrus Experiment Station at Riverside in 1907. The Davis and Riverside campuses have thus been active in every phase of agricultural research for over sixty years and, together with the favorable climate, largely account for the extraordinary success of the state's agriculture. As an example, the mechanized methods of rice growing developed at Davis have reduced the number of man-hours needed per acre of rice from around seven hundred in the Orient to seven-and-one-half in the Sacramento valley. The very successful wine industry, started by European immigrants in the late nineteenth century, owes much to the experts on soils, ecology, and pesticides, mainly on the Davis campus. Altogether the net increase in agricultural income in *one* year more than repays what the state has put into agricultural research in *all* the years since the work started.[3]

The third consequence has been the placing of major federal contracts with the university. Contracts and grants from the AEC, the Department of Defense, the National Science Foundation, and the National Institutes of Health are made to individual investigators, but the overhead accrues to the university. At present the proportion of overhead averages 44 percent of the salaries and

[3]*Fiat Lux*, The University of California, (1967).

wages component of each project. Many millions of dollars per year come to the university through the overhead of grants to individuals, and the regents are able to use this as a special fund. The outstanding examples are the Los Alamos and Livermore Laboratories.

In 1930, Ernest Lawrence presented to the National Academy of Sciences his concept of the cyclotron, a device for accelerating the electrons in a beam to very high energies. A few months later he built a cyclotron which produced eighty thousand electron-volts, and by the end of 1931 one million electron-volts was reached. New and successively larger cyclotrons were then built, leading to the establishment of the Radiation Laboratory on the Berkeley campus. The work there led to the discovery of new radioisotopes which have proved invaluable as tracers in biology and medicine. Furthermore, Edwin McMillan discovered the first trans-uranic element, neptunium at the laboratory in Berkeley, and in 1941 Seaborg produced and identified the highly fissionable plutonium. As a direct result of all this productivity, when the government, in 1943, decided to set up a laboratory for research on nuclear energy weapons, it naturally turned to the University of California to organize and administer it. Although located at Los Alamos, New Mexico, this laboratory has from the start been run under contract with the University of California, and the staff has included a good number of California faculty as well as graduates from the university's physics, chemistry, and engineering departments.

In 1946, the Los Alamos laboratory's contribution, made under Oppenheimer's inspiring leadership, to ending the war led the newly created Atomic Energy Commission to approach the university again. This time they envisaged a laboratory to study not only nuclear weapons but various aspects of the application of nuclear and thermonuclear power to both war and peacetime problems. The university accepted the responsibility and set up the laboratory in the old Naval Air Station at Livermore. At first this was regarded as a branch of the Radiation Laboratory on the Berkeley campus, but it soon became very much larger and after E. O. Lawrence's death was christened the Lawrence Laboratory. These laboratories have employed many California residents, and they have contributed large sums in contract overhead to the operation of the university. These sums have been used by the regents as an opportunity fund for enrichment and emergencies.

Quite apart from economics, the Berkeley and Livermore laboratories, starting in 1939, made available quantities of isotopes for biological and medical research, with enormous benefits to the public. The Donner Laboratory, built from private funds and presided over by E. O. Lawrence's brother John, has rapidly become a major center for research in the application of physics to biology and medicine. The value of the research results, in the form of human comfort and prolongation of life, cannot be expressed in financial terms. Furthermore, the many students and visiting scientists from abroad who have been trained at the Donner Laboratory for medical work with isotopes have taken back to their institutions all over the world an invaluable residue of respect and affection for the University of California.

Unfortunately, scientific research is now suffering a setback which one hopes is only temporary. Its causes are threefold: (a) decreased federal support to the National Science Foundation; (b) discontinuance of the National Institutes of Health Training Grants; (c) curtailment of all university funds, in the name of economy, by the state legislature. From the viewpoint of state finances and benefits, this is false economy. If the starved goose stops laying its golden eggs, the loss to the people of California will be very serious.

Neil Smelser's analysis of the role of the state colleges in the educational hierarchy stresses their somewhat anomalous position. The state colleges are less universalist and egalitarian than the junior colleges, yet they are not able to offer the advanced degrees and research facilities of the university. The scientific and technological industries of the state, and the role of the university in fostering them, have an important bearing on this anomaly. The state, to support its heavy involvement in applied science, needs a steady flow of young people with the highest grades of technical skills. Such semi-scientific professions as machinist, electronics repairman, glassblower, dental mechanic, musical instrument maker, technical printer, as well as skilled craftsmen in many fields, are greatly needed and in general underrepresented in this state. Although the idea is not likely to be popular, the conception of the state college's role should be revised; instead of aiming to provide general academic education at an intermediate, subuniversity level, they might better plan frankly technical and vocational training. This would take them from their present uneasiness and frustration in a rather ambiguous role into a role in which they could be preeminent and in which their students could develop a strong sense of competence and self-esteem. For there is nothing so satisfying as feeling that one can do a job really well. The state colleges (now to be called state universities) need feel no frustrating competitiveness with the university if they were to devote themselves to top quality technical training, leaving the more purely academic pursuits — for which at the moment there is a lessened demand — to the university. Indeed, this emphasis should perhaps have been theirs from the beginning.

It should be noted in passing that the demand for the title *state university* rests on a false parallel with such institutions as the state colleges, now state universities, of Michigan, Oklahoma, or Pennsylvania. For these were specifically founded to provide training in the agricultural and mechanic arts, and only broadened their role to cover the general arts and sciences area as the demand for agriculturists decreased in the 1940s and 1950s. The California state colleges were not envisaged primarily as agricultural and mechanic arts schools but as a second level of general academic institution. The change of name appropriate for such schools in other states has little meaning for the California colleges.

In proposing this role for the state colleges, I am not downgrading the work they could do. What they could provide is not mere technical training; it is something new and something very much of today. For in place of the union-type workman who will do only the specific tasks he has learned to do, they could produce men who not only can *do* but also *understand* — the carpenter who knows something of the growth of trees, the master plumber who has taken courses in hydrodynamics, the radio repairman with a double major in electronics and music. Thus California might pioneer in bringing up a new generation trained in using *both* head and hands. Long ago Christopher Marlowe wrote (and it could be still true today):

> O what a world of profit and delight,
> Of power, of honor and omnipotence,
> Is promised to the studious artisan.

Relative Growth in Humanities and Science

by HARVEY BROOKS

STATISTICAL BACKGROUND

There appears to be a widely held assumption that the natural sciences and engineering have grown disproportionately in comparison to the humanities in the universities. It seems therefore desirable at the outset to examine the validity of this assumption. In fact, if relative emphasis can be measured by Ph.D. output, there is little to support it. The output of doctorates in the natural sciences and engineering has remained close to 50 percent of the total output of doctorates in all fields since the beginning of the twentieth century, and the output of bachelor degrees in the sciences and engineering has been about 25 percent of the total of all baccalaureate degrees, despite the dramatic growth in total numbers.

Table 1 shows the ratio of all Ph.D. degrees granted in the period 1960–1966 to the total granted in the period 1920–1960 for the whole country and for selected universities. The second row of figures shows the ratio of the average number of Ph.D.s per year in the later period to that in the earlier period — more than a factor of 4 overall, and ranging from 2.7 at Harvard to 4.3 at Stanford. The 1960–1966 period is when Ph.D. production soared, owing primarily to the demographic effects of the postwar baby boom. If there had been a large shift in the distribution among fields, it should show up in the relative distribution for the 1960–1966 period compared to the 1920–1960 period.

Table 2 shows such a comparison for the country as a whole, and for the same selected universities in four fields: the natural sciences and engineering taken together, the social sciences, the

Table 1
INDICES OF GROWTH OF PHD OUTPUT 1920–1966

	Total	Berkeley	Harvard	Columbia	Stanford	Illinois
Degrees 1960–66 / Degrees 1920–60	0.625	0.592	0.404	0.355	0.645	0.60
Degrees/yr. 60–66 / Degrees/yr. 20–60	4.16	3.95	2.69	2.37	4.3	4.0

Table 2
DISTRIBUTION BY FIELD OF PHD OUTPUT

		Nat. Sci. & Eng.	Soc. Sci.	Arts and Hum.	Professional
Total	1920–60	49.1%	15.8%	16.2%	5.4%
	1960–66	49.6%	16.0	14.0%	9.6
Berkeley	1920–60	59.0	16.0	15.75	9.3
	1960 66	60.5	15.6	12.3	11.4
Harvard	1920–60	22.1	23.4	31.0	13.5
	1960–66	24.9	20.8	28.0	17.9
Columbia	1920–60	22.2	14.5	18.3	45.0
	1960–66	22.3	18.8	20.4	38.5
Stanford	1920–60	41.4	12.6	16.0	31.1
	1960–66	56.0	12.2	13.9	18.0
Illinois	1920–60	67.8	11.5	12.8	7.8
	1960–66	63.3	10.9	11.2	14.6

arts and humanities, and the professional schools, including business, religion, and education. Psychology is included with the social sciences for the purpose of this tabulation, and agriculture, health sciences, and engineering with the natural sciences. Table 2 shows that the proportion of Ph.D.s in the natural sciences and engineering has remained nearly constant, and that the small drop in the arts and humanities results primarily from the growth in doctoral programs in professional schools, principally education. This general pattern is fairly uniform over all the individual schools illustrated, except at Columbia, where the humanities and social sciences have grown, apparently at the expense of the Ph.D. education. The old-line private universities, typified by Columbia and Harvard, show the smallest absolute percentages in science and engineering and the largest in the humanities and social sciences. Most changes, in each institution and overall, have taken place within rather than between the broad areas. Nationally the trend has been a doubling of the percentage of Ph.D.s in engineering and the professional areas. This appears to have been at the expense of the physical and life sciences, and, to a slightly lesser extent, of the arts and humanities. At the major state institutions it appears to have taken place mainly at the expense of the life sciences and humanities, but the effect has been small in relative terms.

Thus, the image of a dramatic growth of the natural sciences and engineering at the expense of the humanities is simply not supported by the data. The only detailed financial and faculty data available to me are for Harvard, which may be somewhat atypical in view of the relatively small proportion of graduate students in the sciences and the general practice of not supporting faculty salaries out of federal funds. At Harvard the natural sciences and engineering have shown the least faculty growth of any of the major areas in the faculty of arts and sciences. In the twenty years between 1950 and 1970, tenure faculty grew only 36 percent in the natural sciences, but about 56 percent in the humanities and more than 65 percent in the social sciences. Junior faculty numbers grew much more rapidly, but the percentage growth was still least, by a considerable margin, in the natural sciences and engineering.

A financial study of the three areas for the first fifteen years of President Pusey's administration at Harvard indicated that the percentage growth in budget for the three areas during this period was about the same when government contract funds were included in the calculation for the sciences. Thus the main effect of federal funding at Harvard appears to have been to facilitate the transfer of university resources to the humanities and social sciences. In general, the budgets of the Harvard libraries have increased somewhat faster than outside funds for sponsored research in the sciences.

The pattern at Harvard may, as I have said, be somewhat more favorable to the humanities than the pattern at the universities of the California system, but analysis of the Ph.D. pattern shown in Table 1 does not indicate that it is likely to be very different. The question that naturally arises is why there has been such a perception of relative advantage and growth in favor of the sciences, felt at almost all universities. This may be a question of "relative deprivation" as explained by Smelser. Although the relative size and affluence of the three areas has remained fairly constant during the period of rapid growth, the sciences started from a larger base, and consequently there has been an increase in the *absolute* difference between the sciences and the humanities. This may have made the poverty of the humanities more obvious, although it has not changed relatively. Moreover, the increments in support to the sciences and, to a lesser extent, to the social sciences have provided fringe benefits — such as travel funds, research assistance, and computing services — which improve conditions for scholarly work. Indeed the fact that science faculties may have grown *less* rapidly than other faculties means that, because the growth in funding has been about the same, the support per faculty member has increased relatively. At all events, there is little question about the feeling of relative deprivation in the humanities.

OCCUPATIONS OF PH.D.S

There is a wide difference in the postdoctoral activities of Ph.D.s. In the physical sciences and engineering, less than 50 percent of the Ph.D.s enter university employment, although more than 30 percent go into industry. However, with the rapid growth of graduate education during the 1960s, the percentage going into university or college employment increased, and the percentage going into industry declined from 44 percent in 1958–1960 to only 30 percent in 1964–1966, and is probably even less currently. In the life sciences, about 58 percent of the Ph.D.s go into academic employment, and the next largest employer is foreign government or industry — about 16 percent in 1964–1966. For the social sciences, the postdoctoral employment pattern is very similar, but nearly 90 percent of the arts and humanities Ph.D.s go into academic employment. Thus the humanities look almost wholly to the academic system for reward and recognition. Graduate education in the humanities is part of a closed system, with little necessary for response to any external constituency or clientele.

Even more significant is what Ph.D.s in the various areas list as their principal postdoctoral activity. In the physical sciences and engineering, no more than 28 percent go into positions where teaching is the primary activity, whereas more than 64 percent go into positions where research is the primary activity. The distribution is almost the same for the life sciences. In the social sciences, we find that about 30 percent find their primary posdoctoral activity in research and about 48 percent in teaching. Finally, in the arts and humanities, we learn that 70 percent of the new Ph.D.s find their primary employment in teaching and only 9 percent primarily in research and scholarship — a striking contrast to the natural scientists.

Smelser's model assumes that in the academic system, status and privilege are strongly attached to research and scholarship; the most prestigious institutions are those in which research is more important than other educational functions, and all other institutions strive for the same status. The statistics quoted above suggest that a similar status hierarchy might be found in the broad areas of knowledge, according to the degree to which their apprentices can aspire to ultimate careers in research. In this respect, the relative deprivation of the arts and humanities is striking and may explain the greater involvement of humanities students and faculty in campus activism. It is harder to determine the significance of the greater employment of humanities Ph.D.s in academic positions. The fact that the physical sciences and engineering must be more responsive to an external clientele may also have a considerable influence on the sense of relative deprivation of other areas; the scientists feel more wanted by society. In any event, these employment patterns have to be taken into consideration in Smelser's model.

STYLES OF SUPERVISION

There is a considerable difference in the pattern of student–faculty relationships in the sciences compared with that in the social sciences and especially in the humanities. This difference in graduate work style is also reflected in some of the statistics. For example, the median time elapsed between the B.A. and the Ph.D. is 6.3 years in the physical sciences and engineering, 7.3 years in the biological sciences, 8 years in the social sciences, and 10 years in the arts and humanities. During the thesis period, between the master's degree and the Ph.D., the relative difference is more striking: 4.1 years in the physical sciences, and 6.2 years in the humanities. The median time, however, is not the whole story. There is a much greater spread of such time for the humanities than for the natural sciences; the social sciences are intermediate. Thus about 41 percent of the students in the physical sciences finish in five years or less after the B.A., 30 percent in the life sciences, 24 percent in the social sciences, and 14 percent in the humanities. In education, only 4 percent receive a Ph.D. within 5 years of the baccalaureate. Thus, expectations are much more uniform in the sciences than in the humanities, in part because many — perhaps most — people in the humanities write their theses while already holding teaching positions.

One result of this pattern, which is also reinforced by tradition, is that theses in the humanities are written with much less faculty supervision than natural science theses. Most supervisors in the natural sciences see their graduate students once a week and often much more frequently. Usually they are collaborators, and the student is a true apprentice researcher. In the humanities the student is much more on his own, attempting to be an independent scholar in his own right. This partly reflects the fact that there is less collaboration in the humanities. Team research is not an established pattern in the humanities, but is commonplace in the natural sciences, especially in physics and engineering. I am not suggesting that these differences in pattern are either good or bad, only that they must affect the attitudes and perceptions of students and faculty in relation to their scholarly activities and their status in the university pecking order. The humanities student feels less a partner and more a subordinate than the science student, even though the former may have more apparent intellectual independence.

These patterns of student–faculty relationships to some extent reflect the nature of career development in the disciplines. The peak of intellectual productivity seems to be reached earlier in the natural sciences than in the humanities, and especially in theoretical physics and mathematics. Merton and Zuckerman have associated this with the degree of codification. The more a body of knowledge is codified or structured, the more quickly it is possible to arrive at the frontier where a creative and original contribution to the advance of the field is possible. This high correlation between age structure and degree of codification is undoubtedly one of the reasons why it takes longer to get the Ph.D. in the humanities. The lack of financial support for graduate students also plays its part, as shown by the fact that the *registered* time to the Ph.D. in the natural sciences and humanities shows much smaller differences than does the *elapsed* time. But the scholar in the humanities takes much longer to be recognized as an equal, and there is less uniformity of judgment about major contributors. In an age where the status and privileges of youth in relation to its elders is becoming a major political issue, the relationship between age and scholarly recognition becomes a phenomenon of increasing significance in the political structure of the university. Although the scientist is more closely scrutinized by his supervisor, he can look forward to earlier scholarly independence and recognition, and he may also find recognition outside the closed system of academia. All of these factors exacerbate the feelings of deprivation and inferiority of the scholar and teacher in the humanities.

These problems will be aggravated as the rate of expansion of academic faculties declines. Conditions in the physical sciences have approached more closely those in the humanities. But today universities are not expanding at the rate they did in the sixties, and the phenomenon of the seventies is the drying up of the job market for university Ph.D.s. Although the plight of the scientists and engineers has received the greatest publicity, the actual situation among humanists seems to be worse. Perhaps this merely reflects the fact that the physicists have been the darling of the media for so long that their troubles are more newsworthy than those of historians. But the main point is that for the first time in twenty-five years, the United States may be producing a cadre of frustrated intellectuals, people who cannot find employment commensurate with their capacities, training, and aspirations. At present, this group is likely to have more representatives among the humanities than among the sciences, if only because the humanities graduates are more restricted to academic employment. I have often wondered about the extent to which student unrest in the last half of the sixties might be explained by an almost subconscious anticipatory reaction to the lack of career opportunities for the student educated in the liberal arts tradition. This tradition, which represents the highest status in the value system of the university, seems to be increasingly disjoint with the career opportunities society is prepared to provide in the present decade.

Educational Articulation, the Transfer Process, and the Transfer Student

by G. J. MASLACH

The single system of higher education of the state of California is divided into three parts. The separate parts are loosely coupled by an educational articulation program which insures the transfer of qualified students from one school to another. The transfer process is defined explicitly in the admissions circulars of the state colleges and the university. It is my thesis that the effectiveness of our total system is measured in large part by the record of these transfer students. Although each part of the system often proclaims its size and growth, and thus its need for added budgets, there is seldom record or praise of the quantity or quality of the transfer output, which alone makes the California system unique. In this article I intend to record in detail the successful operation of one type of student transfer, engineers from community colleges to the university; to identify a few of the advantages the process offers to the transfer student; and to describe the institutional and personal efforts necessary to make the system work.

THE ADMISSIONS PROCEDURE

Before giving numerical data and comparative figures of scholastic achievement, I would like to review the basic admissions policy of the university, especially as it pertains to transfer students. Although the policy has often been publicized and is well stated in the admissions circular, it is suprisingly vague in the minds of students and staff in all segments of the state educational system.

The admissions circular clearly and specifically states the requirements for admission with advanced standing, for both

Californians and nonresidents. The preferential statement relating to transfer students is often repeated: "Each campus will give the highest priority in admission to qualified transfers from California public community colleges who have completed two full years of transferable academic work (84 quarter units). With due regard to the composition of the student body, applicants who are residents of California will receive preference over nonresidents."

EDUCATIONAL ARTICULATION

The articulation process was started in 1932, when the president of the university, Robert Gordon Sproul, appointed a University of California Junior College Conference Committee. The concept was expanded with liaison committees, each representing a given discipline, and the effort is now known as the Articulation Conference. The first notice of an Engineering Liaison Committee appears in November of 1947, with the following explanation of purpose by Dean L. M. K. Boelter of the College of Engineering at UCLA:

> The committee was established primarily for the purpose of making all schools in the state which offer pre-engineering training a part of a unit working together toward the common goal of producing the proper number of well-trained individuals to go into the junior year in engineering training. The primary function of the committee would be to serve as a center for the exchange of information. . . .
>
> One of the most important items . . . is the advising of students. Advising methods, therefore, would make a good study topic. Another important subject for study has to do with the philosophy of instruction. . . . An exchange of course description and outlines of curricula in the schools would be valuable. Also a discussion of plans for changes before such changes are put into effect would be valuable so that there would be understanding as to why the changes are made.

Over a period of twenty-four years, the committee has demonstrated a consistent, common dedication to these goals. The committee is best described by the following excerpt from a discussion of the university transfer policy for engineering students:

> Mr. Boelter suggested a change in the university's upper-division admission policy, with respect to engineering students, which would permit a variation of approximately ten units from existing lower-division requirements. This proposal would give the

junior colleges sufficient leeway to prepare for Berkeley and UCLA and, at the same time, to conduct a certain amount of experimentation with courses in their own pre-engineering programs.

In 1959, the Engineering Liaison Committee was re-formed and enlarged to officially permit the participation of state college representatives; the initial and early efforts at curricular coordination from 1932 to 1959 involved only the community colleges. Finally, in 1965, the common lower division concept for engineering students was refined to reflect the desires of all public institutions offering engineering education. Since 1965, the major concern of the committee has been maintenance of enrollment in all units, especially the community colleges, in the face of an unprecedented proliferation of new institutions.

The scale of the problem is evident from the fact that six campuses of the university, fourteen state colleges, and over eighty community colleges now offer elements of the common lower division engineering program. Approximately 2,000 full-time students are enrolled in the lower division of engineering at the university, and 4,000 students are enrolled in the lower division of the state colleges. The community college engineering transfer and technician programs together enroll 36,000. The best measure of size and interaction of the community college segment is the fact that approximately 1,000 students transfer to four-year institutions each year.

The one major accomplishment of the Engineering Liaison Committee was the concept of the common lower division program, one which could be taught in all three segments of the total system of higher education in California. The program has not remained fixed for twenty-four years and was never completely common. Sufficient flexibility was provided, and some subjects have been removed while new courses were added. The important feature of the common lower division is the assurance it provides that transfer will be possible at the junior year for a "second chance" student, or at anytime in the first two years for the student originally eligible as a freshman in the University of California.

THE RECORD OF SUCCESS

Beginning with the files of students who were listed as juniors in the fall semester of 1963, the College of Engineering at Berkeley examined the records of 1692 students, 590 of them first-term transfers from community colleges and 1102 "native" students who started at Berkeley or transferred prior to the sophomore year. We wished to develop comparative data for successful completion of degree requirements, time required to graduate, and grade-point average nearing graduation, not only for those students who started as freshmen at Berkeley, but also for those who were eligible or ineligible as freshmen but chose to go to a community college for their lower division work. The data represents a 100 percent sample spanning eight years. The most useful data follows Berkeley's change to the quarter system in 1966, but does not include the most recent year, where many students are still enrolled and the data are thus incomplete.

The first measure uppermost in the minds of students and their former instructors is "How many failed?" Of 190 students who transferred since 1966, when the change to the quarter system involved major curriculum revisions, 4 transfer students have been dismissed, or about 2 percent. Of 489 students who either started at Berkeley as freshmen or transferred earlier than their sophomore year, 7 were dismissed, or 1.63 percent. Both the absolute low dismissal rates and the comparison of two separate groups are revealing: not only does Berkeley engineering *not* dismiss people wholesale, but the community college transfer is almost indistinguishable from the "native" student.

To move to the positive side, "How long did they take to get the B.S. degree?" Of all 530 transfers who could have graduated since 1963, only 26 are still enrolled, or less than 5 percent. Of this total, 5 are taking three years or more, less than 1 percent of the original 530. All others will probably complete their work in two and a half years. Thus the overwhelming number of transfers graduate in less than three years, or approximately 67 percent in exactly two years. This performance is almost identical to "native" students, of whom 66 percent complete the upper division in two years and less than 1 percent take more than three years.

A more detailed comparison of transfer students and "natives" is best shown in tabular form. The question always arises, "How do the 'eligible' transfer students (those who could have entered Berkeley as freshmen) perform compared with the 'ineligible' (those "second-chance" students whose high school record did not qualify

them for freshmen admission to Berkeley) and 'native' students?"
The accompanying table records the technical grade-point average
for courses taken as a junior or senior.

		Transfer	
Entering	Native	"Eligible"	"Ineligible"
1963	2.76	2.80	2.68
1964	2.92	2.72	2.72
1965	2.86	2.91	2.70
1966	2.94	3.12	2.77
1967	3.01	2.83	2.74
1968	3.06	3.05	2.97
1969	3.17	2.94	2.99

TECHNICAL GRADE POINT AVERAGES COMPARED

Obviously all the students are doing well, with approximately
50 percent of the "natives" meeting graduate school entry requirements, 45 percent of the eligibles doing so, and 40 percent of
the second-chance transfers able to go on for higher degrees.

ADVANTAGES OFFERED BY THE TRANSFER PROCESS

What are the advantages of the transfer route? First there is
the matter of cost, including the possible expenses of living away
from home for two or more years. Often the student must give up a
part-time job near home when he moves. Second, the community
college is the place where students undecided about their career
can risk taking courses not closely related to their proven skills.
Third, the liberal withdrawal privileges offered to students at
community colleges aids in their search for a career without
penalizing them with failing grades. Fourth, the admissions circular provides for two units of high school work that can be removed.
Engineering transfers often come to the university without the two
language units required in high school, and humanities students
come minus two math or science units. Fifth, transfer students
usually come with more than two years of community college work
and often with more than the maximum of 105 quarter credits
accepted by the university. With a 180 quarter-credit degree requirement, these students have a time advantage over "native"
students in completing the last two years; in essence, seven quar-

ters of credit can be transferred. Sixth, advanced community college students study in small classes and get a great deal of individual attention. The average mathematics class in the sophomore level at Berkeley has 250 students, but the same class in most community colleges has 15 to 25 students. Although other fringe benefits can be cited, the above advantages are constantly in the records of transfer students.

METHODS OF ENCOURAGING THE TRANSFER PROCESS

If the transfer student does not suffer in the process and if there are advantages in this route to a university degree, why aren't more students attracted to this method of education? The experience of the College of Engineering at Berkeley reveals two necessary conditions for a flow of students to start and be maintained. The most important is agreement as to a common lower division program which can be taught with a minimum of special facilities at the community colleges and adhered to at the university. A sincere, demonstrated commitment to be part of such an agreement is the one indispensable condition for insuring the success of the transfer student. Such commitment requires that community colleges receive not only catalogue statements but course outlines, sample tests, and problem assignments with solutions, together with text choice and planned coverage. Students are reassured if they know that a given course in the community college catalog is the direct equivalent of the same offering at Berkeley, and this directs them in their transfer thinking.

There should also be proof that only two additional years of study are required for transfer students to obtain their first degree. The 180 quarter-credit engineering degree requirement at Berkeley is truly divided into equal parts with no hidden upper division university or college requirements. In addition, an open elective should be provided in the first quarter of the junior year, so that transfer students can make up a single deficiency without losing time in the upper division. Such an opening exists in all curricula of the College of Engineering at Berkeley.

Although these commitment and mechanistic proofs of compliance are necessary and reassuring to the potential transfer student, they are not in themselves sufficient. The institutional agreement must be reinforced with a personal encouraging contact, preferably by the dean of the college. Between 1950 and 1966, the transfer rate of engineering students to Berkeley rose rapidly until 1958, and then dropped just as rapidly. The agreement was being rigorously adhered to, but no personal contacts existed beyond the yearly meetings of the Engineering Liaison Committee. Starting in 1966, a program of visits, scholarships and financial aid, brochures, and personal advising was organized. In a five-year period, the dropping rate of transfers was reversed and now the College of Engineering at Berkeley admits five times as many transfer students as in 1966, a number equal to the previous peak year of 1958.

The success of this campaign merits some discussion of its methods. In the main, this effort consisted of my visiting community colleges and speaking to students, counselors, and leading staff. The first visits managed to slow down the trend away from Berkeley, and they also taught me, the visitor, what kind of information was needed to strongly influence apprehensive students. A great number of myths about the university must be dispelled by factual data. I am no longer shocked to hear many students and counsellors express surprise that the university is not planning to become a graduate school exclusively, or that there is considerable room for the transfer students, or that they are not dismissed in great numbers. Not only the data cited above, but detailed records by name of former transfer students have helped to dispel these often morbid myths.

The very fact that the dean of a college of the university would travel, year after year, to interview a small group of students far from Berkeley was heartening. In five years I have visited over sixty community colleges, with the same reactions everywhere and the same increased transfer rate. After a group session, I often spend several hours examining transcripts and advising individuals. The many advantages of going to Berkeley are often forgotten by university faculty: not only academic advantages, but the possibility of scholarships and financial aids, cooperative study programs and loans. All this may sound rather mundane, but such information and encouragement is especially important to minority students who form an increasing part of the community college population. The increased number of minority graduates from engineering at Berkeley — five black Ph.D.s in 1971 — can be directly traced to these visits to community colleges and state colleges.

In addition, the College of Engineering at Berkeley prepared a brochure aimed at encouraging the community college student. This and other material is sent to each applicant with a personal letter, and those admitted receive a second packet of material and a congratulatory personal letter. A third round of correspondence follows registration, including detailed advisory material. This attempt to personalize the university may be as effective as the visiting program in encouraging students to choose engineering at Berkeley.

Once a year, in February, the College of Engineering invites all potential transfer students and interested faculty from the community colleges to spend a full day at our campus. This event gives the transfer students at Berkeley the opportunity to serve as guides and ad hoc advisors, and the Berkeley faculty an opportunity to explain their work and curricula offerings in detail. Community College Day is a large-scale program with more than one hundred community college students participating.

Obviously, all of this activity has been mutually rewarding. The university gains quality students in a field where it is superbly equipped to teach. The transfer students receive the best advice and encouragement. The community colleges obtain a feedback of information on their students which evaluates their teaching effectiveness. Everybody gains, no one loses. There is no doubt in my mind that this form of liaison between the community colleges and the university should be extended to other disciplines. Only then will the Master Plan of Higher Education for the State of California become totally effective.

Higher Education in California: An Irenic View

by ROSEMARY PARK

The university has long been recognized as the most durable and the most fragile of organizations. Both qualities are apparent in Neil Smelser's analysis of this unique social structure as it is manifested in the higher education system of the state of California. The stresses now so visible within that system are shown to be the inevitable result of the incorporation of two different values in the structure — values which do not appear to be integrated any longer by a comprehensive and accepted purpose for the entire system. In effect, higher education today is not susceptible of further definition than the operational one; it is what we do in the system. An examination restricted to an analysis of the relations between the constituent parts may push aside this more basic question of purpose and could tend to foster the illusion that durability is conditioned by the continuing coherence of the strata. Actually the boundaries of the system are permeable, subject to the generalized osmosis of a biological model rather than of a mathematical one, and unrest in the surrounding ecology is apt to be immediately evident within the structure of higher education and to result in varying degrees of internal imbalance.

Higher education is only one of the basic institutions of our society which suffer from recent seismic instabilities. Forms of government, business organizations, ecclesiastical landmarks, and other eleemosynary institutions are all being challenged to examine the values they incorporate and their adequacy to new times. Too often, it seems to me, the field of higher learning offers itself as a scapegoat, ready, if not anxious, to assume all the sins of the people and to attempt to bear them away to some irrelevant outer desert. Instead of such romanticism, we need to realize that higher education cannot and should not attempt to isolate itself from the general cultural reevaluation and, further, that higher education has no supreme guilt, but only shares with other established structures in the uncertainties of the times.

That higher education has been subject to attacks and to internal stresses is the result of influences from the surrounding culture as well as of any inherent faults, and testifies to the centrality of the institution in today's world. An irrelevant structure would have been passed over. Unlike other epochs in the history of higher education, the symbiosis of education and society is increasingly close today. Higher education as the basis for the knowledge industry has furnished a unique momentum toward affluence and into a postindustrial age. During these years of expansion, competitive excellence and egalitarian opportunity were important and proper values to institutionalize in an educational system, as California has done. Now, in times approaching stability in conventional enrollments, there may be a question as to whether these values in their present incorporations are adequate, either to secure continued support in the state or as accepted goals within the system. This is not to imply that competitive excellence and egalitarian opportunity have been achieved and can be deemphasized, but rather that they require supplementation today, or reinterpretation. If innovation can be achieved which could more nearly articulate the purpose of the system as a whole, then these traditional qualities may be discovered to be continuing and significant characteristics to perpetuate in a durable structure.

To examine such a possibility, an appraisal of recent innovative activities and their genesis is indicated. Recurrent in the criticism of almost all institutions today is the charge of impersonality, which is difficult to interpret when directed against the university. At no time in its history has higher education provided more services directed toward enhancing the personal well-being of students than it does today. Even for faculty members, assistance of many kinds unknown to earlier generations is provided to relieve them of routine tasks and permit more private time. Secretarial pools, departmental assistants, teaching assistants, and research assistants, as well as insurance programs and faculty clubs, are among the programs of universities, as are counseling facilities for students which assure privacy and confidentiality, health services, activities staffs, and student union buildings. Useful as these bureaucratic adjuncts are to the individual, they are not what the student refers to when he complains of impersonality. He speaks rather of the process of learning, which no longer seems to him to represent conviction about the nature of the end product. He suspects that the system does not know what an educated person is, and he is not satisfied with the implication of the statement, "If you have been through our system, you are an educated person." In requiring particular learning experiences of him, the university is forcing him into a meaningless, impersonal mold, he thinks. And his radical mentors tell him that process can only be to the advantage of an evil military–industrial complex which waits to destroy his selfhood in its lethal embrace.

To test this hypothesis that there is no definition at the center, the student exerts pressure on the boundaries set in the degree programs, demanding now a diminution in the number of courses, now an excision of laboratory science, or foreign language or history, now pass–fail grading. Because there is apparently little conviction about what characteristics are exemplified by the educated person, most of these student suggestions are complied with for a variety of reasons, perhaps correctly. A logical consequence is the skepticism now abroad in the land about the B.A. degree, which is interpreted increasingly as a meaningless cachet forced upon unwilling youngsters who aspire to influence in social or economic life. Neither the students nor the public are as sure as they once were that higher education knows what it is doing. Left without a vision of what the process is planned to foster, the student substitutes his momentary interests for an accepted framework of knowledge, and proclaims that the institution is depersonalized when it occasionally refuses to sanction his individual plans.

Very often, however, the institution acquiesces and permits the establishment of, for instance, so-called experimental courses. Most of these are initiated by students; some are almost taught by students or, if not, then by faculty members who share the student skepticism about the present educational process and are willing to believe that impersonality will be erased if knowledge can be an experience, not a discipline. The results of some of these courses have been extraordinary in the energies released for learning at optional rates. Occasionally and ironically quite traditional conclusions were reached, like "People can't use freedom if you *give* it to them." But for students the most significant aspect of such courses has often been the satisfaction derived from beating the system or nonsystem and introducing a personal element of choice and creativity into an imposed and to them meaningless pattern.

The faculty response has been similar. At the university, responsibility for the conduct of these innovative courses rests with an academic senate committee which is charged with facilitating the transfer of successful courses to regular department offerings. For many reasons, some of them budgetary, such transfers have been minimal. A cynic might say that the faculty was, like the student, seeking a way around the system, and so devised the senate committee as an instrument for short-circuiting student complaints while appearing to welcome innovation. A more charitable gloss would be to adduce that the recentness of these committees on the campus has so far precluded careful study of the effects of these courses on the teaching methods of regular offerings. Perhaps it is too early to determine whether the charge of impersonality has been affected by the willingness of authority to permit such innovation.

It is not only in the curricular area that attempts have been made to respond to the assessment of impersonality in the university's operations. On several campuses, in California and elsewhere, a new office has been created, that of ombudsman. He represents a combination of the fatherly dean of the old residential college, who could shrive the guilty and support the weak, and a modern efficiency expert. In a landscape of bureaucrats, he alone keeps no records, belongs on no organizational chart, and has no Parkinsonian aspirations. More extraordinary still, he has no power when all around him are flaunting theirs. To both the administration and the student, he is first a person and only secondarily an official. Theoretically, of course, the administrative system should work to the genuine enduring interest of students and faculty members, and should not require the intervention of a nonmember to function efficiently. Undoubtedly the ombudsman will improve the system as he guides his clients through, and by his success will decrease the need for his activity. At the moment, however, he is seen by administration and students alike as a way outside and around the system, a personal, not a bureaucratic, aid. Like most experimental courses, he represents an innovation which effects no basic change in the existing organization and must therefore be interpreted as palliative rather than genuinely therapeutic. However useful in given areas and for selected individuals these two successful internal innovations have been, they do not seem to me to satisfy the basic need for a greater conviction about the purpose of the total system of higher education, and consequently they do not provide the kind of innovation which a successful integration of that system would require.

Uncertain as we may be about the definition of the educated person today, we do not suffer from the same uncertainty in assessing the formation of the professional or expert, at least not in the same degree. The university's excellence, by virtue of which it stands in competition with other universities on the national scene, is related almost entirely to its success in the training of experts. This success is attested to by professional board examinations and the testimony of peers in seeking positions and in inviting graduates to migrate. Within the system in California, it is the university's competence in training professionals and specialists which has led to the status it is accorded and, correspondingly, the jealousy it inspires. This competence is so respected that the charge of impersonality that is rife in the undergraduate area is less common in graduate and professional schools. The excitement of a research ambience and the camaraderie between student and faculty in the laboratory and in the seminar, as well as the necessity to be prepared to support oneself immediately on completion of the degree, seem to result in acceptance by the student of the university definition of the specialist as the end of the graduate school process. In this area both the student and the public are more ready to concede that the system of higher education may know what it is doing, and impersonality or lack of basic conviction is seldom charged.

For the system as a whole, some consequences may be drawn from this relative assurance about fundamental aims at the professional level. One of the problems that Smelser identifies in the California situation is the unfortunate incorporation of excellence almost exclusively in the university, and the invidious judgments which therefore adhere to the other segments of the system in their own eyes. A greater cooperation between these segments in educational matters might reduce this unrealistic, unconstructive tension. For example, a natural cooperation between the university and the junior colleges in the training of paraprofessionals can be identified. Because both institutions have other assignments in California besides this interest in professional educators, closer association in this one area would not necessarily weaken the autonomy of either the junior colleges or the university, an autonomy which is well protected by statute. Obviously cooperation would be conditioned and certainly enhanced by geographical propinquity. A university professional school could concern itself with the development of paraprofessionals in a nearby junior college, on the basis that they need exposure to some of the same training experiences as the professionals for whom the university is responsible and with whom these junior college students will subsequently work. The concept of excellence claimed by the university could then to be associated with the paraprofessional programs in which the university and the neighboring junior colleges had cooperated. Such joint endeavor seems particularly reasonable when the obligations of the specialist of all types are being continually modified by the results of research, most of which originates in the university. Formerly, vocational training had suffered from the tendency to educate for industrial and commercial and for semiprofessional circumstances which had characterized the recent past rather than the present and future. Today, the useful relations which many junior colleges maintain with local industries and communities help to prevent obsolescence in training programs. Information from these nonacademic sources would enrich the university's own soundings in the community, and together both institutions might do better in their formation of professionals and paraprofessionals than either does alone.

Extrapolating further from the competence of the university in training specialists, it would be possible to devise a quite different relation between the undergraduate and graduate programs within the university. For several years now, the elapsed time between entrance into graduate training and its conclusion has been a problem in California and elsewhere. To meet this difficulty, it has been suggested that a preporfessional stem be introduced into undergraduate education, with the intent of anticipating some of the work required for the professional degree and thereby reducing the time and funding needed to complete it. Skillfully planned, such experiences might exploit the need for commitment of the younger generation, particularly if arrangements were made for observation of professional situations and practical experience with limited responsibility. For the small number of students who can make a tentative professional choice at the beginning of their undergraduate years, a cooperative sequence involving professional schools and undergraduate programs would be an important educational option. A program of this type would necessitate the maintenance of a lower division at the university which can be defended on other grounds as well.

Further consequences arise from the emphasis on the creation of experts as the unique function of the university. It has become increasingly clear that the professional man continues to require further training today if he is to keep up with the work in his field. In the past this has been an individual responsibility. Today educational institutions are attempting to help maintain professional competence by instructional sequences for mature men and women. In addition, the emergence of large groups of women who require further education at the conclusion of their full-time family responsibilities defines a new group of students, to which can be added men and women who wish to change occupation in mid-career. In effect, the responsibilities of a higher educational system are not fulfilled today when it has given degrees to a selected group of younger citizens. Instead, its problems have only begun, because some of these citizens will be back in a few years, and they may be more precise in their educational needs, if less dramatic than the younger students who complain of impersonality.

The needs of the mature professional will be met in part by the university professional school, which can furnish reports on the latest research and its relevance for practice. But as one views the professions today, it is evident that this kind of instruction alone will not be entirely adequate because the urgent problems of the professions concern more than specialized competence. Matters of public policy are involved, and of personal ethics. Which patient is to be given the heart transplant? Should legal cases be tried on TV to assure a public trial? Are teachers paid too much? Why should public money support the arts? The professional school will seldom have ready answers to such questions, and this lack may lead the mature student as well as the undergraduate to doubt whether the degree he has earned represents anything but minimal competence in a specialized field. In the future, both younger and more mature students may expect the system of higher education to respond to concerns of this type, reexamining the meaning and substance of our present degree system.

If we accept for the moment the possibility that our present degree structure may be antiquated in some aspects and that a new type of educated man may be evolving, then any system of higher education will find, as in the past, that its responsibility is not discharged by providing solely for the training of experts and for the maintenance of this expertise through life. I have suggested that the younger generation is no longer convinced that there is substance to the program frameworks required for our degrees, all of which are interpreted as arbitrary and imposed. It is therefore important to discover with what kinds of innovation the youth culture supplements the university degrees. Their charge is impersonality and lack of humaneness, and so it is understandable that encounter groups and other forms of sensitivity training appeal strongly to them, and that many of their proposals for experimental courses involved these techniques. Rather than being the well-rounded gentleman of the eighteenth century exemplified by Thomas Jefferson, the educated man of the twenty-first century will be narrowly trained in one area or field but, if the younger generation has its way, he will be a humane expert. The educational question remains to be answered: "How does one train the humane expert?"

The form of supplementation which the new culture recommends, its communes and its sensitivity groups, can hardly be regularized in a special curricular offering. But there may be areas presently covered by the curriculum which could be developed to foster the forms of humaneness that might characterize a new type of educated man. Most obvious are the fields of the humanities and the arts, which do not depend on pure rationality for understanding. Recently Jacques Barzun, with his usual elegance, defined the humanities as "the study of man through an enjoyment of the deliberate works of his mind." Study through *enjoyment* may at first seem contradictory. But enjoyment is the essence of much literature and the arts, although the word *enjoyment* has seldom if ever been seen in college catalogues — partly because there is nothing more difficult than teaching another person *enjoyment*. It is interesting how much the word *literature* meant to our forefathers, who established literary funds in the early colonies long before research funds were thought of. The study of the humanities, properly taught as an entrance into enjoyment and not just expertise, may be one way today to imbed our excellence in humaneness. This is only a beginning, but it helps us toward a definition of the human type which higher education must develop in response to the criticism of impersonality today.

If I am right and we need to respond to the new culture's need for humaneness, then obviously humanities courses at all levels of the higher education system will not be adequate, however helpful they may be. I come to the romantic conclusion that there is no bureaucratic way, no simple curricular rabbit to be pulled from the institutional hat amidst applause, which can meet the new concern with humaneness. Rather, as institutions we need to state this concept of humane expertise as our goal, and leave it up to each stratum, each level of higher education, to implement this aim in its own way. Operationally I suppose the advising system of the institution would have to be alert to a variety of ways in which this concept could be implemented. The courses or learning experiences in the area of expertise will be rigorous and subject to the correction of professional accrediting boards. Whether it is possible to give courses which aim at humaneness and sensitivity with the same kind of rigor, I do not know. Many accomplishments of the new culture dissolve in sentimentality on examination, and we have all known the ignominious fate of music appreciation courses from our own youth. They were a haven for the dilettante and the intellectually somnolent. If it is possible to make clear the extreme pedagogical difficulty of teaching another person sensitivity and enjoyment, perhaps new courses could be constructed which would provide an enlargement of enjoyment, of empathetic understanding.

In the process of developing such courses, the testimony of students is essential. It is necessary to understand where they are in their artistic interests and to enlarge these horizons by the experiencing of other forms of art which can be interpreted not only as subtly contrived accomplishments or, as Jacques Barzun says, "as deliberate works" of the human mind, but also as examples of a type of experience widely shared by all human beings now and in the past. Empathetic understanding related to community problems can also be developed through the study of the social sciences. However, in both the humanities and the social sciences, the student needs to understand that the institution is consciously trying to find a new type of learning which will give meaning to the concept of humaneness that higher education wishes to foster without in any way denigrating the importance of rationality and disciplined learning.

In the formation of the expert, the student contributes little by his testimony except perhaps to explain how he experiences the course and learning sequences — too hurried, too slow, too lacking in structure. If it is possible to give programmatic reality to the concept of the humane expert, then a student would experience not only the rigor of developing expertise but the creativity of defining more precisely the idea of humaneness. A more mature and responsible student might result than the resentful "expert *malgré lui*" that we turn out today.

If the formation of humane experts for a postindustrial society is our educational purpose in a system characterized in California by competitive excellence and egalitarian opportunity, what relationships would exist between the constituent parts — the university, the state colleges, and the junior colleges? The present suspicions and tensions seem to me unconstructive, and I have accordingly suggested that the university professional schools and the junior colleges might collaborate in the training of paraprofessionals. The increase in specialized knowledge required of various occupations today makes the separation of the professions and the occupations not as simple a task as it once was. At the moment the university is responsible for training professionals, and there seems to be no educational or economic justification for changing this charge. Development of innovative forms of expertise in the new areas of specialized activity connected with the communications industry or publishing, with transportation and construction, with public order, for example, could well be the task of the state colleges. In some instances the university has established nonteaching research centers which study aspects of these problems. These centers might develop connections with state colleges or, where they do not rely upon the expert knowledge of a number of university departments, they might even be transferred entirely to the state college interested in adapting training programs to implement research findings. For many years the state colleges have been primarily responsible for the training of teachers up to the college and university level. The university's programs for this field, where it shares responsibility with the state colleges, have been research oriented, although not entirely so. With this situation as a model, perhaps other professional and emerging professional areas could be devised with joint effort.

This mutual cooperation through the system is logically sound but practically difficult to achieve, because the separate segments unfortunately sense that the hierarchical nature of education tends to accord status only to the most advanced level. This may have been more true before recent attacks on higher education — from within and without — selected the university as their target. It is now clear to all that the summit of the system was even more vulnerable than other areas, which for a variety of reasons were less often exposed during the years of unrest. The necessity for innovation was accepted grudgingly at the university level as a consequence of disturbances, and a variety of measures were introduced with only moderate success. The assumption, however, that in educational matters the university was not only excellent but right was found to be at fault. It is therefore easier today to discuss how the system of higher education can serve the state than it was before 1964. And so this moment in time should not be let pass lest we all freeze back into unconstructive rivalries which confuse and do not serve the state. Some of the cooperative educational ventures should be examined further. And it may also be the time, for instance, to examine the governing boards of each segment to see whether they should be enlarged by the presence of both students and faculty members, in the hope that adversary relations are not the form of educational communication in this state. In many organizational structures today, representation on governing boards is yielding to participation by those who know most about the process because they work at it every day. In higher education, I believe the public interest must be paramount. But the internal health of our institutions would be improved if it were admitted that professors and students, who know the institutions well, can interpret the public interest at least as well as those who know the public interest from the vantage point of one profession or one industry. The difficulties of administering large systems today require an openness and a willingness to innovate which were not as necessary when the goal of the system was clearly set and the separated segments knew their places and their duties. In the student disruptions, a great tradition of value-free learning was challenged before there was any clear outline of a new educational ideal. To prevent increasing the fragility of the remaining structure of higher education, cooperation and listening will be required by both generations; that is, not only by students and faculty, but also by governing boards and those presumably governed. The durability of the systems of higher education in California and elsewhere may depend on our capacity to foster new curricula and new forms of governance and new internal relationships within the parameters of the Master Plan.

For this task the moment is propitious, particularly if out of the local search for individual institutional prestige could emerge a pride in the system as a whole, and not just pride in one segment. Now that the university has a clearer sense, through its efforts to establish ethnic programs, of the difficulties facing those parts of the system which have primary responsibility for implementing the egalitarian ideals of the structure, it could more sympathetically assist those institutions in developing areas of mutual concern. Now that the state colleges and junior colleges have seen the public travail of the university, they too may more properly evaluate their own importance and more successfully develop the pride in their own achievements which leads to excellence. They do not any longer have to be like the university to be excellent.

In this irenic view, I have suggested that the system of higher education in California needs to establish a definable goal which can characterize the efforts of the total structure. By identifying this goal as the formation of humane specialists or experts, I have attempted to unite the necessity for specialized competence today with the concern of the new culture for humane sensitivity. To realize this aim, each segment has a unique role, aspects of which can properly be discharged by cooperation on a regional basis. But most fundamental for the success of the innovations necessary to implement the new aspiration is a renewal of pride in the system as a whole. This can develop first as local concern for the excellence of one's own institution or level. But if the public is to awaken again to the enthusiastic support which made the California system the envy of other states, then our local patriotism will not suffice. The bitter experiences of the recent past have given us all a respect for the duties and achievements of the other parts of the system. It is on this foundation, and on a determination to make higher education better able to serve a postindustrial society, that our innovations should be undertaken and our pride established.

The Public and Higher Education in California

by JOHN VASCONCELLOS and PATRICK CALLAN

Our commentary will deal primarily with the value questions Neil Smelser raised in his analysis. We particularly want to address the conflict between egalitariansim and competitive excellence and the implications of those values for planning the future of California higher education. In our initial comments, we discuss our impressions of the general cultural and social context of higher education in the 1970s. We are in a period of remarkable and unprecedented differentiation of values which must be taken into account as we ponder the future. In the latter part of the commentary, we suggest some specific implications of this value differentiation for higher education.

I

As Rosemary Park has suggested, excellence and equality must be reincorporated or redefined to be operative values, with operative meanings, relevant to our place in time, in our culture. We agree. Almost everything about us is changing — our world, our society, our institutions, and our people. And each of us must wonder what *excellence* and *equality* mean for human beings sharing our culture today.

Institutional change and crisis are the hallmarks of our times. Many of our important social institutions — the family, church, school, government, and the university — are either besieged financially, rapidly losing the people's allegiance, or finding their very legitimacy challenged. Throughout our society, we are in a time of radical change, accompanied by a remarkable loss of credibility among those persons and institutions which have traditionally been the sources of value, authority, and power. Higher education and the university are not immune to this change, and their future must be explored in the light of their intimate relationship with our entire cultural transformation.

We find our society existing at this point in history between conflicting cultures, each experientially grounded and each with its own value system and ethic. Although the diversity of persons and views is very great and simplification can be hazardous, we believe the contemporary cultural conflict can best be understood as the clash of two cultural models. Let us refer to them as the old culture and the new culture. The old culture was generated in a world of scarcity — most notably from our basic struggle for survival and from the insecurity of the depression. The new culture has been more recently generated — since World War II — in a time of affluence (the problems of distribution notwithstanding).

For persons whose gut experience is scarcity, the moral imperative is competition; but for persons whose gut experience is plenty, the moral imperative is sharing. The old culture emphasizes work, intellectuality, accumulation, elitism, and conformity. In more difficult times, these values were necessary for personal and collective survival. But the new culture rejects the work ethic, rejects conformity, is more sensuous in its orientation, more democratic, and more trusting of diversity, feelings, and the human body.

Such different cultures, with such different moral imperatives, result in contrary attitudes and values about almost everything — the value of human life, freedom, responsibility, war, peace, consciousness, drugs, marriage, sexuality, God, religion, pleasure, property, emotions, the human body — even human nature and human potential — and, likely, even about excellence and about quality. The most fundamental divergence has to do with the nature and value of human life. The implicit bias underlying the traditional culture and its institutions is that man is evil, depraved, sinful, or — at best — neutral, and that he must look to institutions, authority, religion, education, and the like to save him. The new culture assumes man's fundamental and spontaneous responsibility and trustworthiness and sees the old culture's institutions, with their negative assumptions, as the greatest threat to personal wholeness and integrity.

It is ironic that the achievements of our old culture and its traditional values, along with the sacrifices and generosity of its people, have helped give birth to a new and different culture. Beyond this irony is the painful realization that the experiences and perceptions of many persons who have grown up in this new kind of world — in the past twenty-five years — are radically different, in their expectations as human beings, in their attitudes, and in their most deeply held values. It is not so much a matter of choice, nor a matter of preference, nor a matter of right and wrong that underlies our split cultures, but rather a matter of experiencing the evolved character of our world. And along with affluence we have technology, automation, universal education, rapid transportation, and the mass media — all leading to an evolving consciousness, an evolving character of humanity. This takes shape as something very different in the way human beings experience life, how they think, how they feel, how they believe, how they hope, and even how they love.

No wonder we recognize a cultural crisis and an institutional crisis. Our institutions, including the university, were conceived and constructed out of the old experience, the old culture, the traditional ethic — and they served them well. In fact, though, our institutions served traditional values so well that they evolved a new world, a new experience, a new culture, a new consciousness, and a new ethic.

Along with the new experience, and probably as a result of universal education and the mass media, there exists a curious, and by now obvious, demystification process. It is much like the way science in the past served to demystify religion, and all the world was transformed as persons began to see through old myths of power, authority, and truth. Today, in similar fashion more and more persons are unwilling to accept without argument, to swallow whole, what is told them by persons in positions of power, command, and governance. Questions are being asked, little is taken for granted, the burden of proof is often on those in authority.

And along with the new experience comes a process of *horizontalization*, especially the horizontalization of institutions. Our traditional institutions depend on a model of someone up above, with power, truth, and answers, making the decisions for all the rest of us and handing these decisions on down, often in the form of rules for us to follow. In our society today such vertical authority is under attack within most of our traditional institutions — family, religion, work, government, and education, including the university. The new-culture persons are much less willing to accept from on high what some authority says is true, or right, or what you ought to do, or how you ought to be; instead, there is a thrust from the bottom that is upending almost every institution in our society.

And along with the new experience of our radically changed external world comes a radically different experience of our internal world. Throughout history, we have lived in a world of scarcity; as a result, man chose — in order to survive — to limit himself, to suppress his body and his emotions in order to concentrate all his energy in his intellect and thereby encounter and conquer the threatening environment.

Now, in this new world which we have created and entered, man can relax some, let himself be and become more whole, functioning not only through his intellect but as a complete person of mind and body and emotions, functioning holistically. Franklin Murphy, former chancellor of UCLA, has characterized this evolution as man now choosing to become the being of "I feel, therefore I am."

Somewhere, somehow, in this movement out of an old world culture, we see emerging something new in the way human beings experience and envision themselves — a radically different way for human beings to see human nature, potential, values, relationships, and institutions.

II

What are the significant implications for the future of our institutions, for the future of the university?

First, we must recognize that the tensions between excellence and equality are endemic to our entire society. From our legislative–political perspective, the conflict between these values seems to be present in all our public institutions and public policy processes. It is not surprising, then, that we have institutionalized this tension in our system of higher education.

It is important to recognize that Americans have always defined both excellence and equality in terms of competition. Just as excellence has usually meant competitive excellence, equality has meant equality in competition. Richard Hofstadter made this point well when he stated that "American traditions . . . show a strong bias toward egalitarian democracy, but it has been a democracy in cupidity rather than a democracy in fraternity."

The problem with competition is that it tends to imply a single standard of excellence and a single standard of equality. This works reasonably well when there is concensus about values and standards. But it breaks down when there is disagreement and polarization about values. Today there is in our society and culture just such a breakdown of concensus. And the times demand a rethinking and restatement of the meaning of *excellence* and of *equality.*

The most basic assumptions and premises about human life are at issue here. It is from what persons experience of themselves and their lives that they derive their vision of man and human nature and human potential; thus it is from their vision of man that they derive conceptions of excellence and equality. And it is in a society divided over the nature of man and the meaning of life that we are now faced with the necessity to reexamine our values and their relationship to institutions of learning.

Second, it might be hoped that the university could be the place where both models — of culture and of man — could be tested, and where a valuable dialogue between new and old would occur. But the university is so much a part of the traditional culture that it shares most of its assumptions and, for the most part, resists the notion that there might be another legitimate model.

The university is the servant of the traditional culture in at least three important ways: for one, in its exclusive emphasis upon intellectuality, abstraction, and theory. There is little regard for experiential learning, little respect for the affective domain of human life. The university fragments man just as its disciplines fragment knowledge. The affective and cognitive are split, and as a result, it is forgotten that the whole man may be greater than the sum of his separated parts. (Yet recent research demonstrates the relationship of affective and cognitive development.)

In addition, the university assumes that most persons learn at the same rate in the same sequence — the *lockstep* so much discussed recently. This is basically an industrial assembly line model of learning, which relies on an external uniform standard rather than on the needs and wants of the individual person. It also implies that the institution, and not the persons served, knows best what its clients need.

Moreover, the university is elitist. In its educational processes, the university has perpetuated the socioeconomic dominance of the haves while doing little for the have-nots. California's Master Plan provides a good case study here. Despite our claims that higher education provides an avenue of social mobility, we persist in using culturally, economically, and socially biased admissions criteria that exclude most lower- and lower-middle-class persons from our "better" institutions. The same holds true in research, where universities and their faculties have served the powerful (agribusiness, the Department of Defense) and, in so doing, have helped perpetuate a socioeconomic order stacked heavily in favor of those with wealth and power. We are suggesting that the new culture challenges our universities to become genuinely person-centered and pluralistic — not only in its intellectual dialogue but also in its teaching, learning, and research.

Third, our difficulties are not simply the simpler ones of different thinking; rather, they are the more complex and painful ones of different feelings, and different visions, and different values. This is true throughout our society. The conflicts on our campuses, in our streets, cities, and ghettos are conflicts of differing experiences, perceptions, and values. So we cannot expect our path to be comfortable or easy.

Fourth, it is in our institutions of higher education that this cultural revolution has been experienced most painfully, because it is precisely within them that the persons and aspirations of the new culture collide with the traditional way things have been.

In *The Pursuit of Loneliness*, Philip Slater suggests that higher education may be hopelessly caught between the new and the old cultures. The persons who pay for colleges and universities are mostly persons of the old culture, who will not continue to pay if higher education caters to the perceived needs, wants, and goals of new-culture persons. But if higher education refuses to cater to the new culture, young persons may well destroy or abandon it (there is already much evidence of both). If Slater is correct, the universities are in danger of being destroyed in the collision of the two cultures.

However, there is another possibility. The universities could become the place where our society learns the value of tolerating and respecting and encouraging diversity. If we can envision and realize this possibility, the conflict between excellence and equality may be much less severe than we have imagined. And because these are indeed revolutionary times which (to paraphrase Lincoln) respect neither old lines nor old laws, we may ultimately come to the place where excellence and equality converge. Somehow, then, discovering how to bridge this gap between cultures is a life-or-death adventure for our public institutions of higher education.

Fifth, we must confront and accept the realization that there is no going back. There is no way to abolish television, or technology, or universal education — and these are precisely the forces and conditions that bring us into a new world, with its new culture and new persons. Because the old balance cannot be revived, we must discover and strike a new balance.

Sixth, in so doing, we must recognize that persons at the bottom of our society, who have not shared equally in opportunity (for whatever reason), have now seen, for the first time, what they are missing. The availability of television and other media in every home, in every city, in every part of our country, has let every person at the bottom see what others have. And they are constantly urged to want and to expect and to struggle for those very things. And besides the thrust toward material equality, we have the liberation movements — Black or women or gay or Chicano or children or whatever.

The have-nots — materially or psychologically — aren't going to be put aside or ignored; they are here to stay, and they deserve to stay. What they are probably doing, most profoundly, is proposing and reaching for a new operative definition of *equality* (what does it mean to be equal as a person?) — a definition that recognizes the inherent and equal value and worth of each individual human being and the inherent right of each person to be himself.

Seventh, we must recognize that it is not only those persons at the bottom who are envisioning themselves and life and human existence in a new way. At the same time we find those students, our pride and joy, who have done the very best in school, who come to "the best" of our educational institutions, experiencing and envisioning life in a new way. The most sensitive of our better students are the persons who are most readily sharing in the attempted redefinition of *equality*.

They are asking our society and higher education to redefine *excellence* and adapt to pluralistic models of excellence. Certainly, the traditional model and traditional learning experiences should be available to those who wish to pursue them. But other models should be available, including noncompetitive models which recognize that: (a) learning and growth are valuable in themselves; (b) learning and growth are often best judged by the learner in relation to his own life, rather than by comparison with the achievements of others; (c) experiential learning is as valuable as purely intellectual learning; and (d) affective and cognitive learning are inextricably interrelated. And they may well be searching out another new and operative definition of *excellence*. What does it mean to be an excellent human being, what does it mean to be a person?

Thus we have, at this point in time, persons on the bottom and persons on the top reaching toward a new vision, a new search, a new ethic. Persons at the top and bottom are moving away from allegiance to institutions toward allegiance to persons. They are moving away from elitism and competition and moving toward a more democratic society. This ought to be recognized as a rejection neither of excellence nor or equality, but only of our traditional idea of these terms, in a search for new and more human meanings for both.

Eighth, we must recognize, and nourish, the movement of our society away from elitism (although not away from excellence) and toward equality. We have already experienced some movement away from a social, political, or religious elite. More powerfully now, we are experiencing a rejection of racial elitism and of sexual elitism — each so deeply ingrained in so many of us and in our public institutions.

But there is another elitism which is now being questioned — our bias about who we are as human beings, and about the respective values of the various parts of ourselves as human beings. For many years, Western man has assumed the elitism of intellect over body. We have so elevated the intellect as the measure of a person that we readily judge and categorize him by measuring his intelligence quotient. And the university is the very embodiment of this most basic elitism — no wonder it is experiencing so much challenge and conflict and pain. We must now examine the origins and the appropriateness and the ramifications of the mind–body split which underlies Western culture. This examination is not intended to separate out our intellects; rather, it ought to elevate our bodies to their existential place as coequal partners of the whole human being.

Ninth, Rosemary Park suggests that the problem of institutions is the lack of consensus about the definition of an *educated man*. Far deeper and more vital is the lack of consensus about the nature of man, and about the meaning and value of individual human life.

III

The answers are not clear, but each of us must begin by asking the right questions. Those questions and our responses must fully recognize and accept all the human reality of our times.

We must recognize ourselves, and all other human beings, and all that is happening within and between and to human beings today. In times of scarcity, persons need to curtail themselves, and conform and fit together artificially, in order to survive; in times of affluence, they can and will be more unique and whole and diverse.

In times of ignorance, persons could be kept down; in times of universal education and mass communication, persons must be encouraged up! Individual persons are bringing themselves, with their minds and bodies and feelings and needs and wants, to institutions of higher education. They will be differing persons, with differing experiences, needs, wants, goals, and expectations. The true criteria for higher education is whether it will respond to each of them, to their individuality.

The real challenge for higher education today is whether it is ready and able and willing to envision a new model of man, and to recognize and respond to the new man and woman knocking at its doors.

Epilogue: The University "Bundle": A Study of the Balance Between Differentiation and Integration

by TALCOTT PARSONS

This paper grows out of a dialogue between Neil Smelser and myself about his study of the California state system of public higher education during the last twenty years. The university system in California has been conspicuous for its broad organizational syndrome — what Smelser calls the bundle. This syndrome has especially characterized the elite sector of the American system of higher education generally, concentrating on the "full" university. Smelser has expressed considerable skepticism about the viability of this syndrome, which he believes is largely responsible for the state of "functional overloading" and results from what he calls a "resistance to differentiation."

I am inclined to regard this functional overloading of the university as mainly a consequence of its extremely rapid growth, including a generous measure of inflationary pressure (see Chapter 7 of *The American University*). It seems substantially less likely that it results, as Smelser suggests, mainly from what he calls "resistance to differentiation." By this latter phrase he mainly refers to resistance to the separating out of the various components of what we are calling the bundle. He speaks especially of the possibilities of the organizational separation of teaching from research, and of the separation of what in California terms is called lower division teaching from the last two years of the undergraduate program. He does not, so far as I am aware, stress the undesirability of a continuing association between faculties of arts and sciences and professional faculties in the same universities.

There have also been external sources of overloading, especially of the faculty role, as well as of those internal to the university. I think here of the vast increase in interinstitutional communication and citizenship, through such media as conferences and the development of the activities and size of professional associations, especially though not exclusively in the disciplines. The typical elite university professor has indeed become a man who is subject to a multiplicity of demands.

It is very difficult to judge how much of this involvement should be regarded as excessive. A good deal of such involvement in the recent past probably should be. The main object of the present paper, however, is to argue what in a sense is the obverse case — namely, that great benefits accrue to the modern university system from the connectedness of the various components of the bundle.

The aim of the present paper is to probe more deeply into both the nature and the functional significance of the bundle. It thus constitutes a kind of epilogue to the book, *The American University*, on which I recently collaborated with Gerald Platt.[1]

It seems best to begin with an outline of the bundle. The first primary characteristic is the prominence in the typical high-level American university of a faculty of arts and sciences. Such a faculty is normally organized as a set of partially independent departments, each of which focuses on one of the well-recognized intellectual disciplines. Such faculties cover the range of these disciplines, which are conventionally grouped into three main categories — humanities, natural sciences, and social sciences. Although there are overlappings, this is structural uniformity. Some units are organized for research and teaching on other bases than disciplines, but they are on the whole secondary to the main departmental structure.

In addition to their range of intellectual content, such faculties are multifunctional in another principal respect: they combine research and teaching. A highly conspicuous feature of the American university in its development during the present century has been the institutionalization of the research function as fundamental to the professional role. Research is no longer carried on by

[1] Talcott Parsons and Gerald M. Platt, *The American University* (Cambridge: Harvard University Press, 1973).

interested amateurs, but is highly professionalized. At the same time, most such professional research is not carried on in specialized research institutes outside the university, but as part of the academic professional's role within the university. The function most closely associated with research itself is graduate training of future members of the academic profession who typically will be researchers and teachers. An important part of this function is carried on through various modes of formal and informal apprenticeship.

Another prominent feature of the bundle is that the faculties of arts and sciences typically are engaged in general education, primarily at the undergraduate level. In part this undergraduate teaching has been oriented to certified qualifications for later occupational roles, but on the whole it has been declining in relative importance and is less prominent in the higher prestige institutions than the lower. Of course, one important function has been to qualify students for entry into both graduate school and postgraduate professional schools. The undergraduate college within the university was not displaced by graduate schools; rather, a kind of symbiosis has developed between the two. Organizational forms vary, but this is clearly a central pattern.

Another conspicuous feature of the American university is the absorption into the university of such professional schools as law, medicine, and engineering. These have increasingly become integral parts of the university, although they retain some autonomy. There has also been a notable development in recent decades of new professional schools in such fields as education, administration, and social work. The professional schools in general, and increasingly, have also institutionalized research as part of the professional role structure of their faculty members, and this in particular binds them to faculties of arts and sciences.

In addition to these formal, structural aspects of the bundle, there are two other important features. First, although there is no formal organizational component especially concerned with the function of supplying knowledge, competence, and cognitive standards to that diffuse group called intellectuals, there is no doubt of the universities' importance in an interchange with outside elements. Some members of university faculties can rightly be classified as intellectuals. The same term, however, can be applied to others, such as writers, journalists, politicians, artists, or generally interested citizens. Most of them are college graduates, and they are likely to be in close touch with currents of thought within the universities. In the present century the universities have developed a central role in this context which did not exist to the same degree in the nineteenth century.

The final characteristic of the bundle is more highly formalized; namely, the existence of a ramified nexus of relationships, dealing with intellectual subject matters, which operates across the divisions into particular university units. Perhaps the most conspicuous aspect of this nexus is the set of national and international associations concerned with particular disciplines. Such associations started to develop at about the same time that the university structure was taking shape, in the latter nineteenth and early twentieth centuries. In addition to associations organized around particular disciplines, a considerable number were built on cross-disciplinary bases. The existence of this nexus means that the typical university faculty member is in rather intensive communication with colleagues outside his own institution, both within his own discipline and in wider relationships. For example, the members of such organizations as the National Academy of Sciences, the American Philosophical Society, and the American Academy of Arts and Sciences include not only representatives of a variety of disciplines and people attached to a variety of academic institutions, but a significant minority whose occupations are not academic.

Clearly, the bundle which constitutes the typical American university nexus has two primary aspects. It embodies a rather sharply differentiated institutionalization of functions that are concentrated on cognitive concerns more or less for their own sake. This is particularly true of research, at least in some sectors, and of graduate training of future academic professionals. The relatively high differentiation and consequent autonomy of this "core" complex, as Platt and I have called it, is both characteristic and relatively recent in the present state of development.

And there is also a complex set of concerns and interests that brings the university in contact with nonacademic sectors of the society. The two massively formal ones are the undergraduate college and the so-called professional schools. The great majority of college graduates will not become academic professionals, and the great majority of professional school graduates will not teach but practice. A substantial proportion, probably a considerable majority, of "intellectuals" are not academic professionals either, and this dual reference of the academic system is vital.

SOME THEORETICAL CONSIDERATIONS

The remainder of this paper will be concerned with the parallels between the modern economy and the cognitive complex institutionalized in the modern university. It is an essential keynote that these two subsystems of action will not only be compared, but that they stand in a relation of developmental succession to each other. That is, the modern economy was largely a product of the Industrial Revolution, and some features of it became a primary storm center of social conflict and preoccupation of ideological discussions, centering notably about the roles of labor and capital. The rise of the cognitive complex to a position of comparable centrality is a culminating consequence of the Educational Revolution, as we have called it. This, notably at the level of the role structure of higher education, has become a storm center of disturbance and a primary focus of ideological preoccupation centered on the status of cognitive standards, of the academic profession and of students. The shift has been from an adaptive level within the social system — the economy, to the adaptive level in the general system of action, with special stress on the *cultural* level.*

There are important structural differences in the economy between the units primarily concerned with the production of goods — manufacturing — and those primarily concerned with mediating economic to noneconomic sectors of the society — sales organizations. We suggest that there is a parallel distinction of organizational type in the cognitive complex. Research is the function most directly concerned with the production of new knowledge. Teaching, as a function, is more concerned with mediating the output of this knowledge to various categories of the population not equipped simply to take it as it emerges from the research process. Platt and I have developed a concept originating in a characteristic of professional schools which we apply to other mediating functions of the university. This is the concept of the

*On this background, see *The American University*.

clinical focus, the mobilization of relevant knowledge for the effective performance of some function other than the pursuit of knowledge itself. This concept is especially relevant in the field of medicine. Obviously the organization of knowledge in a clinical context is very different from that of intellectual disciplines.

The so-called science of medicine is not itself a discipline, but a body of knowledge put together for its relevance to the medical practitioner and drawn from many different disciplines. One reason why the intrinsically intimate relations between law and the social sciences have been hampered is that law is primarily a clinical discipline especially concerned with the settlement of cases, and its mode of organization cuts across that of the social science disciplines. There are parallel factors in the reorganization of knowledge appropriate to the undergraduate teaching functions and the output which is relevant to intellectuals.

Clinically relevant knowledge, however, is still subject to the fundamental cognitive canons of validity, although the standards of significance vary somewhat from the primarily cognitive focus. Cognitive interests have to be combined with noncognitive in this whole range of applied or articulated contexts. The valuation of health is not a cognitive interest, nor is the valuation of satisfactory settlement of disputes and maintenance of normative social order which are the double focus of law. Given the importance of the clinical contexts, what constitutes the social machinery of mediation between the core aspects of the academic system and these other partially, if not primarily, noncognitive contexts? The range of clinical foci are analogous to the problems of sales organization in the market systems.

In a second basic parallel to the economy, generalized symbolic media of interchange play a crucial part in the academic system — both internally and in its relations with the outside world — analogous to the economic role of money. Because knowledge is primarily focused in the cultural system, which is related to society at the level of the general system of action, Platt and I have given great prominence to *intelligence*, which we conceived as a generalized symbolic medium of interchange with functions comparable to those of money in the economy.[2] This unfamiliar use of

[2]*Ibid.*, chap. 2.

the concept of intelligence is distinct from its more common meaning as a trait of the individual personality.[3]

As a generalized medium of interchange we conceive intelligence as circulating. It can be acquired by individuals — for example, through learning, and it is spent as a resource which facilitates the solution of cognitively significant problems. It should, however, be clearly distinguished from knowledge, just as money should be distinguished from concrete commodities. The parallel to the point that money has no "value in use" also applies to intelligence. We may say that a person has more than the usual intelligence, but this should be understood as being parallel to the statement that a man has more wealth than others. In neither case is this category of "possession" a trait of his personality.

The cognitive enterprise is institutionalized at the social level, and a primary aspect of its institutionalization is the modern university with the bundle structure. At the social level the university and its subunits, as well as some of the interuniversity associations, constitute communities. Therefore, we have paid special attention to the generalized medium, at the social-system level, that is particularly concerned with the integrative functions centered on various kinds of community within the larger society.[4] This generalized medium we have called *influence*, and we have tried to combine the treatment of intelligence on the one hand, and influence on the other.

We conceive all generalized media, like money, to be contentless. The idea that money has no value in use, but only value as a medium of exchange, is very familiar from the work of the classical economists. Similarly, intelligence is not knowledge but the capacity to mobilize what it takes to produce or command knowledge and the other primary outputs and factors of the cognitive system. Intelligence can be converted into influence, and sometimes vice versa, through the *institutionalization* of cognitive functions in social organizations. So far as this occurs, cognitive excellence and cognitive achievement will acquire institutionalized *prestige* — the primary institutional way that influence as a medium acquires its legitimacy and justification. Those with pres-

[3]*Ibid.*, see especially chap. 2 and the Technical Appendix.
[4]Talcott Parsons, *Politics and Social Structure* (New York: Free Press, 1969).

tige have access to influence, and through influence the capacity
to persuade others of the merits of their positions on various matters. But we do not *conceive* influence to be intrinsically persuasive, as items of concrete information may be. It is, rather, a way of
securing control over intrinsic persuaders, like information or
commitments to action, and over factors of persuasiveness.

As a social structure, the university is differentiated by the
relative primacy of cognitive functions, but within this conception
it has all the primary features of an institutionalized complex. Cognitive function is primarily anchored at the cultural level. For this
reason, in our classification of social subsystems we place the university in the "fiduciary" system. As an institutional complex, the
university holds fiduciary responsibility for the maintenance,
transmission, and development of knowledge in particular, and of
cognitive functions and resources in general.

Finally, we should outline the units in the nexus of relationships where intelligence and influence have a combined relevance.
First, there is intensity of concern. This is at its highest level for
the academic professional as an individual, and for departments,
faculties, universities, scholarly associations, and the like as collectivities. To become an academic professional is to accept a major
stake in implementing the standards central to the cognitive function — a far greater stake than other occupational groups impose on
their members, and the same applies *pari passu* to academically
specialized collectivities.

Intensity in this sense may be regarded as the primary index
of level of commitment to the values of cognitive rationality, the
paramount value-pattern institutionalized in differentiated
academic organizations. Among the manifestations of intense
commitments in this direction are high valuation of knowledge and
competence and high respect for the standards of cognitive validity
and significance. It is, above all, in the intensity of their commitments to cognitive values that the special position of faculty members — especially senior faculty members — in the academic system is grounded. That commitment underlies the institutions of
both tenure and academic freedom. The relative disadvantaged-
ness of students in these respects is grounded in the recency of
their involvement in the academic world and the fact that, for most

of them, this involvement will be temporary and not — as it is for academic professionals — a career commitment.

The second unit is the extensive nexus within which the combined intelligence-influence medium can be effectively used, parallel to Adam Smith's famous idea of the "extent of the market." An important part of our argument rests on this nexus and the possibilities it opens up for the analogue of Smith's division of labor: namely, the differentiation of the components of the cognitive complex. These possibilities constitute a particularly important condition for a high level of the "gross cognitive product."

A fundamental theorem of modern sociology states that the unit of a social system always has multiple modes of participation, never a single mode. This means that an individual will be involved not in one role but in a plurality of roles. Thus, even if he is a specialist in cognitive functions, he will have other roles — familial ones, for example — in which the cognitive component is less salient. Hence it is important what modes of articulation occur, between the involvements of units in the cognitive complex in relationships where cognitive considerations are crucial and those other participations and interests where the cognitive component is less important.

RESEARCH AS THE STORM CENTER OF ACADEMIC DISTURBANCE

The prominence of the research function has played a great role in the development of the modern American university, particularly in recent years. Indeed, in one set of aspects, the recent phase of the educational revolution may be considered parallel to the Industrial Revolution. The primary social disturbances generated by the Industrial Revolution were focused on the status of labor, on the one hand as a role or a category of concrete human beings, and, on the other, as a factor of economic production. Out of these disturbances came a very powerful ideology, broadly called socialism, which gave birth to some extremely important social movements and had immense repercussions in the intellectual world. Its most influential version was formulated by Karl Marx.

Two key concepts of Marxist theory are particularly relevant to the present problem — the *alienation* of labor and the *exploitation* of labor. (These have recently been greatly clarified by

Anthony Giddens and Jeffrey Alexander.[5] Marx relied heavily on the general framework of utilitarian thought and also on some classical economic theorists, notably Ricardo. The alienation of labor consisted, above all, in the treatment of *labor power* as a commodity. The reasons for the exploitation of labor were that labor was the sole source of production (that is, the only important factor of production), but the laborer did not control the production process and did not own either the means of production or its resulting commodities.

Neither of these propositions is acceptable to the main currents of economic theory today. Labor is not, like commodities, a *product* of the process of economic production — that is, a category of output — but is a *factor* of production. Commodities — or *goods*, in recent usage — are now considered the result of a combination of production factors of which labor is only one element; the others are land, capital, and organization. Therefore, it is not theoretically legitimate to identify a category of economic output with a category of factor in a plural-factor process. The error goes back to Ricardo, who did not have an adequate analysis of the determinants of economic value or utility on the demand side of the supply-demand relationship. The discovery of the principle of marginal utility would later solve this problem.[6]

As Alexander[7] has shown, Marx treated the functioning of the capitalistic economy as wholly dominated by the play of economic interest, within the utilitarian framework of theoretical analysis. The development of capitalism, according to Marx, suppressed a crucial aspect of precapitalist society — what can perhaps legitimately be called *Gemeinschaft*. Marx repeatedly refers to the social character of labor and labor's alienation from its rightfully social character. But it can be argued that, from the point of view of the structure of society, the crucial event was that labor became a

[5] Anthony Giddens, *Capitalism and Modern Social Theory* (Cambridge: Cambridge University Press, 1971), and Jeffrey Alexander, "The Transcendence of the Utilitarian Paradigm: An Essay on Marx, Durkheim, and Weber" (as yet unfinished Ph.D. dissertation, University of California, Berkeley). See also, Neil J. Smelser, *Social Change in the Industrial Revolution* (Chicago: University of Chicago Press, 1959).

[6] Cf. Joseph A. Schumpeter, *History of Economic Analysis*, edited from a manuscript by E. B. Schumpeter (New York: Oxford University Press, 1954).

[7] Alexander, *op. cit.* (n. 5, above).

mobile factor of production. This was institutionalized especially in the separation of the context of economic production, the factory, from the kinship-oriented household. Most sociologists today regard this as a process of differentiation. Marx overwhelmingly regarded it as a process of destruction of the nexus of solidarities in which the worker had lived.[8]

In stating that research was the storm center of recent and current academic disturbance, we meant research as the spearhead of the differentiation of the cognitive complex relative to other sectors of the society, but particularly of the fiduciary subsystem in its special relation to culture. It is most closely analogous, in the economy, to that sector of differentiated "capitalistic" enterprise which grew prodigiously under the factory system. The clear primacy of economic orientation in the factory parallels the clear primacy of cognitive considerations in "pure" research, which has thus brought about complex repercussions on the other element of both society and culture in which cognitive factors have been prominently involved.

In closer parallel to the industrial case in Marx's time are what Platt and I have called *cognitive standards of validity and significance*. This is *not* a category of cognitive output, but a primary *factor* in making qualitatively improved cognitive output possible. It occupies a similar position to that of labor as an economic factor of production. As such, it is an input to the cognitive system from the cultural complex, just as labor is an input to the economy from the fiduciary system of society. The cognitive output parallel to commodities is what we call knowledge, as a category of cultural objects, whereas commodities are a category mainly of physical objects evaluated for their economic utility. Cognitive standards are those, for the social sciences particularly, analyzed by Weber in his studies of the problem of objectivity in social science knowledge,[9] notably the "schema of proof" formalized by Von Schelting.[10] This set of standards is at the heart of the great con-

[8] Robert Bellah, "Intellectual and Society in Japan," *Dedalus* (Spring 1972), pp. 89–115.

[9] Max Weber, "Objectivity in Social Science and Social Policy," in *Max Weber on the Methodology of the Social Science*, trans. and ed. Edward A. Shils and Henry A. Finch (New York: Free Press, 1949), chap. 2, pp. 50–112.

[10] Alexander von Schelting, Max Weber's *Wissenschaftslehre* (Tubingen: J.C.B. Mohr (P. Siebeck), 1934).

troversy about value-free social science, or science in general, which parallels the famous controversy about the alienation of labor. The idea of value freedom in Weber's sense, discussed very specifically in *The American University*,[11] is widely judged a derogation of the dignity of culture in general. Nor is it far-fetched to say this parallels the conception of labor treated as a commodity. A factor in the generation of a category of outputs is being confused here with the outputs themselves. The confusion stems from the feeling that it is illegitimate to treat cognitive standards as a mobile resource clearly differentiated from other components in the production of knowledge, and to treat knowledge distinct from other components of culture.

There is then the tendency to impute to the modern cognitive world the idea that only firm adherence to these cognitive standards produces valid and significant knowledge. This notion is parallel to the famous labor theory of value, which alleged that labor alone created commodities. On the contrary, cognitive standards constitute *one* factor in the generation of knowledge and the other cognitive outputs. The other factors are first the *valuation*, based on cultural premises, of cognitive rationality, which is *not* identical with the substantive standards of cognitive validity and significance. Second, there is the *motivation* of researchers to solve strictly cognitive problems, which cannot be taken for granted as a simple function of the existence of the standards themselves. Finally, there are the *affective meanings* of cognitive pursuits, as compared to the other alternatives open to units in the social system. A special combination of all four sets of factors is needed to produce valid and significant knowledge — no one of them alone is *the* agent of its creation.

Current ideological controversy, then, concerns the alleged alienation of man's cultural heritage by subjecting it to the discipline of cognitive standards, a discipline analogous to the economic discipline of the labor factor. The same ideological controversies involve an idea of the *exploitation* of cultural standards by pressing them within the mold of this discipline, and the alleged suppression of alternative possibilities, notably in moral–political and expressive directions.

Such alienation is from a matrix parallel to that of

[11] Parsons and Platt, *op. cit.* (n. 1, above), chap. 2.

Gemeinschaft as the alleged basis of the solidarity of precapitalist society. Because the primary focus now has been transferred to the level of the general theory of action, rather than to that of the social system as such, the central concept of this matrix is probably an aspect of the cultural system, and was formulated in a famous and major concept of Weber's.

Weber called it *Gesinnungsethik*, as contrasted with *Verantwortungsethik*. The latter is easily translated as "ethic of responsibility." *Gesinnungethik* is difficult to translate appropriately — perhaps "ethic of sentiment" is adequate. Weber distinguished between these two types mainly with respect to their separate attitudes toward the consequences of decisions to act. What characterized *Gesinnungsethik*, Weber said, was the refusal to consider or take responsibility for consequences. Morally one was obligated to "do what was right" from the point of view of some pure and absolute standard, and to let it go at that. If the action in question had morally objectionable consequences, in Weber's religious terminology, the responsibility for them was God's, not man's. The ethic of responsibility, on the other hand, involves responsibility for consequences, even if indirect and unintended. The relevance to the present context lies in the fact that, in order to take responsibility for consequences, one must *know* what they are, and this knowledge is subject to the canons of *cognitive* validity and significance. The apostle of *Gesinnungsethik* can afford to be non- (if not anti-) intellectual, provided he is subjectively certain his position is right, but the apostle of the ethic of responsibility cannot afford this luxury. To act ethically he *must* be concerned with cognitive matters. This was Weber's own ethical position, and it was surely a very powerful motive for his pursuit of intellectual problems. Weber also felt great concern, in his extensive discussion and documentation, about the major role of *Gesinnungsethik* in social and cultural history.

It is quite clear that the ethic of responsibility postulates a much more highly differentiated cultural, social, and psychological orientation to problems of the moral legitimacy of action than does the ethic of *Gesinnung*. The apostle of the latter can merge moral–evaluative and expressive standards — my use of the term *sentiment* above is meant to suggest this — and either eliminate cognitive considerations altogether, or accept simplistic and cognitively dubious formulae. (Compare with Erikson's remarks, in his *Daedalus* paper on youth, about the "totalistic" stance of many young radicals today).[12]

Characteristically, radical and revolutionary movements postulate a "dedifferentiated" version of the main culture of our time. This was certainly true of the radical (Communist) wing of Marxian socialism — and certainly of Marx's economic theories — and we think it is also true of the radical opposition to the contemporary university system.

FORMAL STATEMENT OF THE CORRESPONDENCE BETWEEN MARXIAN IDEOLOGY AND CONTEMPORARY ANTI-UNIVERSITY IDEOLOGY

In the previous section, I argued that there is a very striking formal similarity between the Marxian analysis of capitalism, both as economy and as society in the sense of *Gemeinschaft*, and the analysis (much less sharp and systematic than Marx's) by some New Left spokesmen of contemporary alienation, with special reference to the role of the cognitive complex. This formal similarity throws a bright light on the structure of felt strains and their symbolization in the current and recent academic situation. In sum, parallels are as follows:

First, the emergence by differentiation of the research complex from the more general matrix of cognitive concerns, especially teaching, seems analogous to the differentiation of factory production from those modes imbedded in relatively diffuse community settings, such as the peasant community and the town handicraft system. Second, the analogy to the role of factory labor is the use of clearly differentiated standards of cognitive validity and significance as the standards defining satisfactory research. From our formal analytical point of view, the use of these standards constitutes one of the primary factors in the generation of knowledge and other cognitive outputs.

This is a mode of implementing values of cognitive rationality which is directly parallel to economic rationality. Furthermore, as a formal factor in the genesis of knowledge, the use of cognitive standards occupies a place analogous to that of labor as a factor in

[12] Erik Erikson, "Reflections on the Dissent of Contemporary Youth," *Daedalus* (Winter 1970), pp. 154–176.

economic production. Third, parallel to the sense in which Marx saw labor as alienated, we may speak of a more recent version of this concept as the alienation of the research-dominated intellectual worker from control of intellectual output and of the intellectual product itself. This extrusion from control allegedly subordinates the primacy of noncognitive factors to the interests of those who are bound by cognitive standards. As we have suggested, the matrix of this differentiation is what Weber called *Gesinnung*. Furthermore, the primary aspects of *Gesinnung* are a diffuse, undifferentiated combination of moral–evaluative and expressive concerns with "religious" concerns. This pattern clarifies what is often meant by *relevance* as a criterion of knowledge and cognitive procedures. From the point of view of dissident ideologists, relevant knowledge and its relevant pursuit would essentially subordinate cognitive considerations to moral–evaluative and expressive ones, thus turning the tables.

Fourth, as we have noted, interpreters of Marx[13] have laid great stress on the equation in Marxist thought of labor and commodities. There is, however, a theoretical difficulty in treating labor as a kind of commodity: in later post-Marxian economic theory, labor is a factor of production, whereas commodities are a category of economic output.

In the case of the cognitive complex, the parallel lies in the tendency to make absolute the relevance of purely cognitive standards by equating cognitive concerns specifically with knowledge, which is a kind of a scientistic orientation. The relationship is established by the concepts of economic rationality on the one hand and those of cognitive rationality on the other.[14] The *discipline* of these sets of rational standards is allegedly the focus of alienation in the two cases.

Fifth, the one-factor theory in the generation of relevant output is closely connected with these points. In Marxism, it is the famous "labor theory of value," the theoretical device for denying significance to the other factors of production and for equating labor and commodities. In the cognitive context there is a tendency to confuse what for Weber were the canons of the objectivity of knowledge, especially in social science, with the factors involved in

[13] For example, see Giddens, *op. cit.* (n. 5, above).
[14] See Parsons and Platt, *op. cit.* (n. 1, above), chap. 2.

the *social role* of the seeker after knowledge — the *Wissenschaftler*, in Weber's term, inadequately translated as scientist.[15] The factors in the scientist's role which are suppressed by this one-factor theory are the values of cognitive rationality itself; the motivations not only of the scientist but of the student to learn — that is, to engage in cognitive learning; and the affective meanings of the manifold alternatives in the commitment of action resources which relate cognitive to noncognitive considerations.[16] This is particularly crucial in the socialization of what Platt and I call the educated citizenry.

Sixth, there is also a close parallel to the Marxian theory of exploitation. Not only is the worker allegedly made into a kind of production machine by capitalism but the surplus value of his output is appropriated by his employer. The institutional mechanism through which this occurs is the ownership of the means of production and of the product by capitalists as their private property. All that is left to the worker in his disadvantaged, competitive position — disadvantaged because he owns neither the means of production nor the product — which is only permits the subsistence of the workers and their reproduction, so that they will not be depleted in one generation. The institutional analogue of private property in the Marxian scheme is, in the dissident academic ideology, the control of cognitive resources by the academic profession, above all as institutionalized in tenure and academic freedom in a stratified manner. It is contended that the professional component, notably tenured senior faculty, have vis-à-vis students a monopoly of control through which they enforce the primacy of cognitive discipline on the academic community as a whole. The political component of the structure of the firm, in the Marxian account, parallels the stratification of the academic community into a superior component of faculty members and an inferior one of students. Students, it is alleged, are compelled by the competitive structure of the system to suppress their noncognitive interests in favor of rigorous cognitive discipline; and even here, control of the primary output of the process, notably knowledge, is appropriated by the superior

[15] Max Weber, "Science as a Vocation," in *From Max Weber: Essays in Sociology* ed. H. H. Gerth and C. Wright Mills (New York: Oxford University Press, 1946), pp. 129–156.
[16] Parsons and Platt, *op. cit.* (n. 1, above), chap. 4.

class and put to uses about which the producers — partly in the role of students — have little, if any, decision-making power. I should link this with the frequent indictments of the university's "complicity" in the interests of the "establishment." It is also implied that students are "forced" to learn primarily in order to become, in their future occupational roles, instruments of the establishment.

The parallel does break down at one crucial point. The only possible analogy to the proletariat in Marxian thought is the student body. The proletariat, however, was treated as a class* in the sense of a transgenerational status group in which the typical individual inherited the manifold of opportunities open to him and would be expected to pass it on to his children. In this sense, of course, the student's status is not a class status, except in the sense that class influences the opportunity for higher education, but this is changing. The basic point, however, is that the status of student is a temporary one which has been overwhelmingly concentrated in one rather small sector of life, the postadolescent.

The consequences of this presumptively illegitimate subjection to cognitive discipline would have to be understood differently from the subjection to the discipline of capitalistic rationality. It would be a kind of diffuse and pervasive penetration of the culture as a whole with the values of cognitive rationality, and it would extend the exploitative subjection of the nonrational components — notably the moral–evaluative and expressive components — inculcated in student years, into the entire future lives of those concerned. It is somewhere along these lines that Marcuse's notion of the "repressive tolerance" of modern societies is to be interpreted. In the Marxian conception, even without tight monopolistic control, the institutionalization of private property in the hands of "capitalists" beat the "formally free" workers into an exploited proletariat. Similarly, even though the academic system is formally free in some respects, a repressive discipline is allegedly imposed on students, and if the socialization process is sufficiently effective, its consequences will permeate the whole of their future lives, and hence the society as a whole.

*That students do constitute a class in this sense has been asserted by some, for example Jerry Farber in *Student as Nigger*. For the reasons stated here, however, I cannot regard his position as acceptable.

Seventh is an aspect of the parallel that is particularly crucial to the problem of the bundle's significance. It will be remembered[17] that, in Marx's view, the division of labor was a primary aspect of the trap into which the worker fell to become the victim of alienation and exploitation. The principal reason for Marx's abhorrence of the division of labor was its relation to a system of *instrumental* interdependence in the market nexus. To be truly independent and free, the worker would have to escape this dependence on others. Expropriation from ownership of the means of production and of products was the index of this state of enslavement.

The bundle (with some modest extensions mentioned earlier) is the analogy in the cognitive world of the economic division of labor. One crucial property of the bundle is its high degree of *differentiation*, both of cognitive subject matter within the disciplines and of functions in relating cognitive content to various societal interests. This differentiated system is a highly integrated nexus analogous to the economic market system. The two important media of intelligence and influence constitute primary mechanisms of this integration. We have argued[18] that just as Adam Smith's concern with the "extent of the market" referred not only to the division of labor but to the conditions of productivity in the economy as a whole, so the extent of the bundle is not only a factor in promoting a high level of differentiatedness, but is also a major factor among the conditions of a high level of cognitive output for the cognitive complex as a whole. But this highly differentiated bundle creates a state of affairs which is analogous to the combination of a high division of labor with extensive markets. In such a state many plural units are interdependent, not specifically on the level of instrumental, but rather of cognitive–communicative, interdependence.

This point is important to the much discussed concept of relevance. As in all ideological discussions, the dissidents tend to make a sharp either–or dichotomy between relevant and irrelevant knowledge. But so essential is interdependence to the bundle that

[17] Giddens, *op. cit.* (n. 5, above); and Ralf Dahrendorf, "On the Origin of Inequality Among Men," in *Social Inequality*, ed. A. Beteille (London: Penguin Modern Sociology Readings, 1969).

[18] Parsons and Platt, *op. cit.* (n. 1, above), chap. 8.

no such sharp dichotomy makes sense. This is illustrated by the relation between the relatively pure intellectual disciplines, on the one hand, and the clinical focus of the organization of knowledge and competence, on the other. For the purpose of relatively pure research, items and subbodies of knowledge have one sort of relevance to each other. For the purposes of clinical practice in the professions, they have another. Although these two sets are not incongruent, they are definitely differentiated. It is not cognitively legitimate to transfer from one context to the other without taking account of the differential contexts in which the various items are relevant.

In this connection, there is a very important sense in which the development of increasingly *theoretical* levels in the cognitive system have become focal to the storm center of cognitive disturbance. Daniel Bell has asserted the special importance, in the postindustrial society, of theoretical knowledge.[19] Theory is a level of cognitive generalization which produces relevance, in our sense, in a much wider range of contexts than those in which more specifically empirical statements of fact can be relevant. We think it significant that the prominence of the bundle at the organizational level of cognitive enterprises has roughly coincided in time with the rapidly increasing importance of theory in the culture of the cognitive system itself.

DIFFERENTIATION AND DEDIFFERENTIATION

Another very important aspect of the parallel we have been drawing has to do with levels of differentiation. The Marxian scheme of the economy suppressed several primary aspects of theoretical differentiation which subsequent economic theory has strongly emphasized. We would like to suggest a parallel in the understanding of the cognitive complex. For the economy there are three types of Marxian failure to recognize differentiations. As we have noted, the first is the differentiation between a factor of production and a category of economic output, as in the famous allegation that labor has become a commodity. The second is the differentiation between plural factors of production, which is denied by the theorem that labor alone is the source of production.

[19] Daniel Bell, "The Cultural Contradictions of Capitalism" *The Public Interest* 21 (Fall 1970), pp. 16–43.

The third is the failure to discriminate categories of economic output, notably goods and services. Although service belongs under the same rubric of output as goods, it is very clearly differentiated from goods. We should also clearly distinguish service as a category of output from labor as a factor of production. Service is a result of combining the labor factor with land, capital, and organization factors.

Much current ideology about the cognitive complex makes absolute cognitive standards as value-free, and identifies the primacy of cognitive standards with knowledge as output. We treat cognitive standards — that is, standards of validity and significance — as a *factor* in the development of cognitive outputs, not as a category of output in itself. Knowledge, however, is a category of output. Cognitive outputs are made possible, not by cognitive standards alone, but by the combination of cognitive standards with three other major factors: first, the values of cognitive rationality, which are different from standards of validity and significance; second, the person's motivation to cognitive learning, which is not a simple function of the existence of either values or standards or both together; and finally, the affective meanings of the alternatives contained in a manifold of possible social participations, which includes the devotion of personal and collective resources to cognitive concerns. We think it very important to note that there is not just one category of cognitive output, namely knowledge, but that there are others as well, particularly *competence.* Knowledge is an output to the cultural system and becomes incorporated in it as a type of cultural object. Competence, however, is an output to the personality system and is internalized as part of the personality structure.

The result of such analysis of factors, categories of outputs, and modes of relation between the sets makes it necessary to define some complex distinctions and interdependencies. Only in that way can we do justice to the complexity of the cognitive complex in its internal structure and its various modes of articulation with the noncognitive aspects of the action system.

We have been using Marxian ideology and the ideologies critical of the modern university system as a theoretical foil. It is not our purpose to judge the strength of either ideology in the process of social development. Rather, we have used the conceptual structure of these ideologies to illuminate the structural complexes of the organization of action with which they deal. Both ideologies postulate and advocate a far less differentiated system than the one already developed when the ideologies were promulgated, and which they have attacked as corrupt. We think have been able to ascertain the precise points where differentiation is considered undesirable: notably, the plurality of factors in economic production and in cognitive output, and the differentiation of types of output.

Both ideologies want to replace the current differentiated structures with an idealized system in which both the differentiation and the alleged evils would be eliminated or at least greatly minimized. This would necessarily have a highly deflationary effect on the generalized media of interchange involved. Gregory Grossman, one of the principal authorities on the Soviet economy, speaks of the "demonetization" of the Soviet economy.[20] Another major consequence is to ignore some fundamental cost factors in economic production. As Marshall Goldman has shown, this particularly applies to land costs and capital costs.[21] It would seem to follow from our parallel that the implementation of the New Left ideology would have a highly deflationary effect on the media of intelligence and influence. It would also ignore the cost factors involved, particularly in motivation to cognitive learning and the values of cognitive rationality.

I would like here to emphasize that in *The American University* Platt and I laid great emphasis on the sense in which *all* generalized symbolic media of interchange are subject to inflationary and deflationary disturbance in ways which are strictly parallel to the comparable economic disturbances in which the monetary system is at the center. In particular we devoted a major chapter (the seventh) to inflationary and deflationary processes involving intelligence on the one hand and influence on the other as these two media are involved in the academic system. We have argued especially that, when viewed against the background of a long inflationary process, the recent student disturbances could be interpreted as in considerable part a deflationary crisis with respect

[20] Gregory Grossman, "The Politics of Economic Reforms: A Comment," *Survey* 70/71 (1969): 165–168.

[21] Marshall Goldman, *The Spoils of Progress: Environmental Pollution in the Soviet Union* (Cambridge, Mass.: MIT Press, 1972).

to the media both of intelligence and of influence, with some relations to those of affect and value commitments.

It thus seems highly significant that movements dominated by Marxian ideology, especially more radical Communist ones, have not achieved political power in any of the highly industrialized societies. Their great successes have been in the underdeveloped world, which included Russia in 1917. We think there may be a parallel in the special appeal of the New Left ideology to youth and particularly to students. Because the socialization of youth has not yet been completed, they are analogous to an underdeveloped economy, and for them the ideological simplification has strong appeal.

The parallel between the Marxian diagnosis of capitalism and the recent dissident diagnosis of the educational revolution helps explain both the strikingly persistent use of Marxian themes and rhetoric by the New Left and the different emphases of the two ideologies. One sharp difference is the neglect of technical Marxist *economic* theories in contemporary discussion. Although there is a conspicuous nostalgia for the "working class," there is an equally conspicuous absence of any precise analysis of this nostalgia. As Erik Erikson notes, the New Left is content with asserting the common "dependency" of workers and students.[22] They speak of alienation, but in a different sense than Marx, discarding his special reference to the labor role in favor of fuzzy generalizations about personality. And there is also a subtly important difference between Marx's "exploitation" and contemporary "repressiveness." Finally, the value accents are inverted. Marxism defiantly asserted the value of "materialism," although qualified by the adjective "historical." Today, however, one prominent reason for the indictment of contemporary society is its materialistic character. Perhaps we can legitimately relate this inversion to the shift in concern from the economic to the cultural level.

Let us turn to the ways in which the development of "free enterprise" economies has taken the historical course that has proved to be an alternative to Communist revolution. Because our interest has focused on labor, we suggest that the alternative has emerged mainly through the development of a complex system of *occupational* roles.

[22] Erik Erikson, *op. cit.* (n. 12, above).

Two crucial points must be considered at the start. First, there has been a process of structural differentiation, between labor as a category of factor input and service as a category of economically valuable product output. Labor inputs have had to be combined with other economic factors to make them valuable. This has occurred primarily through the channels of socialization and formal education, which, *among other things*, have been processes of creating economic value. It is further significant that, although Marx confined the category *labor* to those roles specifically controlled by the owner of the firm, the occupational role has become a much wider category, including the institutionalized managerial functions and high-level professional functions as well as routine labor functions. The professional role-type particularly has become a kind of a model prototype for the changing body of occupational roles. One aspect of this change, of course, has been the great proportionate reduction of the unskilled labor force. This has been accompanied by a rise in the level of qualifications for an increasing proportion of jobs. Occupational roles then, as forms of service, are performed in contexts of organization that have both political and community aspects. The associational structure of university faculties and departments, for example, is an important example of solidary social community. Furthermore, the academic community includes students in complex ways.

Parallel to their economic views, the dedifferentiating cultural revolution would minimize, if not destroy, the autonomy of the cognitive complex by incorporating it into a diffuse matrix of *Gesinnung*. But alternatively, this process of differentiation can be carried even further, uniting the patterns of integration into a differentiated structure that can bind them together. To achieve this, it is essential that cognitive standards be considered as a *factor* in cognitive output, and not a category of such output. That factor should then be treated, institutionally as well as theoretically, as one among a set of factors of cognitive output. Beyond that we would stress the development of competence as a learned and therefore internalized aspect of the individual personality, which can attain high levels of excellence only through a relatively prolonged and complex educational process.

We must also stress the importance of integrating the competent personality in a community-type societal nexus that is highly differentiated both internally and from other aspects of the society, such as the economy and polity, and in which affect as a medium of interchange plays a prominent part. The articulation of competence and the affectively controlled nexus of social community are, we think, the principal answer to the charge that modern society and particularly its intellectual community is inherently alienative.

If this alternative to the cultural revolution is — as I personally believe — the probable way of the future, I scarcely mean to imply that the way will be smooth and harmonious. It is very likely that the prominence given to the cognitive complex — research and higher education — will continue to be a highly disturbing force in our society and culture. Therefore, its internal development and its complex relations to the rest of the society are likely to be turbulent. This has been true of all the great structural changes in the evolution of modern society.

The educational revolution is by no means complete. The complex developmental process will continue to involve many changes in structure, including changes in the composition of the bundle. Our use of ideological themes, however, and of the parallel between Marxist ideology and the current dissident attack on the cognitive complex, seem a useful way of highlighting some problems in the nature of the system that are vital to understanding the changes and tensions it has generated. But other approaches are also valid, and this essay is intended not as a program for action but as a paradigm of interpretation.

I referred to the work of Max Weber earlier. It is perhaps appropriate to conclude this discussion with a reference to the very much broader concept of the process of rationalization, which was a central preoccupation of Weber's work, particularly in his later years. Although his analysis was indeed different from Marx's, they can be linked through the concept of rationality. For Marx, the discipline of economic rationality, enforced on capitalists by the market and on workers by the capitalists, was a focal source of evil in the capitalist system. Robert Bellah, commenting on Marxism's strong appeal to Japanese intellectuals,[23] speaks of Marx's "nostalgia for *Gemeinschaft*."

On quite a different level, Weber was deeply disturbed by the

[23] Bellah, *op. cit.* (n. 8, above).

process of rationalization, which produced what he called an "iron cage."[24] Weber had a different but comparable nostalgia for something akin to *Gemeinschaft*. But by Weber's time, the rationality factor in the organization of the economy had become one, albeit very prominent, instance within the much larger process of rationalization as a whole. Weber himself strongly emphasized the factor of *bureaucracy* in the structure of the economy and elsewhere in the society. He was also on the threshold of seeing the vast significance of the cognitive complex at the cultural levels, as well as the significance of social organization. In the half century and more since Weber's death, however, the development at the cultural level has proliferated immensely.

Without that proliferation, the themes discussed in this paper would not have been as much at the center of contemporary preoccupation. I think it fair to say that we have been experiencing a sociocultural crisis comparable to the crisis that accompanied and followed the Industrial Revolution, which Neil Smelser has analyzed.[25] In my view, Weber, at the time of his premature death, was in the midst of working through some of the crucial problems arising from that vast social and cultural change, the educational revolution, and its ramifications through the entire society and culture. This essay will, I hope, prove a modest contribution to what, in the spirit of Weber, we may call both the value-free and the objective understanding of these changes.

[24] Max Weber, *The Protestant Ethic and the Spirit of Capitalism*, trans. Talcott Parsons (London: George Allen and Unwin, 1930).

[25] Smelser, *op. cit.* (n. 5, above).

[26] Neil J. Smelser, *Essays in Sociological Explanation* Englewood Cliffs, N.J.: Prentice-Hall, 1968).

Index